A Sea of Misadventures

STUDIES IN MARITIME HISTORY

William N. Still, Jr., Series Editor

Recent Titles

*Iron Afloat: The Story of
the Confederate Armorclads*
William N. Still, Jr.

*To California by Sea:
A Maritime History of the Gold Rush*
James P. Delgado

*Lifeline of the Confederacy: Blockade
Running during the Civil War*
Stephen R. Wise

*The Lure of Neptune: German-Soviet
Naval Collaboration and Ambitions*
Tobias R. Philbin III

*High Seas Confederate: The Life and
Times of John Newland Maffitt*
Royce Shingleton

*The Defeat of the German U-Boats: The
Battle of the Atlantic*
David Syrett

*John P. Holland, 1841–1914: Inventor of
the Modern Submarine*
Richard Knowles Morris

*Cockburn and the British Navy in
Transition: Admiral Sir George Cockburn,
1772–1853*
Roger Morriss

*The Royal Navy in European Waters
during the American Revolutionary War*
David Syrett

Sir John Fisher's Naval Revolution
Nicholas A. Lambert

Forty-Niners 'round the Horn
Charles R. Schultz

The Abandoned Ocean
Andrew Gibson and Arthur Donovan

*Northern Naval Superiority and the
Economics of the American Civil War*
David G. Surdam

*Ironclads and Big Guns of
the Confederacy: The Journal and
Letters of John M. Brooke*
Edited by George M. Brooke, Jr.

*High Seas and Yankee Gunboats:
A Blockade-Running Adventure
from the Diary of James Dickson*
Roger S. Durham

*Dead Men Tell No Tales: The Lives and
Legends of the Pirate Charles Gibbs*
Joseph Gibbs

*Playships of the World: The Naval Diaries
of Admiral Dan Gallery, 1920–1924*
Edited by Robert Shenk

*Captains Contentious:
The Dysfunctional Sons of the Brine*
Louis Arthur Norton

*Lewis Coolidge and the Voyage
of the Amethyst, 1806–1811*
Evabeth Miller Kienast and John
Phillip Felt

Promotion—or the Bottom of the River
John M. Stickney

*A Sea of Misadventures: Shipwreck
and Survival in Early America*
Amy Mitchell-Cook

A Sea of

MISADVENTURES

Shipwreck and Survival in Early America

~

AMY MITCHELL-COOK

THE UNIVERSITY OF SOUTH CAROLINA PRESS

© 2013 University of South Carolina

Published by the University of South Carolina Press
Columbia, South Carolina 29208

www.sc.edu/uscpress

Manufactured in the United States of America

22 21 20 19 18 17 16 15 14 13   10 9 8 7 6 5 4 3 2 1

Library of Congress Cataloging-in-Publication Data

Mitchell-Cook, Amy.
A sea of misadventures : Shipwreck and survival in
early America / Amy Mitchell-Cook.
pages cm
Includes bibliographical references and index.
ISBN 978-1-61117-301-7 (hardbound : alk. paper) —
ISBN 978-1-61117-302-4 (ebook) 1. Shipwrecks—America—
History. 2. Survival at sea—America—History. I. Title.
G525.M564 2013
910.9163'0903—dc23
2013015879

This book was printed on a recycled paper with 30 percent
postconsumer waste content.

PRECEEDING PAGES: *My Child! My Child!* and *They're Saved! They're Saved!*,
companion prints engraved and published by John C. McRae, N.Y.,
ca. 1855, courtesy of the Library of Congress. CHAPTER OPENING PAGES:
Americae sive qvartae orbis partis nova et exactissima descriptio, by
Diego Gutiérrez, 1562, courtesy of the Library of Congress.

CONTENTS

ILLUSTRATIONS

PREFACE

The image of shipwreck has long been a part of recorded history. Every maritime society collected tales relating to maritime disasters, castaways, and those who simply disappeared. The horror of shipwreck, the excitement in the human drama, and a fascination with faraway lands riveted readers as doomed sailors and passengers prayed for divine mercy. Such enthusiasm continues with popular reality shows, box office hits, and a plethora of books concerning survival and the ability to "beat all odds."

My interest in shipwrecks stems from several years employed as a nautical archaeologist. As an archaeologist, I worked with the remains of vessels decades or even centuries after their final voyages. I recorded ships' hulls as they lay on the bottom of various rivers, bays, and oceans; I took photographs of construction features and labored over waterlogged artifacts in the conservation lab. Analysis did not end underwater, and I made some of my best discoveries in the archives, carefully scrutinizing stacks of historical documents. In fact, as an archaeologist, I spent more time conducting historical research than diving underwater.

Historical analysis as part of archaeological research, however, was limited. Much effort went to detailing a ship's life, finding the various ports where the vessel called, looking at its captains, and trying to determine if the vessel ever participated in an "exciting" historical event. In addition to the ships' histories, such reports focused on the material remains and the methodology used in recovering them. Although this is certainly a valid format within the field of archaeology, this research fails to examine a pivotal moment in a ship's history: shipwreck.

This is not to imply that historians have focused on shipwrecks either. Similar to archaeologists, historians often emphasize the tale of a specific vessel. They learn about its crew, its cargo, and perhaps the places it sailed. And yet, like archaeologists, historians often neglect to examine what happens when a voyage ends in failure. Relegating shipwreck to the final chapter or even a lowly epilogue, historians typically offer little analysis concerning the actual moment of shipwreck.

This book is an attempt to fill that gap. My research examines the period between when a ship is sailing and when it becomes a submerged cultural artifact at the bottom of the ocean. What happened as men and women struggled to stay alive? Why did some survive while others did not? How did survivors react to unimaginable circumstances? The answers I found were surprising. I assumed that societal and cultural standards fell apart and all hell broke loose. I thought that mutiny and cannibalism occurred randomly among desperate sailors. I was wrong.

ACKNOWLEDGMENTS

This book would not be possible but for the numerous individuals who offered their support. First and foremost I would like to thank William Pencak, Anne Rose, Matthew Restall, and Lorraine Dowler at Penn State University for their advice, support, and invaluable criticisms. I would also like to extend my gratitude to William Joyce, Paul Gilje, and Lisa Norling for commenting on specific areas for helping me smooth out various rough patches. To the anonymous reviewers who added to and refined my manuscript, I thank you for your thorough comments. To my colleagues at Penn State University and at the University of West Florida, I thank you for your support and patience in commenting on various chapters and providing numerous essential libations when needed. I would also like to acknowledge the assistance I received from several graduate students at the University of West Florida, primarily Tom Barber and Paul Zielinski.

For fellowship support I must recognize the generosity of the John Carter Brown Library for the William Reese Company Fellowship. Their outstanding holdings and amazing staff gave my project a much-needed jump-start. In addition I would like to thank the Peabody-Essex Museum, the RGSO, and the Department of History at Penn State for the Hill Fellowship. Several institutions generously opened their archives: William and Mary, the Massachusetts Historical Society, Mystic Seaport, the Mariners' Museum, the Rhode Island Historical Society, Hay Library at Brown University, and Gloucester Archives Committee.

Portions of this book appear in other publications and are reproduced here with permission from Mystic Seaport Press and from *Coriolos* for portions of chapters 4 and 5. Chapter 4 appeared as "Negotiating Power: Status and Authority in Anglo-American Shipwreck Narratives" in *Pirates, Jack Tar and Memory* (Mystic Seaport Press, 2007), and chapter 5, "To Honor Their Worth, Beauty, and Accomplishments," appeared in *Coriolos* (June 2011).

My greatest debt goes to my family, who stood by me and supported me each step of the way. I thank you for your patience and encouragement.

PROLOGUE

Life at sea was never easy. Extreme weather conditions, hard work, bad food, and dangerous working conditions made even a calm day difficult. Many sailors lamented their time at sea. Some acted out with drinking or violence, others deserted at the first possible chance, and yet a few turned inward and wrote letters or kept journals. For example, the logbook of the *Cashmere* (1838), reveals how one sailor viewed his time at sea:

> Home, yes this is my home, but what a home! The only difference between it and a home in an American states prison is that here now I have a chance of escaping imprisonment by being drowned, that's some encouragement certainly and instead of eating salt fish ourselves, we may possibly become food for the fishes of the salt sea.
>
> It is now one week since we left Boston. . . . How long before I shall see that coast again! Perhaps a year—perhaps never—At any rate how many thousands of miles must I sail before I again see it. How many dangers of the sea and land must I escape.[1]

Unfortunately such fears were often realized as fair winds and calm seas gave way to storms and rough water. A bad situation became worse when a ship foundered or hit bottom, forcing sailors into small lifeboats or to take refuge along hostile coastlines.

Shipwreck was a real possibility. Estimates gleaned from several sources suggest that 4 to 5 percent of voyages ended in disaster.[2] While this number may sound low, given the sheer number of voyages at any particular time, 4 or 5 percent represented a real threat to mariners and the ships they sailed. In addition this number does not take into account the number of ships that limped into port with leaky hulls, torn sails, and half-starved sailors.

Frontispiece, J. F. Layson, *Memorable Shipwrecks and Seafaring Adventures of the Nineteenth Century* (London: Walter Scott, 188?)

Survivors of shipwrecks and storms related their adventures and provided graphic details concerning how some met their demise while others survived. Filled with narrow escapes, starvation, and all sorts of terrifying exploits, these stories were part of a strong oral tradition within the maritime community. But they were more than yarns told in a favorite bar; many stories expanded beyond seafarers to become a popular form of literature for landlubbers as well.

This book examines printed shipwreck narratives from the seventeenth century to the early nineteenth century and their place in American history. Although, of course, shipwrecks occurred at sea, accounts describing them reflected land-based perceptions and ideologies. The narratives expressed issues of hierarchy, race, and gender that revealed society's attitudes toward aspects of religion and labor. Rather than debate the veracity of the tales, this research is a cultural and social analysis of these moments in crisis that places the image of shipwreck within the broader context of North American society.

The most surprising element of the published accounts was that during and after shipwrecks, status and authority remained intact. Only after the immediate danger subsided, and as survivors began to take stock of the situations, did individuals sometimes improvise more flexible, and temporary, arrangements to fit the emerging circumstances. Yet the end results were always ones of stability, where traditional understandings of social order were reestablished.

Published shipwreck narratives were meant to be popular and to appeal to a broad audience. Printed as cheap, or street, literature in the form of broadsides, chapbooks, or poems, they were affordable to all levels of society. In general they were short stories, running from a few paragraphs to several pages, and gave precise accounts from the voyages' inceptions to the rescue of remaining survivors. Advances in printing technology and the increase of worldwide commerce expedited publishing in the nineteenth century and allowed for the creation of larger anthologies, but later editions were almost always merely adaptations of earlier shipwreck accounts. The published narratives afforded a public platform that individuals used for a variety of purposes: to obtain money, to express religious beliefs, or simply to create interesting stories. Their use as popular literature implies that authors and publishers manipulated, qualified, and adapted the stories to make best-selling books.[3] Although this malleability suggests that some information in the narratives is less than accurate, it does not diminish their value. Rather this factor increases their significance because the authors and publishers crafted their stories to appeal to a broad audience, and therefore the stories reveal much about the social and cultural context of that time.

Although the narratives exhibit time-specific elements, incorporated in them was a level of cultural continuity that allowed for their sustained popularity. As newer shipwrecks added to the overall body of literature, older narratives underwent numerous reprints. Take, for example, the well-known story of Pierre Viaud, who wrecked off the coast of Florida in 1766. The tale reported that he and other survivors fought Indians, encountered wild animals, and dealt with every hardship imaginable. After twenty-four days they made their way to St. Augustine, and eventually Viaud sailed to New York, where he spent several weeks recovering. The first edition was published in Paris in 1768, and a second edition went to press in 1770 in Bordeaux. The first English version appeared in 1771, and from there additional reprints included editions in 1774, 1798, 1799, 1814, 1935, and more recently 1990.[4] The basic story remained unchanged with only minor abridgments to the original narrative. The numerous reprints also demonstrate the continued popularity of the shipwreck genre and that at some level the stories appealed to audiences over time.

Such continuity suggests that the narratives remained true to their original story and, despite subsequent editions, related events as told in the first printing. This standardization appears in several narratives, and each exhibits little or no change over time. Modifications typically reflect a distancing of the narrator from the story, usually seen in a shift from first person to third. Other alterations are abridgments that do little to take away from the original story but probably cut printing costs.

Perhaps shipwreck narratives appealed to a broad audience because they provided exciting stories of human endurance and ability. Rather than depressing accounts of death and deprivation, the narratives presented something positive. The printed accounts transformed the chaos of shipwreck into an ordered and understandable event in which aspects of gender, status, and religion remained solid. Even in shipwreck's most extreme situation, cannibalism, survivors maintained social hierarchies in deciding the order of sacrifice.

The emphasis on maintaining social order may also reflect authorship, and not just efforts to produce best sellers. Captains, officers, or passengers rather than ordinary seamen wrote most of the accounts. Despite the popular notion of the captain going down with his ship, many high-ranking officers lived to tell their tales. From tracing sixty published narratives to their original printings, it appears that two-thirds were written by such individuals.[5] This authorship creates a definite class bias, one that directly relates to the narratives' ultimate creations. It is not surprising to see the narratives suggest a continued sense of order, as that would best suit those used to traditional power. Rather than social mobility, the published accounts provided a conservative message that confirmed a sense of place.

American society and culture, however, did not remain static from the seventeenth to nineteenth centuries. Gender, status, and religion shifted over time to incorporate movements such as the Enlightenment and romanticism; the beginnings of the Industrial Revolution also altered how early Americans viewed themselves and one another. The narratives too adjusted to the changes; yet nevertheless they remained conservative. Flexibility expanded temporarily if the situation required it, but individuals who experienced shipwreck rarely overstepped established boundaries.

Despite the narratives' continued consistency, they do reflect broader social shifts over time. For example, in the seventeenth century published accounts of shipwreck stressed religion and God's involvement in both causation and redemption. By the eighteenth century emotional sympathy for the victims increased, and the actions of specific individuals who rescued survivors became an important theme. The stories were secularized, stressing human ability and benevolence rather than divine intervention in effecting salvation. Enlightenment rationality and inquisitiveness brought to the narratives a level of apparent veracity through detailed descriptions of how ships were wrecked and the methods survivors used to persevere.

By the nineteenth century the narratives had diverged into two main groups. One consisted of abridged versions of earlier shipwrecks. These accounts lacked emotion and drama and were typically in a third-person perspective. Such stories read like newspaper accounts with only the "facts" presented. The second group offered dramatic tales replete with the horrors of survival. These stories often directly confronted the audience to elicit an emotional response. At the same time a religious emphasis returned. Seventeenth- and eighteenth-century features combined as narratives merged a sense of God's involvement and the need to follow his will with the importance of human agency.

Many early North American narratives reflected a Puritan outlook, in which shipwreck was a part of God's design and survival was the ultimate reward for belief.[6] Often attached to sermons or used as jeremiads, narratives provided lessons for moral and spiritual behavior. They explained the terrifying and random event that had meaning to both participants and readers.[7] By the mid-eighteenth century shipwrecks lost some of their theological goals as the Enlightenment brought forth more secularized language. While God sometimes intervened in human affairs, a universe where God remained aloof gained greater currency. At this time American colonists weighed the conundrum of free will versus providence and to what extent each played a role in their lives. The event of shipwreck provided an excellent format for debating the two ends of the spectrum as issues of human ability, predestination, God's will, and the forces of nature affected how individuals viewed the world around them.

Following this cosmic understanding, chance elements such as the weather explained most shipwrecks, death, and survival. For example, Benjamin Franklin narrowly escaped shipwreck in 1757; rather than praise God for deliverance, he instead saw the need for more lighthouses.[8] By the early nineteenth century providence and chance gave way to the belief that intelligent human activity, including technical knowledge of ships, ocean currents, and personal resourcefulness, determined whether a ship sank or not. But human agency and know-how did not totally replace earlier beliefs; instead Calvinistic theology, situated in popular religious faith, continued to explain wrecks alongside a deepening belief that human ability offered positive effects.

In addition to religion, one of the more important themes found throughout the narratives concerned gender. Overall the stories taught men and women to remain "proper," even in chaotic situations. Women's roles were usually minor and always secondary to the main events. Men took control while women protected the children and themselves and prayed to God for mercy and divine guidance. Female passengers remained pious and obedient as they waited for men to decide the best course for survival. Women who did not survive this catastrophe became heroines who sacrificed their lives for the preservation of husbands, children, and most important, their reputations. In fact few women survived. These women became models for female readers by validating idealized feminine behavior, whereby submissiveness, restraint, and piety came to represent a woman's inherent strength and superior morality.

Shipwreck narratives also validated specific forms of male behavior by praising capability, leadership, and bravery. Heroes of shipwrecks displayed polite manners and the general characteristics of a good husband.[9] The stories once again reassured their audiences that their understandings of cultural order were unshakable.

Race rarely entered into shipwreck narratives. The accounts seldom mentioned the presence of Africans or African Americans, and very few black individuals wrote these accounts. White survivors authored most narratives, probably for white audiences, and so left out or minimized the actions of black crew members. Slaves and servants appeared in some narratives, but usually as minor characters with no active voice. As such, they typically went down with the ships and rarely survived. Due to their bravery or extraordinary behavior, however, a few black individuals did come to the fore, but they emerged only temporarily and never threatened social order.

Published accounts of shipwreck related that social stratification remained intact.[10] In shipwreck social order was preserved as the captain or highest ranked survivor organized and guided the survivors to safety. After the fear of immediate survival passed, this officer continued his leadership, though a lowly sailor or passenger might rise to meet the new demands. The narratives suggest that class had its rewards, as many times deference permitted officers to enter lifeboats ahead of common seamen. Rather than go down with the ships, captains, officers, and gentlemen passengers often lived to tell their versions of the stories.

Although a crew could legally refuse to follow the captain once the ship was lost, such incidents seldom transpired and then only when the crew lost respect or confidence in the captain's authority. Mutinous behavior did occur, but rarely to the fullest extent, and men who participated in such events met with death and disaster. Even on such occasions captains or officers regained control when the crises passed. A wise captain balanced authority with sympathy; he listened to the crew's fears but never lost control.

6

By such means, hierarchies remained but were flexible in their reactions to temporary crises.

Shipwreck narratives not only reflected societal and cultural beliefs but, to an extent, also asserted national pride. American and English sailors did not steal, desert, murder, or otherwise take advantage of the situations. They remained loyal to the communities and demonstrated positive natural character. In contrast, for example, Portuguese narratives exposed personal greed, laziness, and efforts at self-preservation. Rarely did a captain and crew remain loyal to a vessel, let alone to one another. Sailors stole precious goods as they rushed away from the boat, with barely an expression of regret to those left behind. In spite of such failings, Portuguese narratives revealed how ships' companies survived regardless of the presence of these individuals. The moral and physical strength of the Portuguese reflected on the state as a whole, allowing the Portuguese to triumph in the end.

Economic and legal concerns obviously influenced the impact of shipwreck and the overall creation of a shipwreck narrative. Most ships carried some form of cargo, which was frequently insured as it represented a sizable investment to merchants, shippers, and owners. Fear of losing money was an ever-present threat for many captains, most of whom owned shares of the vessels. Maritime law and marine insurance guaranteed owners, captains, and sailors that in shipwreck due process would protect cargoes and wages. Acting responsibly and doing what was most logical to save the ship and cargo proved a captain's loyalty to inquisitive audiences (and courts). As they reached shore, survivors used both published and unpublished avenues to justify and explain their conduct or to avoid litigation from angry insurance companies. The legal and economic contexts required that sailors be interested and that in such events captains and crews fulfilled their customary duties or compensation would not be forthcoming.

Similar to deliverance tales, such as those of Native American captivity and escaped slave narratives, shipwreck was more than a physical disaster.[11] Written both to entertain and to educate, the narratives helped readers discern acceptable social behavior, offered lessons for spiritual instruction, and provided information on how to survive in a time of crisis. Overall published accounts transformed a potential moment of crisis into a positive and ordered event that appealed to a broad audience.

∾

An attempt is made in this book to bring the event of shipwreck fully into maritime and American historiography. As shipwrecks occurred, individuals struggled against nature as well as one another to stay alive, and in the process they revealed societal and cultural themes that ultimately exposed what it meant to be human and living in early modern Anglo-American cultures. Shipwreck narratives were not merely tales; they were strong indicators of American society and culture, imparting a conservative view that substantiated the need for order based on gender, status, and religious expectations. In a period of social mobility and flux, authors provided a sense of stability and order. Even though shipwreck was a moment of crisis, the narratives reassured audiences that traditional understandings of society and place persisted.

Published narratives, given their detail, stand at the core of my research. This project utilizes one hundred accounts of shipwreck from the late seventeenth century to the mid-nineteenth century.[12] The earliest account dates to the 1660s, with the first American-published narrative printed in Philadelphia in 1697. I ended my research with 1840 because in the early nineteenth century accounts of shipwreck began to focus on steamship explosions. The printed narratives shifted blame to faulty machinery or inadequate captains rather than interpreting shipwrecks as a form of divine punishment. Mid-nineteenth-century anthologies centered on human fault and the growing humanitarian effort to improve safety rather than portraying shipwreck as an act of God or nature.

My synthesis of published and unpublished sources provides the first systematic study of the role of shipwrecks in North American colonial and early national culture.[13] Rather than presenting the radical sailors who promoted a general tendency toward democracy and social mobility, as often seen in maritime culture, these stories remained conservative in their approach to society.[14] They advocated traditional place and deference that reassured audiences that stability and order remained, even in times of crisis.

. I .

FACT OR FICTION?

The Publication of American Shipwreck Narratives

I am so far from ever wishing to appear before the public in the character of author, that I had long resisted the importunities of very many
of my friends, who, from time to time, earnestly requested me to write,
and publish a narrative of the wreck of the Oswego, and of the subsequent sufferings of myself and crew among the wild Arabs. At last I
have been prevailed upon to do it; and am encouraged with the hope
that my narrative will meet with candor, and be of some benefit to
mankind generally, and more especially to sea-faring men exposed
to the like awful calamities.[1]

Survivors of shipwrecks often wrote about their experiences, and they did so
for a variety of reasons—to make money, to demonstrate God's presence, or
simply to find a sense of closure. Beyond such personal motives, these narratives furnished excitement and adventure as well as practical suggestions
concerning proper survival behavior that authors hoped would appeal to
eager audiences. As with other popular forms of literature, such as captivity
or travel narratives, accounts of shipwreck blended reality with fiction to
produce a harrowing and affordable form of amusement.[2] "So long as there
had been newspapers, murders, along with such other evidences of man's
depravity or ill-fortune as treason, highway robbery, forgery, piracy, shipwrecks, epidemics, and catastrophic storms, had been news."[3]

Shipwreck narratives are typically first- or secondhand accounts that focus primarily on the shipwreck events and their immediate aftermaths. German, French, Spanish, Portuguese, British, and American narratives exist

in almost every major archive. The narratives for this study date from the sixteenth century through the 1840s. Recorded shipwreck narratives, however, continue to be printed up to the present decade. Some are single broadsides or pamphlets; others are collected anthologies or are embedded individually in larger tales of adventure.

Structured as short stories rarely more than twenty pages long, the accounts provide condensed scenarios of events from the voyages' inceptions to their ultimate demises. As one of several varieties of street literature— pamphlets, tracts, and chapbooks—the narratives supplied a cheap means of entertainment and of disseminating information. A chapbook consisted of a sheet folded into several uncut or unstitched pages, while a broadside was a large, single sheet with material printed on one side; broadsides could be posted on buildings or left on tavern tables for patrons to read.

Chapbooks and broadsides represented the most common means for telling shipwreck disasters until the nineteenth century, when decreased costs permitted longer accounts published in greater quantities.[4] Early collections do appear, such as Increase Mather's *An Essay for the Recording of Illustrious Providences* (1684), but are rare. By the nineteenth century collected anthologies, including the anonymous, *Remarkable Shipwrecks: or, a Collection of Interesting Accounts of Naval Disaster* (1813), and Archibald Duncan, *Mariner's Chronicle* (1804–8), had become commonplace.[5]

British colonists in the New World were not lowly illiterates trying to eke out a living in the wild American forests; they read and owned books, created libraries, and began founding colleges. Colonists of all social classes looked to the printed word for guidance, news, and entertainment; "the printed word thrived in early America, because so many early Americans were, indeed, devoted readers."[6]

There was a high rate of literacy in the colonies. According to some estimates, in New England 60 percent of white males were literate in 1660 and 85 percent were literate in 1760, with percentages in the remaining colonies slightly lower. Of course literacy varied according to area, age, and gender, with women having a much lower rate. For example, women's literacy rose to approximately 45 percent by 1700 but then stagnated, rising only slightly by the end of the eighteenth century.[7] Furthermore individuals in taverns and at home read news, stories, and other forms of literature out loud, so even the illiterate had access to printed material.

Publishing began early in the colonies. The first press in America was established in 1639 in Cambridge, Massachusetts.[8] During the seventeenth century the colonies of Virginia, Maryland, Pennsylvania, New York, and Rhode Island also began presses; the remaining colonies established them in the eighteenth century.[9] At first royal governors regulated and restricted material for publications.[10] Primarily used for tracts, almanacs, sermons, catechisms, and official government pronouncements, the early presses generated few works of popular literature, except those reflecting a strong religious emphasis.

Colonial printing tended to be expensive and slow, and many printers relied on supplies from England. The need to import such items as ink and type limited North American printers' ability to expand production. Practical problems such as a scarcity of labor and a lack of light at night also hindered output.[11] Not until the nineteenth century, with improved technology and mechanization, did printing move beyond this initial phase toward mass production.[12]

Without adequate resources to print a large amount of material in North America, colonists imported many books through the seventeenth and eighteenth centuries. Such books were expensive, and varying levels of literacy and incomes often prevented a high number of sales.[13] The longer the book, the less likely it could be printed or sold in the colonies. To alleviate this problem, publishers and printers often shortened popular works to make the material more cost effective. Publishers found that short, single narratives were ideal for American printers.[14]

Although the American Revolution spurred a taste for printed material, only in the nineteenth century did advances in mechanization alter the book-making process. Low incomes and expensive printings had previously prevented many from purchasing larger works, forcing bookstores to serve select individuals who could afford imported books from London.[15] By the nineteenth century publishers who had previously produced only a small amount of material consolidated into larger printing houses able to generate a greater volume.[16] The use of paper labels instead of embossed leather and machine versus hand-bound books helped decrease prices and improved availability and distribution.[17] From the perspective of readership, printing now entered the realm of mass marketing as printers recognized the demands of an increasingly literate population rather than catering to the tastes of a few gentlemen or clergy.[18] Tied with increased literacy rates and expanded printing capabilities, American printers found ready markets for publishing.[19]

In the early decades, when printers acted as publishers, authors, and booksellers, many presses were part of households rather than independent shops, with wives and families providing needed labor.[20] The printers-publishers linked authorship with manufacture and finance with distribution, creating a complex and often clouded process. The role each person played through the early nineteenth century is difficult to determine, and the texts provide little assistance. In addition in many early works printers omitted

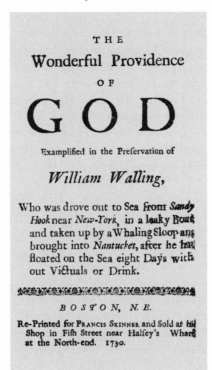

THE

Wonderful Providence

OF

GOD

Examplified in the Prefervation of

William Walling,

Who was drove out to Sea from *Sandy Hook* near *New-York,* in a leaky Boat and taken up by a Whaling Sloop and brought into *Nantucket,* after he had floated on the Sea eight Days without Victuals or Drink.

BOSTON, N. E.

Re-Printed for FRANCIS SKINNER and Sold at his Shop in Fifh Street near Halfey's Wharf at the North-end. 1730.

Title page, William Walling, *The Wonderful Providence of God,*
Early American Imprints, series 1, no. 3373

authors from the title pages, suggesting that authors were subordinate to the printers.[21]

To complicate matters further, private individuals, who were neither authors nor publishers, often commissioned narratives. For example, the *Shipwreck of Ann Sanders,* Providence, Rhode Island, was "printed for Z. S. Crossman, 1827." Monsieur Crespel's *Travels in North America* was "printed by and for Sampson Low, Berwick Street, Soho, 1797." Who were these individuals? How, if at all, were they connected to the story? Perhaps these accounts fit within the larger trend of publishing, in which even into the early nineteenth century anonymous authors paid printing costs and hoped to recoup profits through subscriptions.[22]

Although authors might have been absent, most narratives at least identified narrators within the first few paragraphs. Often these narrators-survivors were "respectable," such as officers, captains, or gentlemen passengers, thus contributing to the stories' authenticity. First-person narratives comprise approximately 70 percent of the accounts used in this study. These stories were the most personal and dramatic, allowing the readers to relive the ordeals through survivors of the original events. In a letter to his mother (which became a part of the narrative), Lieutenant Archer described the events preceding the loss of the *Phoenix* (1780) off the island of Cuba: "As soon as I was below, one of the Marine officers called out: 'Good God! Mr. Archer, we are sinking, the water is up to the bottom of my cot.' Pooh, pooh! As long as it is not over your mouth, you are well off; what the devil do you make this noise for? I found there . . . nothing to be alarmed at: . . . 'Come, pump away, my boys. Carpenters, get the weather chain-pump rigged.' 'All ready, sir.' 'Then man it, and keep both pumps going.'"[23]

The first-person accounts drew the readers into the story as the ship encountered every storm, wave, or disaster. An author could frame shipwreck "as a 'scene,' making his reader the spectator to a drama of terror and pain."[24] According to the anonymous *The Mariner's Chronicle* (1834), "so like the vicissitudes of a whole life, are all his voyages, that we read the details of his route, even his day log-book, with a fellow-feeling of interest and anxiety. Then we have the enjoyment of his adventures, without their danger."[25] Audiences had all the thrill but none of the pain.

Second-person narratives were also common, accounting for almost 25 percent of accounts studied. The survivors related the events to the authors, and then the authors described the stories to the readers. Again, the narratives identified reliable sources to assure a level of authenticity. Though not as emotional as the first-person accounts, these narratives retained a high level of drama, once again allowing the readers to relive the events through the survivors' descriptions. Aboard the brig *Tyrrel* (1759), on its way from New York to Sandy Hook, the chief mate, T. Purnell, provided this account: "Her lashings being cast loose by order of the captain, and having no other prospect of saving their lives but by the boat, Purnell, with two others, and the cabin boy, who were excellent swimmers, plunged into the water, and with great difficulty righted her, when she was brimful, and washing with the water's edge. They then put the cabin boy into her, and gave him a bucket that happened to float by, and he bailed away as quick as he could."[26] Although dramatic and exciting, the use of secondhand knowledge removed readers from experiencing the shipwreck fully.

Only a few narratives lacked any association with a survivor or knowledgeable individual. Obviously these accounts were also the most emotionally distant. The readers had to assume the stories' authenticity without relying on the reputation of survivors' versions. This method was probably the least popular because these accounts potentially failed to create empathy for individuals within the narratives.

Common motives, such as justification for an author's survival, need for money, and moral vindication, clearly affected the final stories. Barnabas Downs of Boston, who wrecked aboard the *General Arnold,* prefaced his 1786 narrative by offering his gratitude to his creator for salvation and requesting that the public purchase it to alleviate his "distressed' circumstances: "When any Remarkable circumstances take place in a man's life, he feels commonly a disposition to communicate them to the world: If they have been deliverances from great and signal disasters, he will make this communication from a principle of gratitude to the Being who hath protected and preserved him."[27] Judah Paddock added to his 1818 advertisement (the quotation that begins this chapter) that "it is no part of my object to enrich myself by means of this publication; the clear profits from, (should there be any) are to go otherwise than to my own private emolument."[28] The authors not only hoped to provide useful and entertaining tales but also sometimes added a level of altruism to sell copies.

The desire to make money was frequently the publisher's or printer's motive rather than the author's. The following title, lengthy even by colonial standards, of a 1684 anonymously written narrative gave away the whole story, and yet in doing so it continued to entice potential buyers: *Strange News from Plymouth, or, a Wonderful and Tragical Relation of a Voyage from the Indies: Where by Extraordinary Hardships, and the Extremities of the Late Great Frost, Several of the Seamen and Others Miserably Perished: and for Want of Provision, Cast-Lots for Their Lives and Were Forced to Eat One Another, and How a Dutch Merchant Eat Part of His Own Children, and Then Murdered Himself Because He Would Not Kill His Wife: with the Miraculous Preservation of George Carpinger, and English Seamen, and the Dutch Merchants Wife, Now a Shore at Plymouth.*[29] The title assured readers that the narrative contained exciting and gruesome events sure to titillate the senses, and to sell books.

In addition to presenting an exciting story, many accounts provided useful information regarding survival in the open ocean or on deserted islands. Reading such anecdotes, audiences who found themselves in similar situations might increase their chances for survival. William Bligh included such useful information when he wrote of how in 1789 he survived for thousands of miles in an open boat after mutiny on the HMS *Bounty:* "With no prospect of getting our cloaths dried, I recommended it to every one to grip, and wring them through with saltwater, by which means they received a warmth, that, while wet with rain, they could not have, and we were less liable to suffer from colds or theumatic complaints."[30] Throughout the narrative Bligh included beneficial advice regarding survival at sea.

Captain Prentice, shipwrecked off Cape Breton in 1780, deliberately inserted useful information in his narrative. Stranded during the winter, he advised his crew to keep moving so as to prevent their extremities from freezing and putrefying (which did happen to several crew members who failed to listen). The resourceful men poured water over their leaky dinghy to freeze up the cracks, allowing them to reconnoiter the coast for possible assistance. Additionally they warned others to be careful of local flora. The shipwrecked crew created concoctions from indigenous plants but without proper knowledge of herbal lore; they "retched for days."[31] Writers included such directions to show the creativity and resourcefulness necessary for survival as well as to furnish information for the next hapless traveler. In addition the information could provide an altruistic justification for publishing that did not stress the desire for profit.

Colonists looked to printed material for news (both local and international), information, entertainment, and in general to understand the world around them.[32] The inclusion of eyewitness accounts, physicians' statements, and information from other authoritative figures added credibility to the news.[33] Several narratives had introductory sections asserting the authors' character and the stories' veracity. Most had one or two letters of recommendation, while others had an inserted preface, introduction, or advertisement in which the story was certified as truth. James Riley's narrative, published in 1818, took integrity to an extreme with letters from Thomas Eddy, friend; Ambrose Peirce, judge of the Supreme Court of the State of New York; Elisha Jenkins, mayor of the City of Albany; Robert Jenkins, mayor of the City of Hudson; and De Witt Clinton, governor of the State of New York.[34] The inclusion of these letters, especially those from well-known and respectable men, lent credence to the narrative's authenticity.

Relying on the narratives' popularity and ability for continued profit, publishers often reprinted the accounts. Several narratives underwent numerous editions, some on both sides of the Atlantic. The shipwreck of the *Nottingham Galley* provides an interesting overview. Within a year of shipwreck, the captain's brother, Jasper Deane, rushed the first edition to press in London in 1711. That same year J. Dutton reprinted the account in London, while in Boston, Cotton Mather added the story to an essay concerning "miserable spectacles."[35] In 1722 the captain, John Deane, printed his own version in London, which he revised and reprinted several times. By 1735 Samuel Wilson had added the story to a sermon in London. A few years later, in 1738, John Deane reprinted his third revision, also in London. The next printing occurred almost a half century after the event when a passenger, Miles Whitworth, published his account in 1762 in Boston. By 1804 Archibald Duncan had added it to his collections of narratives entitled *The Mariner's Chronicle*, and Sir J. G. Dalyell included the account in his 1812 *Shipwrecks and Disasters at Sea*. The narrative found its way into numerous collections throughout the nineteenth century, with printings in 1810, 1814, 1824, 1833, 1834, 1836, and 1842.[36] The story of the *Nottingham* was not the only narrative to undergo such massive reprinting, and several shipwreck accounts appeared in both American and British editions.

Despite the frequency of reprints, an examination of published accounts suggests that few changes occurred within a specific story over time. A comparison of various narratives and their editions reveals that most revisions were slight and reflected only a need to shorten the text or to lower costs. Differences came primarily from omitting minor events or paragraphs that served to shorten the stories' overall length. Such abridgments were popular as they reduced financial hurdles in publishing and printing.[37] In addition they might increase readership by appealing to less educated readers.

By the time a narrative made it into print, several tales had undergone stylistic revisions. Potential audiences shaped the stories' ultimate outcomes by underscoring the dramatic and interesting sections.[38] Without copyright laws, anyone could take a story and use it for his own purposes, potentially obscuring the author's original account. The first federal copyright law went into effect in 1790 and provided copyright privileges for fourteen years. Yet as the travails of early American authors reveal, publishers were hard to police.[39]

The nature of the early book trade limited distribution in North America to networks formed by family, friends, and word of mouth. Additionally an agricultural world with a diffuse population made it difficult to circulate printed matter.[40] Geography remained a problem in the eighteenth century, and only with improved transportation and communication in the nineteenth century did isolated individuals gain greater access to books.[41] A mid-eighteenth-century bookseller named Joseph Condy limited his distribution to individuals who lived along trade routes. Boat, stage, and post riders delivered books and other reading matter to individuals along those routes.[42] Therefore those with geographical access to printed material read, while those removed from regular contact had little exposure to available publications. Much of this literature was local in nature, suggesting restricted distribution in which popular literature supplemented a community network. In the eighteenth century those in power kept information exclusive; those who needed to know about current events did and passed on information as needed to other, lower-class individuals. By the late eighteenth century this began to change when information no longer resided in the hands of the elite.[43]

Population and geography created regional differences in printing capabilities. In New England, Puritans published religious literature that spread easily to a population settled in organized towns. In the middle colonies too the presence of cities and settlements along readily traveled rivers ensured a thriving book trade. In the southern colonies, however, agricultural populations remained dispersed, hindering the movement of news and communication.[44] While New England had institutions, such as Harvard College, that supported local sources of print culture, the southern colonies remained tied to London for a continued flow of literature and information.[45]

Shipwreck narratives support this geographical difference. According to a checklist of shipwreck narratives up to 1860, *all* shipwreck narratives printed in North America prior to 1800 came from presses located in the northern and mid-Atlantic colonies, with Philadelphia being the farthest south.[46] The presence of presses and an available market led to the publication of such literature much earlier than in the southern colonies. After 1800 publishers in both the North and the South generated shipwreck narratives, although the northern presses continued to dominate.

Printers and publishers found numerous uses for these accounts that went beyond their original intent. Shipwreck narratives were frequently attached to sermons or other literature that combined religion with entertainment. The inclusion of shipwreck narratives in Increase Mather's 1684 collection *An Essay for the Recording of Illustrious Providences* began a close relationship between the narratives and print in the American colonies.[47] Similar to Indian captivity tales, shipwreck narratives combined sensationalism with religious instruction; readers could learn proper behavior by imagining themselves within the captives' situations.[48] In this way the narratives became useful and entertaining tools for improving the soul.

Boston's Thomas Thacher used this technique in *A Sermon Preached at . . . the Internment of Eight Seamen* (1795). Eleven men died and three victims were never recovered, but "due to the remarkable interposition of divine Providence," one survived. Thacher compared the lone survivor to Job from the Bible: "And, behold, There came a great wind—the young men are dead—and I only am escaped alone to tell thee." Thacher used this event to warn parishioners, "You may die tomorrow, this day, this moment . . . these men's lives were ripped in the bud . . . consigned to the silent grave." According to Thacher, only through God's tender mercies was this one sailor spared and given a chance to repent.[49]

Although few individuals actually witnessed this funeral, by publishing this sermon Thacher reached a much wider audience and used the narrative's sympathy and symbolism to keep believers along a proper Christian path. Such stories asserted that God may be gentle, but he can also take away life and love at any time. The use of such strong words probably convinced (or scared) many listeners and gave ministers a strong tool to supplement sermons.

This religious purpose was important as print brought the word of God to many. Puritans believed that reading could serve as the means through which God brought salvation to sinners.[50] Literacy and access to the Bible were thus critical, and in response, printers and booksellers often created cheap versions of sermons and religious texts that a wider audience could afford.[51] This trend continued in the nineteenth century, when religious literature flourished and evangelical religion promoted the publication of numerous shipwreck narratives. As with Puritan texts, nineteenth-century evangelicals held strongly to God's presence during shipwrecks. Such intervention provided proof of God's existence for the readers.[52]

Sensationalism coexisted with religious themes and expanded in response to eighteenth-century sentimentalism. At that time narratives began to detail acts of cannibalism and to stress the horror of shipwreck.[53] However, this detail was not gratuitous but helped individuals come to terms with the terror of the events and allowed survivors to "triumph over the forbidden."[54] Sensational accounts of affliction and acts of depravity added to the stories' excitement. Death, despair, and cannibalism increased tension within the narratives.[55]

One example of an individual who did not survive was Nathaniel Gardner, who went mad while struggling to keep a vessel afloat off Nantucket in 1726. William Walling, the only survivor, related Gardner's decline as he raved about various spirits and how the devil tried to take him away. These visions eventually drove Gardner to attempt suicide. Walling warned Gardner: "That if he did kill himself, he would expect nothing but damnation and eternal Misery for his poor Soul, as soon as it Departed from his Body. Why, said he [Gardner] the Devil told me that he would carry me away alive, if I did not kill my self. Then said I, the Devil's ends in persuading you to Self-Murder are, that he might have Power over your Soul." Gardner then asked Walling to hang him so as to avoid the eternal stigma of suicide, but Walling refused. In his madness Gardner became unresponsive and began to drink saltwater, which brought on a fever and flux; he did not live but a day after rescue.[56] Walling, who remained calm and in control of his faculties and put his trust in God, persevered. Gardner let despair overcome his senses and was buried at sea.

Sympathy increased the emotional level in the narratives and drew readers further into the tale. Henry Holden used this tool in his 1836 account. After providing a quick background, he lingered on the moving details of his childhood: "But, in early life, and in the midst of our enjoyments, we were called upon to experience a loss which nothing on earth can supply. My father, after a painful sickness of long continuance, died, and left us with no other earthly protector than our affectionate mother; . . . . we were at that tender age thrown upon the world, and compelled to provide for ourselves as Providence might best enable us."[57] Knowledge of a person's background helped readers become invested in the narrative and perhaps sympathize with shipwrecked victims.

Ann Saunders, shipwrecked in 1826, used this method for her narrative. She too lost her father, and "by this melancholy and unexpected event, my poor mother was left a widow with five helpless children, and without the means of contributing but a scanty pittance to their support."[58] From the beginning her story set a framework of pity and sympathy with which readers might easily identify. Joseph Bailey, master of the *Alida and Catherine* (1750), tugged at the proverbial heart strings with his narrative for a Christian audience: "Its not with a View or design to move any One's Pity or Compassion toward the Unfortunate and Distress'd; neither is it out vain Ostentation that my Name may be recorded, that moves me to write the following Narrative; but it is, as I conceive, my bounden duty toward the Supreme Being, to declare his wonderful Acts of Providence, and tender Mercies towards the most undeserving of Mankind; . . . . I therefore call upon all Christians."[59] Bailey added religion to reveal God's wonders, reasserting his audience's presumed belief in a supreme being. Affliction of all types permeated the narratives, and the victims' perseverance helped make the accounts popular and uplifting.

Shipwreck narratives, despite the tremendous number of deaths, actually imparted a positive outlook that focused on the ability of survivors to adapt and remain in control. For example, Captain Deane described Miles Whitworth, a passenger on board the *Nottingham Galley* (1711), as "a young gentleman, his mother's darling Son, delicately educated amidst so great an affluence as to despise common Food." Under the stress of shipwreck, however, this most genteel man was the first to approach the captain regarding "converting the human Carcass into the matter of their nourishment."[60] In the horrible and terrifying conditions of shipwreck Whitworth sank into the depths of depravity. And yet he endured. Readers might contemplate how they too would react in such a situation. Would they be able to eat rats and pieces of rotten meat? Would they kill another human so that others might survive? Much like murder narratives, shipwreck stories created horror "over the shocking violation of the new sentimental domesticity."[61]

On another level, such detail added to the stories' appeal. A gothic setting, such as "tall cliffs, vast seas, dire chasms, and noble deeds," challenged a reader and filled him "with pity and fear in order to engage his 'sympathy'; to involve him emotionally in the wreck."[62] Shipwreck often occurred near land where large cliffs prevented escape. For example, in 1786 the crew and passengers of the *Halsewell* found themselves in such a situation when the ship struck the rocks on the island of Purbeck, near St. Alban's head: "On this part of the shore the cliff is of immense height, and rises almost perpendicularly. . . . The sides of the cave are so nearly upright as to be extremely difficult of access, and the bottom of it is strewed with sharp and uneven rocks which appear to have been rent from above by some convulsion of nature." The ship beat against the entrance to the large cavern, "but, at the time the ship struck it was too dark to discover the extent of their danger, and the extreme horror of their situation."[63] This narrative had everything: high cliffs, deep caverns, and only a few men who lived to tell the horror of it all.

Terror often threatened to drive people to the edge of madness, and although chaos was a real possibility, the narratives rarely indicated that this happened. For example, after floating helplessly for days, the starving men of the *Peggy* (1766) finally resorted to cannibalism. Rather than randomly dispatching individuals or fighting to see who survived, the crew unanimously decided to choose lots. Even when forced to eat human flesh, individuals acted rationally, within the constraints of the situation. Although the act of cannibalism forced individuals to overcome their instincts, social and cultural standards persisted, though they did not remain solid.

Though the men of the *Peggy* went through the process of choosing lots and selecting a victim, they crossed the line briefly when it came to processing their meal. According to the captain's narrative, "They dragged him [the victim] into the steerage, where, in less than two minutes, they shot him through the head.—they suffered him to lye but a very little time before they ripped him open, intending to fry his entrails for supper, there being a large fire made ready for the purpose; —but one of the foremast-men, being ravenously impatient for food, tore the liver from the body, and devoured it raw."[64] Some people remained in control up to a limit but could take no more. The narratives presented a series of tests that each individual had the potential to fail, thus adding to the story's appeal, as readers must have read with anticipation to find out who survived.[65]

The eighteenth-century man of "enlightened understanding" became the nineteenth-century "romantic man of reason."[66] In reaction to eighteenth-century rationalism, transcendentalism and romanticism brought a renewed emphasis on inner abilities and on the self.[67] Nineteenth-century romance literature warned of the "anti-social character of nature" and its potential sources for disorder.[68] Demonstrating both aspects in a letter to her sister, Sarah Allen recorded her fears of dying while shipwrecked off the coast of Florida in 1816: "And continued the cruel sport of the waves and wind, in a state between life and death, sighing over our misfortunes, certain of our destruction, and yet making indefatigable efforts to extricate ourselves from the perils that surrounded us."[69] In an emotional plea Allen balanced a fear of chaos with human ability as a means to salvation.

With an emphasis on respect for others and bodily restraint, shipwreck narratives served as conduct manuals and a means to instruct individuals. At the heart of late eighteenth- and early nineteenth-century genteel culture were aspects of delicacy, sensibility, taste, and an aversion to coarse behavior.[70] The horror of shipwreck challenged this sensibility. Nathanael Peirce, floating helplessly at sea aboard the *Portsmouth* (1756), had reached the end of his endurance: "In this great Distress, the Master not standing upon Niceties, borrow'd one of the Men's shoes, urin'd into it, and drank it off."[71] In another attempt to elicit sympathy Peirce provided a detailed description of how his body decayed while stranded at sea: "My eyes weak and dazzling, my Limbs hardly enabled me to get on my feet; at the same time, I had bad sores on my ankles, knees, hips, elbows and shoulders and joints of my fingers."[72] In his introduction, Capt. David Harrison of the *Peggy* (1766) warned readers that "the solemnity of this sentiment will not, I hope, terrify the reader of elegance from the perusal of the following pages. — Those who read for mere amusement, will probably find something to entertain them, unless they are too refined to put up in real distress with those circumstances which would possibly yield them most satisfaction in a work of mere imagination."[73] In a time of delicacy and refinement, narratives became more explicit and gruesome, perhaps compensating for the excitement no longer present in the more settled areas where the tales were published.[74]

Sentimentalists sought "to cultivate the reader's finer feelings by appealing to his moral sense and engaging his sympathy."[75] A poem concerning the shipwreck experience of Joshua Winslow (1788) summed up this desire:

> Now let the hardest heart of stone,
> make but our case to be their own
> And view us in this sad surprise
> You'd hear them to lament and cry;
> Twould fill them with ten thousand fears;
> the harden'd hearts would melt with tears.[76]

Authors hoped to elicit sympathy and provide stories that affected even the most stoic readers. Shipwreck narratives presented prime opportunities for survivors to tell their tales of woe. In a supposed fictional shipwreck account, Mrs. Eliza Bradley stated that her story presented an "account of sufferings almost beyond human endurance."[77] Such sentiments were often the seamen's only eulogies.

Shipwreck tales created suspense and reflected the precariousness of human existence. Each ship and its fate stood for a community of believers; "to be cast from the ship is to be cast from the community of belief, to be temporarily excommunicated."[78] Through a combination of divine intervention and human agency, individuals might be saved and brought back to the community. Although shipwrecks removed individuals from comfort and safety, isolating them from loved ones, the stories had a positive message: that those who were virtuous and remained true to societal norms would survive.

This theme went back to the early Puritans, as seen with Anthony Thacher (1635) when his family and his cousin's family sailed for Marblehead and were lost in a hurricane off the New England coast. A few days after the event, Thacher wrote a letter in which he extolled his never-ending trust in God. During the storm his family huddled together in the ship's hold, prayed for deliverance, and waited to die while united as one under God. Only Thacher and his wife survived. Although he lost the rest of his family, Thacher never questioned his faith in God (at least in print); instead he asked God to direct his new life, one that God had seen fit to give him.[79] Rather than wallow in self-pity, Thacher turned to God, believing that the shipwreck was part of a greater design. In this narrative the horror and strife of shipwreck challenged the readers' moral complacency. By following Thacher's lead, readers acknowledged their ever-threatened souls.[80] The strong belief and sincerity presented in shipwreck narratives created models to sustain the readers' convictions and furthered proper Protestant morality.

The Puritans were not the only colonists concerned with religious texts. In fact a relatively high percentage of people in the non–New England colonies could read, though many never read with the intensity of the Puritans.[81] Given their scattered population and a continued identification with England, the colonies to the south did not develop as strong a literary tradition as that in New England. And yet non-Puritan groups such as Anglicans and Quakers did print religious tracts, books, and pamphlets. They too relied on the printed word to reach remote populations unable to attend church or hear sermons.[82] Jonathan Dickinson, a Philadelphia Quaker, titled his 1699 narrative "GOD'S PROTECTING PROVIDENCE MAN'S SUREST HELP AND DEFENCE *in the Times of the Greatest Difficulty and Most Imminent Danger; Evidenced in the Remarkable Deliverance of Divers Persons, from the Devouring Waves of the Sea, amongst Which They Suffered Shipwrack.*"[83] The title alone was enough to challenge readers' moral apathy. Similar to Puritan narratives, his story told of people in crisis who moved from sin to grace, from bondage to salvation.[84]

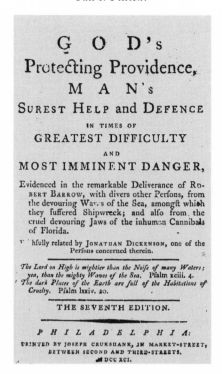

G O D's
Protecting Providence,
M A N's
SUREST HELP and DEFENCE
IN TIMES OF
GREATEST DIFFICULTY
AND
MOST IMMINENT DANGER,

Evidenced in the remarkable Deliverance of ROBERT BARROW, with divers other Perfons, from the devouring Waves of the Sea, amongft which they fuffered Shipwreck; and alfo from the cruel devouring Jaws of the inhuman Cannibals of Florida.

˙ ˙ hfully related by JONATHAN DICKENSON, one of the Perfons concerned therein.

The Lord on High is mightier than the Noife of many Waters; yea, than the mighty Waves of the Sea. Pfalm xciii. 4.
The dark Places of the Earth are full of the Habitations of Cruelty. Pfalm lxxiv. 20.

THE SEVENTH EDITION.

P H I L A D E L P H I A:
PRINTED BY JOSEPH CRUKSHANK, IN MARKET-STREET, BETWEEN SECOND AND THIRD-STREETS.
M DCC XCI.

Title page, *Jonathan Dickenson, God's Protecting Providence.*
Early American Imprints, series 1, no. 46155.

By the eighteenth century cheap literature appealed to a broad audience, especially as leisure became more important. Attitudes toward leisure shifted as society changed from an agrarian base that followed the cycle of seasons to a more urban one in which those with wealth frequently had time on their hands.[85] Benjamin Stout's narrative regarding the loss of the *Hercules* off the coast of Caffraria (1796) emphasized that the story "involves so much interest, as cannot fail to prove extremely entertaining."[86] Essays, poetry, and tales of sensational events appeared in increasing numbers throughout the eighteenth century and into the nineteenth.[87] An account of the shipwreck of the *Bowaniong*, published in London (1812), made sentimentalism central to the story's appeal. The narrative began with a husband dying aboard ship and leaving instructions to a friend to take care of the woman he had secretly married before sailing. The surviving friend related that "the correspondent concludes with the account of the unfortunate fair, whose lover perished with the *Bowaniong;* a summary of which cannot be unacceptable, particularly to the female part of our readers."[88] Aimed at younger audiences, the melodramatic love story identified with, and fed into, a desire for romance and the mourning of unrequited love.

Women in sentimental literature figured more prominently than they had earlier.[89] For example, the only narratives written by women used in this study all appeared in the nineteenth century. Within their narratives each author demonstrated the refinement of the Anglo-American woman and her high degree of piety and virtuousness. At this time reform literature also became popular. Women in nineteenth-century shipwreck narratives often focused on the moral reformation of others, and the sentimental act increased the ability of readers to sympathize with women in the various stories.[90]

The printed narratives helped promote a sense of identity not only for women but also for American society as a whole. They did this primarily through the creation of an "other." Individuals who read these stories discerned what it meant to be English, and later American, especially in narratives in which survivors encountered native populations.[91] The international nature of the maritime world made it easy for authors to point out the failings of others while commending the actions of people like themselves. For example, the ship *Hercules* (1796) carried Americans, Danes, Swedes, Dutch, Portuguese, and Lascars.[92] When disaster struck, the captain recognized that the multicultural and multiethnic crew "require from their commander particular attention. It may happen that by humoring their religious prejudices at a particular moment, an essential service may be obtained." The captain allowed one of the Lascars to make an offering to "his God" by lashing a handkerchief full of rice and "all the rupees I am worth" to the mizen-top mast. Once the "child of prejudice" completed his duty, the remaining Lascars "seemed transported with joy, embraced their virtuous companion, and then labored at the pumps with as much alacrity and perseverance as if they had encountered, before, neither apprehension nor fatigue."[93] The captain's ability to humor others' beliefs allowed the entire ship to survive. In this way the narrative set apart Christians from heathens and situated the Lascars in an inferior position that also demonstrated the efficacy of the captain's tolerance.

Narratives can be taken as a gauge to determine a nation's and citizens' concerns and values; they "reflected the dominant religious and commercial imperatives that are necessary for nation building."[94] In early America national identity was often either linked to or defined in opposition to Britain.

The new nation sought cultural independence and yet depended heavily on England for print culture and trade. Either way, America looked east for identity.

Narratives and tales of wonder added to this connection as popular accounts in England often appeared in the colonies and vice versa.[95] For example, Jonathan Dickinson first published his narrative in Philadelphia in 1699. Within a year T. Swole printed a London edition.[96] In 1817 the first known accounts of the *Commerce* became available in both New York and London, and a year later the earliest stories of the *Oswego*'s wreck appeared in both cities.[97] Most early British narratives used in this study were reprinted several times, and most eventually found their way to American printers. Usually the narratives crossed the Atlantic in the form of collections, such as Archibald Duncan's London edition of *The Mariner's Chronicle* (1804), which consisted of six volumes.[98] American printers reused the stories for single publications as well as for collected volumes. By the nineteenth century, printers incorporated older narratives with newer, American accounts to create their own anthologies. In the 1830s several American collections were printed in Boston and New York as well as in Hartford, New Haven, and Salem.

However, the transfer of culture did not mean that England and America developed exactly alike.[99] The American press published both local and foreign news, often including accounts of shipwrecks. This flow of information provided a means for colonists to learn about one another as well as about events beyond their backyards. Their developing American identity acquired a sense of permanence as individuals took notice of their unique surroundings. While maintaining a transatlantic continuum, a national identity was centered on an ethnically American, Protestant, middling class.[100]

While early narratives were Anglo-American, over time these accounts shifted to create something more distinctly American. Part of this transition was due to the growth and stability of American society. Increased printing capabilities and literacy allowed publishers in America to produce a larger quantity of printed material that helped define an expanding American identity.

The narratives did more than suggest a national identity; they also defined different roles for men and women. The early republic encouraged men to read newspapers and history, while women were expected to read fiction and devotional literature. Believing that the printed word influenced the reader, society deemed women too weak to read anything "substantial." Women could read some history, but only that couched in confessional tracts, conversion stories, and various narratives that displayed rational, virtuous women.[101] Thus when shipwreck narratives portrayed women as moral beings—virtuous, pious, and loyal at the moments of crisis—they reinforced the republican ideal of woman as supportive but passive.[102]

Female readers might place themselves in the narratives, identifying with those struggling to overcome catastrophe. In seeing themselves as shipwrecked, women readers discovered their inherent moral superiority and honesty, becoming socially acceptable yet remaining dependent female citizens.[103] In the narrative of the wreck of the *Kent* (1827), the captain wrote that "the dignified deportment of two young ladies in particular, formed a specimen of natural strength of mind, finely modified by Christian feeling, that failed not to attract the notice and admiration of every one who had an opportunity of witnessing it." When told of the impending wreck, they sank to their knees, clasped their hands, and said, "Even so come, Lord Jesus," and read a portion of the Scriptures to those around them.[104] The values of compassion, sympathy, pity, and benevolence were important middle-class ideals needed to demonstrate the superiority of the narratives' heroes and heroines.[105]

Reflecting ideologies such as enlightenment, sentimentalism, and romanticism, the narratives allowed audiences to come to terms with potentially chaotic and life-threatening events. Whether they demonstrated God's will or human error, shipwrecks provided opportunities for individuals to overcome tragedy and to return to the arms of a supportive and sympathetic public. They promoted a sense of social order where proper women were protected by manly gentlemen. The printed stories stressed a conservative portrayal of society in which each person did not overstep understood boundaries. Despite the subject's chaotic nature, the authors of shipwreck accounts spun positive endings in which those who behaved as good role models survived.

As literature, shipwreck narratives provided hope while embodying adventure and suspense. Readers vicariously traveled to exotic places and endured all forms of tragedy; Joseph Bailey's ship wrecked on a voyage from New York to Antigua, while the crew of the *Oswego* found themselves stranded off the South Barbary coast.[106] In these accounts the sea represented a frontier filled with danger. Treacherous waters, hidden reefs, and vicious sea life meant that many sailors never returned. For example, in 1820 the whale ship *Essex*'s crew had the tables turned when a whale stove in the side of their ship, forcing survivors to endure extreme hardships in three small open boats. Much like today's horror movies or supermarket tabloids, shipwreck narratives created entertaining escapes from reality, diversions from an every-day existence that appealed to a receptive audience.

Geographically the accounts pointed to hazardous areas of travel, cautioning those interested in future endeavors. The large number of shipwrecks demonstrated the importance of accurate charts and equipment and the necessity of learning proper navigational skills. Logbooks, journals, and especially shipwreck narratives provided navigational, commercial, and other data that sailors used for a variety of ends. Knowing the importance of good data, Joseph Bailey included precise coordinates that located the places of shipwreck and rescue.[107] The narratives passed on important information that perhaps helped subsequent sailors avoid falling victim to rocks, reefs, and dangerous waters.

Through these writings sailors and others placed extraordinary events in a recognizable format and, most important, in one readily available to a wide audience.[108] Street literature produced for the masses was cheap, accessible, and entertaining, and it provided both amusing and practical instruction. The narratives commended virtue, self-sacrifice, and bravery on board vessels, while greed and cowardice produced condemnation. Cowardice or naive behavior could result in death, not only for the individual but also for the entire crew and any passengers. Because of these accounts' entertainment value, it is easy to forget that they were grounded in fact. Although published as a form of literature, the various stories must be recognized basically as nonfiction. Authors attempted to reassure readers that "in these Sheets the reader is presented, not with the fictitious picture of imagination, but the bold hand of unsullied truth here records."[109] Fact and fiction combined to create stories that relied on both elements to sell.

Over time the published shipwreck narratives helped foster a sense of community and brought diverse colonies and states into a shared identity.[110] Local and international topics tied together isolated communities, strengthening bonds on both sides of the Atlantic. Increased printing capabilities accompanied expanding commercialism to create a nation that not only read but also defined itself through reading. Literature was a conduit for teaching values to both male and female readers.[111] The popularity of shipwreck narratives reflected what Americans considered important values and provided means of disseminating them.

By the nineteenth century, reading material incorporated the republican ideal of an informed and learned public.[112] Reform movements and reactions to the Industrial Revolution added a new element to narratives that promoted religiosity and social stability and that warned against the hypocrisy of commercial life.[113] Access to publishing defined a burgeoning middle class who read all sorts of publications, from novels to edifying moral tracts. The popularity of street literature, including shipwreck narratives, in the eighteenth and nineteenth centuries allowed a broad audience access to a wider range of printed material.[114] Through such literature the middle and upper classes not only confirmed but also to some extent learned appropriate behavior and social value as Americans.[115]

The Legalities of
Loss, Wreck, and Ruin

Article III: If any vessel, through misfortune, happens to be cast away, in whatsoever place it be, the mariners shall be obliged to use their best endeavors for saving as much of the ship and lading as possibly they can. And in case they save enough to enable the master to do this, he may lawfully pledge to some honest persons such part thereof as may be sufficient for that occasion. But if they have not endeavored to save as aforesaid, then the master shall not be bound to provide for them in any thing, but ought to keep them in safe custody, until he knows the pleasure of the owners, in which he may act as becomes a prudent master.[1]

Shipwreck was a fact of life for all maritime cultures. Although these catastrophic events often happened beyond the sight of land, the consequences of such failures had far-ranging repercussions. Vessels not only carried precious cargoes of human life but also represented financial investments for owners, underwriters, and insurance companies. Businesses, families, and communities relied on successful voyages to deliver needed goods, pay sailors' wages, and maintain commercial well-being.

When a voyage ended in failure, someone had to pay for the lost or damaged cargo, the cost of repairs, and even the surviving crew members' wages. Upon the loss of a vessel, interested courts and insurers asked questions concerning the vessel's seaworthiness, the performance of the master and crew, and whether shipwreck came from human negligence or as an act of God. Apart from the loss of human life, disputes regarding fault, payments, contract, and jurisdiction often fell to the legal system.

A quick perusal of any early modern newspaper reveals that shipwreck was a common event. Sources such as the *Providence Gazette* and the *Boston Gazette* recorded fifteen to twenty wrecks each year during the mid-eighteenth century. Although many entries consisted of only one or two lines each, several provided detailed information about the wrecks and rescues of any survivors. The Gloucester Archives Committee of Gloucester, Massachusetts, compiled a list of shipwrecks from various archival and printed sources for the port of Gloucester. They found that approximately 150 shipwrecks occurred between 1700 and 1799.[2] An examination of insurance records from Massachusetts suggests that 4 to 5 percent of vessels were castaway or lost at sea.[3] Peter Throckmorton, considered a pioneer in underwater archaeology, estimated that until the last century approximately 5 percent of all cargoes were lost.[4] Unfortunately no comprehensive list of early North American shipwrecks exists. But the evidence does suggest that shipwreck happened on a regular basis and that coastal populations were well aware of the risks.

In response to the number of shipwrecks, a body of maritime law developed in the colonial and early republic eras.[5] Captains and crews understood the law and how to use it to meet their needs. Shipwreck narratives and other published material revealed mariners' understanding of the legal system and how those who experienced shipwreck formulated their personal narratives to correspond to legal and economic constraints. Authors went to great lengths to show that shipwrecks were not their fault and that captains and crews did all they could to save the cargoes and ships. Admiralty law and marine insurance reflected the importance that society placed on maritime ventures. The various legal requirements, such as shipwreck narratives, helped transform shipwreck into an ordered event by situating it within a structured legal framework.

Admiralty Law

Some of the earliest known examples of maritime law come from mid-fifth-century B.C.E. Athens, where judges ruled on problems concerning vessels and crews. By the next century commercial maritime tribunals had developed with specialized maritime law.[6] In the early modern world trade expanded, and as ships explored the farthest known regions of the globe, international laws were developed to regulate maritime affairs. England established the Court of High Admiralty in the fourteenth century, primarily to deal with piracy and maritime disputes. Admiralty courts diverged from common-law courts because they "drew upon the ancient authorities and on current

international practice, as well as on the royal decrees and parliamentary statutes, whereas the other courts relied more on the background of common
law."[7] This distinction remains one of the defining differences between admiralty courts and common-law courts.

Admiralty law in the American colonies developed gradually as increased trade and shipping necessitated the regulation of maritime disputes.
In the seventeenth century, without vice-admiralty courts, governors often sat as "admirals" and had the authority to set up special courts when
needed. In many instances, however, they simply tried cases in common-law
courts.[8] Due to the decentralized nature of the colonies, maritime law developed haphazardly, in reaction to localized needs. Frequent warfare and
other factors prevented England from implementing consistent control and
allowed vice-admiralty authority in America to run virtually unregulated.[9]

By 1696 colonial expansion led England to create regular vice-admiralty
courts in the North American colonies. According to Charles Andrews, "the
machinery of enforcement had been almost entirely in the hands of the
colonists themselves. It was decentralized and ineffective, and the Admiralty, with naval administration disorganized and ships scarce, was in poor
condition."[10] In theory the statute of 1696 standardized and reorganized
the admiralty system to keep revenue in the king's hands and illicit trade
under control. However, through the eighteenth century each colony set up
its own vice-admiralty courts.[11]

In the seventeenth and eighteenth centuries Parliament passed several
navigation acts to regulate trade further. To enforce the Navigation Acts,
the jurisdiction of the vice-admiralty courts expanded to allow greater control over colonial plantations. By the mid-eighteenth century eleven continental courts managed American admiralty law.[12] After the French and
Indian War, England reevaluated the North American colonies in terms of
revenue and compliance to the navigation acts. In response to growing illegal trade, in 1764 the Admiralty created a new colonial tribunal, headquar-
tered in Halifax, Nova Scotia, to handle any colonial case, instead of offenses
within a prescribed district. These courts did not last long because of the
American Revolution and throughout the war operated only in British-held
areas.[13]

Almost immediately after gaining independence, the new states created
their own vice-admiralty courts to deal with the issue of British prizes. Under the Judiciary Act of 1789, the Constitution established federal jurisdiction over admiralty or maritime concerns, removing power from the states.[14]
As the United States developed, the demands of expanding trade and shipping dovetailed with the extant capabilities of the vice-admiralty courts, ne-
gating any real need for altering the courts in the nineteenth century.

In the overall volume of vice-admiralty litigation, shipwrecks played a minor role, especially in comparison to other areas such as revenue evasion and prize money. Yet shipwrecks did occur, and both vice-admiralty and common-law courts tried such cases. Procedure in the North American vice-admiralty courts, as well as in the common-law courts, continually evolved as judges borrowed what they thought most relevant from various English systems.[15] Common law allowed each state to develop disparate principles and procedures, depending on different judges. Most day-to-day lawmaking took place at the state level, and judges took into consideration the laws of the state in which each dispute arose. Even when the admiralty courts came under federal control, these judges continued to regulate disputes.[16]

Merchants and seamen preferred admiralty courts to common-law courts, though they were often more expensive. Admiralty courts offered a less complex and faster means of judging cases. Most important, a person could file either in rem (against a vessel or its cargo) or in personam (against a person) to obtain a sympathetic verdict.[17] For example, sailors often banded together to complain about wages or abuse against the boat, in rem, rather than against an individual to obtain favorable results.[18]

Although admiralty courts dealt primarily with cases concerning prize and revenue, the third area, broadly defined as maritime affairs, maritime causes, or local problems, is the most pertinent to this research.[19] This group included salvage, collision, seamen's wages, torts, and fishing rights, to name but a few. Such disputes could be tried in common-law courts, but many sailors, merchants, and shipowners often opted to bring their suits to the vice-admiralty courts.

Shipwrecks often appeared in cases concerning seamen's wages. To sue, a person had to be employed in "the business of navigation and must be necessary, or at least conducive to the preservation of the vessel." Because a master's wages derived from a contract with the owner, a master's wages went before the common-law courts. A mariner's wages, concerning labor performed at sea, went to the vice-admiralty courts.[20] In fact, a sailor's claim took precedence over all others, including cargo and hull damage. For example, while waiting for repairs, the master of the *Margaret* (1795) "disposed of what old cordage was on board to fray the seamen's wages."[21] Even if the voyage ended in total loss, a sailor's wages could legally be "paid out of the fragments of the wreck, if enough is saved to pay them."[22] When shipwreck occurred, the legal system helped mitigate the catastrophe by allowing survivors or families of victims to gain some monetary compensation.

Owners could deny a sailor his wages if during shipwreck a crew member deserted the ship prematurely. According to Richard Peters, "Seamen are entitled, or not, to their wages, in case of wreck, according to the merit of their services in that distressing exigency. Those who do not assist, do not receive their wages."[23] In Richard Henry Dana's 1851 publication *The Seaman's Friend,* the author stated that "if a vessel meets with a disaster, it is the duty of the crew to remain by her so long as they can do it with safety, and to exert themselves to the utmost of their ability to save as much as possible of the vessel and cargo." Dana added, "If they abandon the vessel unnecessarily, they forfeited their wages; and if their leaving was necessary and justifiable, yet they lose their wages up to the last part of delivery and for half the time the vessel was lying there."[24]

Crews by law had to assist with salvage efforts, unless the ships were cast up onshore and the masters or owners hired others to complete the salvages, at which point the owners considered the voyages over and the crews exempt from helping. Also sailors earned their wages only up to the last port before shipwreck. Although a sailor's representatives could demand wages after death, they could sue only up to the last completed leg of the contracted voyage. To complicate matters further, if a sailor died of sickness, his representatives might claim that the sailor would have finished the voyage except for the illness and that therefore the representatives should obtain wages for the entire voyage.[25]

Shipwreck also entered the vice-admiralty courts in cases of salvage, collision at sea, and contract, with salvage and contract more common. Although collision rarely occurred, it often came into the courts under the heading of salvage. Maritime law understood collision "as a dereliction of bounden duty, entitling the sufferer to reparation in damages." In admiralty courts, loss due to collision typically required the "party with the lesser damage paid to the other one-half of the difference between their losses," but not always.[26]

In 1672 the fishing shallop *Hopewell* was at anchor when a larger vessel appeared out of nowhere and "ran them underwater." The shallop was lost, along with two lives and all of its gear. The *True Love,* the vessel that hit the *Hopewell,* picked up the survivors. This case is interesting for two reasons: it came before the Suffolk County, Massachusetts, court (though considered a maritime case); and Chantrell, master of the *True Love,* appealed to the next court of assistants, the upper house of the Massachusetts legislature. Chantrell brought suit against Wood, master of the *Hopewell,* because Chantrell did not think the collision was his fault.

In his testimony Chantrell claimed that his crew could neither see nor hear the shallop until it was too late. He appealed the case and refused to pay damages, "being informed yet tis a rule in admiralty that where losse happeneth not absolutely done by one particular person every individual man payeth his proportional part. . . . the law sayeth that Damage as this done shall be left to indifferent men appointed by the judges, but this was not done." Chantrell argued instead that the accident occurred "through the neglect of the defendant in not using what means he might, having both fyre and candle" to give warning, "they seeing me by the bygnesse of my vessel before I could see them." He also argued that "because the jury giveth the full vallew of the Shallop and goods to the defendant who sues neither as master nor owner of said Shallop so that John-a-stiles (fictitious names of legal parties) might as legally sue Wood, according to the attachment." Wood replied that he sued Chantrell, the master, because he had no one else to sue. Also according to the law, the offending person "shall pay ye damage which is ye Master, ye law doth not say ye Master and Company." Furthermore several fishermen, passengers, and witnesses on land supported Wood's allegation that Chantrell was inebriated. Since on that night of the collision it was brightly lit, reasoned Chantrell, "they minded more a bowle of punch than harkening to ye cry of persons y^t lost there lives." The court denied Chantrell's appeal and ruled for the defendant.[27]

In addition to cases of collision, shipwreck entered admiralty courts through cases of salvage. The technical definition of "salvage" "is the rescue of property from a maritime peril." To apply, it must be effective (the vessel or cargo brought safely into port) and the "danger must be real and imminent." As with most other maritime-related cases, salvage could go before common-law or admiralty courts. Any person who attempted to preserve goods from a ship in distress could, by common law, receive due compensation for his efforts. If the two parties could not come to an agreeable conclusion, then a jury decided the amount. However, according to Francis Clarke's 1838 *American Ship-Master's Guide*, if "the salvage is performed at sea, the Court of admiralty has jurisdiction over the subject, and will fix the sum to be paid."[28] Defendants, plaintiffs, crews, and owners all understood that the law protected their rights and investments, whether shipwreck came about as an act of God or through human negligence. Each aspect of salvage and shipwreck entered the courts through standardized channels and helped bring the chaotic environment of shipwreck under control.

Salvage could occur without an owner's permission if the captain or owner abandoned the wreck; however, if the master remained with the ship, he could refuse rescue, or if he chose salvage, he had the authority to direct its process.[29] Sailors of the ship in danger were already under a legal obligation to save the ship and therefore could not claim salvage. Additionally the courts denied passengers salvage, "it being the duty, as well as the interest, of all persons on board, to contribute their aid on such an occasion."[30] Seamen's behavior during shipwreck affected whether an individual received wages or faced a breach of contract. Following this, the narratives inserted specific details concerning the crews' behavior to demonstrate their cooperation, or lack thereof.

Salvage had standardized rates and rewards, with one-half of the proceeds typically allowed to salvors, but this varied according to factors such as exertion and danger. In *Elias Burger v. Sundry Articles from an Unnamed Brigantine Ashore on Rockaway Bar* (1770, Province of New York), the court awarded a salvage of 50 percent on net value. Elias Burger, master of the *Mary,* saw the vessel stranded on Rockaway Bar and found the wreck abandoned. He spent several days, with the assistance of hired individuals, in removing almost everything above decks. Burger and the owner of the *Mary* filed the libel. The judge's verdict was "that the Libellant saved the several articles mentioned in this Libell with very great Risque and fatigue, and that if it had not been for his Interposition tis more than probable that most part if not all of what was saved from the wreck of the said Brigantine would have entirely perished."[31] For his efforts Elias Burger received half of the proceeds from the sale of the salvaged articles. Under different circumstances Burger might have received a higher or lower percentage, according to effort and risk during salvage.

An interesting argument concerning abandonment comes out in this case. Abandonment did not technically constitute a derelict ship. Rather there had to be no hope of recovery or of the master returning to the vessel.[32] If the master returned or the vessel or cargo was recovered, then the "rescuers" did not receive salvage. For example, in the above case, if the owner had returned during Burger's salvage of the brigantine, Burger would not have received anything for his efforts, or the court might have provided him with a reduced amount for salvage up to that time.

The process of bringing a ship to court was just as complicated as the court system itself. In several colonies the first step required the filing of a libel, usually drawn by an advocate who asked for action or laid out the complaint. The libel was not official until endorsed by the judge. "A warrant to the register authorized the marshal to cite as witnesses those persons who had an interest in the case. In the same way monitions (summons) were served on the claimants in cases of prize and illegal trade, and on defendants in ordinary marine causes."[33] After the libel, courts took custody of the vessel and posted notices on the mast and in several places throughout town. Likewise the courts served monitions on an individual. If he failed to show, the courts posted notices in front of a coffeehouse for a set number of days. The claimant or respondent had several sessions to appear in court. If no claimant appeared, the court judged the ship according to the crew's and ship's papers, and the trial proceeded without him.[34]

Once a trial began, "in all admiralty cases witnesses were examined in private before the judge," although a notary took testimonies for individuals who lived too far away or had to leave for another voyage. The open court then examined this evidence, along with the libel and any other documents.[35] The res (matter) was released if the owner provided a security, or stipulation. Meanwhile in acts of in personam, attachments on property were allowed to prevent a respondent from disappearing. Next came the pleas of advocates, allowing the judge to enter his decree. During the colonial period, the High Court of Admiralty or the King in Council accepted the few appeals that came from the colonies.

One of the admiralty system's benefits was that most trials finished quickly, lasting only one day to several weeks. Regulated fees and costs usually averaged between fifteen and twenty pounds, providing a system that was fast, simple, and relatively inexpensive.[36] As with other aspects of maritime law, costs varied according to labor, level of peril, and value of ship or cargo.[37]

For example, in the *Report of Cases Argued and Determined in the High Court of Admiralty* (1800), in the case of the *Aquila* the High Court of Admiralty tried to determine the rate of salvage. The court condemned the cargo as unclaimed and determined that under the "ancient practice of this Court, as it is submitted, under the true rule of this country, goods found derelict at sea, have been divided by moieties, between the finder and the Crown: this practice is supported by very ancient authority." Laws dating to the fourteenth century stated that the moiety (half) of the thing recovered belonged to the finder but was forfeited if concealed. In the seventeenth century goods were divided between the finder and the Crown. However, by the nineteenth century the goods recovered represented effort and that "an indiscriminate fixt proportion would have in it something of absurdity."[38]

The vice-admiralty courts also acted in an administrative capacity. Once a captain notified the court that a ship had sustained damage, the court (or the governor) authorized a committee to survey the vessel. This survey took into account the level and nature of damages and whether the hull was worth saving, and it sometimes served as evidence for payment on insurance policies.[39] Surveys often supported allegations concerning vessels' seaworthiness and the extent of damages—aspects important for marine insurance claims.

Another form of wreck occurred when a vessel came onshore. *The Shipmaster's Assistant* (1836) provided a detailed example of how this type of shipwreck came to court in various states. Several states employed wreck-masters or specially appointed commissioners to secure salvaged goods, while others, such as Maine and South Carolina, used justices of the peace. Most states held a vessel or cargo for a year (or a year and a day), waiting for the claimants to appear, at which time they sold the salvaged goods. States gave notice in a public format, such as an advertisement in one or more newspapers for a specified number of days. If no one claimed the vessel or goods, the state advertised one more time and then sold the goods at public auction. Salvage came out of proceeds from the auction, with the remainder paid into a public or state treasury.[40]

By the 1830s states also set in motion processes to discourage possible shipwreck (or barratry). According to Blunt's *Shipmaster's Assistant*, in Virginia, for example, "if a person willfully contribute to the destruction of a vessel, or steal from a vessel in distress, [he] shall suffer death." In Georgia a person found plundering a wreck or vessel in distress faced punishment by confinement at hard labor for one to five years, while in Maryland "a person who makes a hole in a vessel, steals a pump or goods from a vessel in distress, or willfully do anything tending to her immediate destruction, he shall suffer death." In addition, if an unauthorized person entered a vessel and hindered or defaced it, that person forfeited fifty dollars, and if he failed to pay, he received thirty-nine lashes.[41]

The laws of New Jersey afforded a very detailed account of legal procedures concerning shipwrecks in that state. Courts of common pleas appointed commissioners, who worked with owners to secure any property. Decisions usually went through arbitration between two freeholders, one chosen by the owner and one selected by the commissioner. If they failed to reach an agreement, they opted for a third person to settle the dispute. A commissioner could not dispose of any cargo with an owner present, whether it was an insurer, a master, or an agent; without an owner present, the commissioner took charge. He had to advertise for four weeks in one or more newspapers, and if the goods totaled more than one hundred dollars, he had to advertise in New York City and in areas around Philadelphia. If no one came forward, the commissioner advertised the sale at public auction for ten to twenty days within the county. Proceeds went to the public treasury, which held them for up to two years, in case an owner appeared and appealed.[42]

Cases concerning salvage, collision, wages, and torts often brought shipwreck into both vice-admiralty and common-law court systems. Whether due to human error or an act of God, financial reparations of shipwreck had to be paid. Ships' protests and other legal documents reveal that mariners understood the law and the necessity of proving innocence in shipwreck. The narratives reflect the importance of the legal system in sorting out what happened and that many survivors went to great lengths to describe what occurred in those final hours. When they were in distress, the law protected mariners and vessels from additional harm. Obviously these laws would not have been necessary if all who plied the sea acted in appropriate and moral ways. But the legal system provided standards of behavior and guides for assistance to sailors and owners in times of need.

Marine Insurance

Through marine contract and insurance, the legalities of shipwreck disputes become clearer. Similar to maritime law, many narratives directly addressed the issue of marine insurance and the need to determine fault. Just as mariners were aware of their legal rights, sailors also understood the necessity of justifying their actions to insurance companies. If crews failed to prove that shipwrecks occurred through bad weather or unavoidable circumstances, insurance companies could withhold compensation to captains and crews. Published narratives reflected this knowledge as authors presented detailed information concerning the wrecking process. Several authors even appended official protests or sworn testimonies to their stories to support their cases.

David Harrison, commander of the *Peggy*, directly addressed the issue of insurance in an appendix to his 1766 narrative: "As I had insured at New York I thought it necessary, for the interests of my owners, to lodge a protest for their indemnity. I had recourse to a Notary Public for that purpose, and have here inserted the papers and attestations which were consequently drawn up, as a proof of the principal circumstances which I have mentioned in the foregoing narrative."[43] Published narratives revealed that authors had knowledge of marine insurance and recognized the necessity of proving their innocence and of placing the blame elsewhere. They also understood how courts worked and the means to negotiate them successfully.

The roots of marine insurance go back approximately two millennia, and there is evidence that owners insured ships as early as the era of the Roman Empire. Although trade and commerce began to flourish in the late Middle Ages, several centuries passed before marine insurance developed in Europe. Eventually, by the sixteenth century, the first steps toward modern marine insurance were taken in England with the creation of the Office of Assurances, which standardized polices and reduced litigation. In 1601 the first English statute relating to marine insurance created a court of arbitration to "hear, examine, order, and decree all and every such cause and causes concerning policies of assurances in a brief and summary course."[44]

By the eighteenth century, expanding trade necessitated a more organized and stable framework for insurance. Insurance companies were formed in response to this need and began to insure specific voyages. Up to that time only loose associations of private individuals (known as underwriters) provided marine insurance. This formalization brought with it a high level of debate regarding corporate versus private underwriters. Until the end of the eighteenth century only two companies were officially allowed to insure marine risks, the London Assurance and the Royal Exchange Assurance. Not until 1824 was the monopoly repealed, allowing the formation of many new companies. In the United States arguments concerning a strong national government versus states' rights along with egalitarian sentiments prevented the creation of companies in the late eighteenth century. Fears concerning corruption and power of large companies continued into the nineteenth century, limiting the power of insurance companies in the United States.[45]

One of the most famous insurance companies is Lloyd's of London, which began as a coffeehouse where those interested in shipping came to meet. By the 1690s it became the main place to discuss the sale of ships, insurance, and other marine affairs. In 1734 Lloyd's published the first "Lloyd's List," devoted to shipping, which printed rates of exchange, notices of departures and arrivals, and prices for goods. These important lists helped underwriters assess risks and determine premiums. Lloyd's split in 1774 when the more serious underwriters acted together to create the New Lloyd's as a company in the Royal Exchange.[46]

Throughout the eighteenth century American insurers continued to rely on English practices, as well as English underwriters, turning to London rather than to individuals in the colonies, although such men were available as early as 1721. The French and Indian War increased the threat of seizure and raised premiums that helped spur the growth of marine insurance in several colonies, creating greater reliance on native underwriters. Marine insurance in America experienced few changes between the Revolution and the last decade of the eighteenth century. Even the Articles of Confederation did little to alter the insurance business in America.[47] By the 1790s increased shipping and commerce spurred the United States to set up independent companies rather than rely on traditional subscriptions by private individuals.[48]

The first true insurance company in the United States was the Insurance Company of North America, founded in Philadelphia in 1794. Problems of seizures, not to mention the threat of piracy, by French and British ships from the end of the eighteenth century to the War of 1812 presented heavy losses for American shipping. Because of the risks, premiums were high; between 1792 and 1802 they averaged 12 percent, demonstrating a tight correlation between insurance and commerce.[49]

Law regarding marine insurance developed slowly. Many insurance policies went through arbitration rather than to the courts, minimizing the need to create a large body of legislation. One of the earliest statutes was the 1601 British Arbitration Act, which established a court of arbitration to handle such cases. Not until 1745 did the Marine Insurance Act pass; the act prohibited speculative insurances and gambling policies (where a person wagered on a loss). Throughout the eighteenth century additional legislation came about, ranging from prohibiting insurance on French property to voiding all blank policies.[50] Law pertaining to marine insurance in the North American colonies paralleled that of Britain through the eighteenth century. After the Revolution the trend to follow English law continued, but popular sentiment stemming from the war allowed divergent developments. American lawyers blended civil law with various European and English influences to create a new form of marine insurance.[51]

At its most basic, marine insurance was a contract between the assured (owners or masters) and the assuree or assurer (underwriters or insurance companies). A contract or insurance policy brought shipwreck under the jurisdiction of maritime law when the assured tried to secure payment for damages or loss. Much like maritime law, marine insurance assisted mariners in shipwreck circumstances. In proving fault, owners and captains minimized their losses and crews found assistance in obtaining wages. The published shipwreck narratives support these uses of insurance when authors attempted to prove that shipwrecks occurred due to circumstances beyond their control.

There were several types of marine insurance policies. Some covered the ship itself (known as a vessel policy), while others insured only the freight or cargo. The typical vessel policy often covered the "body, tackle, apparel, ordnance, munitions, artillery, boat, and other furniture of and in" said vessel, while a cargo policy insured "all kinds of goods and merchandizes, laden or to be laden on board."[52] The contracts varied only slightly, according to the voyage proposed, inflation, and risks involved. Typical policies covered losses by the sea, other vessels, capture, arrests, and detainment by all nations: "And in case of any loss or damage, it shall be lawful for the assureds, their factors, servants, and assigns, to sue, labour, and travel for, in and about the defence, safeguard, and recovery of the said vessel (or goods and merchandizes) . . . without prejudice to this assurance; . . . the assurers, will contribute according to the rate of this sum herein assured."[53] Such policies minimized disputes, and both those insured and insurees were aware of the risks involved.

Many policies ran for specific voyages or set periods of time. Any deviation from an agreed-upon voyage nullified the contract.[54] Deviation became a form of barratry, where courts found the actions of captains or crews as criminal or negligent. According to Steel's *Ship-Master's Assistant,* "If any master, mariner, &c. shall willfully cast away, burn, or destroy, his ship, or procure the same to be done, he shall suffer death as a felon." In setting a ship on fire the guilty person faced execution; damage other than fire resulted in the guilty being "transported to some of his majesty's dominions beyond the seas, for any space of time not exceeding fourteen years nor less than seven years."[55] Deviations from the contract might expose a ship to dangerous waters, extend the length of the voyage, or force a ship to endure storms at sea rather than seeking the protected shelter of port, all of which put the ship at greater risk.

In the New York case of *Jose Ruiz Silva v. Nicholas Low* (1798), Low refused to pay on the policies because he claimed that the vessel deviated from its original voyage. Apparently the *Hull Packet* foundered on its way from Wilmington, North Carolina, to Falmouth, England. A passing ship picked up the survivors and took them to Charleston, South Carolina, where the mate made an official protest. In the mate's protest and in supporting documentation, the assured's agent found evidence that the vessel was on its way to New York when it sank. In August 1798 in New York, the court found in favor of Silva (the assured) for a total loss.[56]

The case went to appeal when the defendant (Low) argued whether a trip to Falmouth by way of New York was different from the voyage insured, and if not, "whether an intention to seek additional seamen in New York would affect the assured's recovery." Two judges agreed that making a trip to New York was not a deviation but rather a logical means to get from North Carolina to England. However, since the *Hull Packet* clearly did not sail with a full crew (hence the reason for detouring to New York), the assured had breached the contract by failing to make the vessel seaworthy for the voyage. The court agreed to grant a new trial based on the issue of seaworthiness rather than deviation. Once again, however, the court found in favor of the plaintiff.[57]

Ultimately if an insurer did not have to pay, then fault lay at a master's feet, whether the issue was deviation, seaworthiness, collision, damage, or total loss. By common law he was responsible for all losses except those resulting from an act of God or a peril of the sea. As related by Clarke's *Ship-Master Guide,* "when a vessel is wrecked, it is the duty of the Master to act as Agent of the best interests of the owner or owners and Insurance Company, and manage the property to the best of his ability."[58] Captains borrowed money on the owners' credit while in foreign ports and hypothecated (essentially pledged) cargoes along the voyages for repairs. Also, "where the voyage is wholly broken up, he may sell the ship and cargo for the benefit of all concerned." But a captain was required to prove that his actions were necessary.[59] Owners and underwriters placed great financial trust in captains' abilities and knew the importance of selecting masters carefully.

As related in *Silva v. Low,* part of the master's duty was to ensure a vessel's seaworthiness. If he failed to do so, no matter what peril the ship encountered, insurance would not cover the damages. The narratives reflect this knowledge, and authors inserted information to settle such questions. For example, in 1766 David Harrison made sure to state that when the *Peggy* left Fyal, "she was tight, staunch, and strong, and had her hatches well and sufficiently secure, her cargo well stowed, and being manned, provided, and properly furnished with provisions, stores, and necessary appurtenances, she thereby became sea-worthy, and in all respects, fitted and complete for such a voyage."[60] Almost fifty years later Judah Paddock added to his 1818 narrative that when he left New York for Cork his ship was "well found in every respect, navigated by fourteen hands, including boys."[61] In general, Harrison and Paddock followed the advice of most sailing guides that a vessel should be "sufficient in all respects for the voyage; well manned, and furnished with sails and all the necessary furniture and that if any loss happens through defects in any of these respects, he must make it good."[62]

In the case of the brig *William and Charles* (1819), the insurers claimed that the vessel was unseaworthy. In a letter to Andrew Dunlap, attorney, they noted that the available evidence suggested "that the vessel failed, and was considered not worth repairing, by wear on the natural decay of her timbers, and not of any injury that had been done by the sea." Given this evidence, the owners should not receive payment from the insurers. However, they went on to state that "if the brig was not seaworthy when she sailed from Salem the underwriters will not be entitled to any part of the premium but if she were seaworthy for the voyage to the Mediterranean and St. Petersburg and yet failed on her voyage home from natural decay (a case hardly supposable) I think the underwriters might then be entitled to the premium till she left St. Petersburg."[63] There was a distinction between "peril of the sea" and daily damage from winds and sea. This difference is important as only through a "peril of the sea" would insurance pay damages.

According to Clarke, "Perils of the sea . . . comprehend all those accidents and misfortunes, to which ships and goods are exposed, at sea, from causes which no human prudence could prevent or control." They had to be extraordinary, above and beyond normal wear and tear of the ocean, and the act of God must be "the immediate cause of loss" to exempt the master.[64] Each contract contained this important peril clause, which typically read as follows: "And respecting the adventures and perils which we, the assurers, are contented to bear, and do take upon us in the voyage, they are of the seas, men of war, fire, enemies, pirates, rovers, thieves, jettizons, letters of mart and countermart, surprizals, takings at sea, arrests, restraints, and detainments of all kings, princes, and people, of what nation condition, or quality soever; barratry of the master and mariners, and of all other such perils, losses, and misfortunes, that have or shall come to the hurt, detriment, or damage of the said vessel, or any part thereof, for which assurers are legally accountable."[65] A master had to prove that a peril in question, whether minor damage or total loss, was unavoidable or beyond reasonable human ability to prevent.

Masters and crews went to great lengths to prove that such shipwrecks were beyond their control. *Every* published narrative provided detailed descriptions of the wind, waves, and how the wrecking occurred. The detailed information justified the crews' actions. For example, in 1715 Capt. Thomas Bilton wrote, "Blowing very hard: The said Pink sprung a Leak, which so increas'd upon her, that this Deponent, and the rest of the said ship's company were oblig'd to quit her, and betake themselves to the boat."[66] David Harrison devoted several pages to describe the weather that ultimately brought about his shipwreck: "to our unspeakable mortification, it came on to blow as hard as ever . . . so that my fore-stay and fore-sheets were not only torn away, but the fore-sail itself rent in pieces; . . . the impetuosity of the storm still continuing, and the seas rolling mountains high, all of us expecting that the vessel would prove leaky, as she strained inconceivably hard."[67] He described storm and shipwreck for another six pages and then went on to relate the horror of starvation and cannibalism. Early in the narrative he set the tone for an unusually strong sea and wind, implying that he and the crew had no hope to overcome the elements.

To determine fault, the courts and insurance companies used a variety of evidence such as ships' logs, protests, and testimonies. Testimonies were originally written interrogatories, though by the late eighteenth century open courts admitted them viva voce.[68] An example of an interrogative in which the defendant was examined on behalf of the plaintiff's request concerns the schooner *Greek,* driven onshore in 1829.[69] At the time of this questioning, the vessel was still onshore. The lists of questions included the following:

1. What is your name, age, residence, occupation or profession?
2. Do you know other parties in the said case, and how long have you known them or known of them?
3. Have you any and what knowledge of a vessel called the *Greek?* If so, state when and under what circumstances your knowledge of said vessel commenced?

4. Do you know whether on or about the 16th day of March last or at any other time when the said schooner was wrecked, or in any degree damaged or injured, by any or what cause?

5. Do you know whether said Schooner came ashore on or at any time, and when stranded upon any part of Long Island? If so, declare fully and particularly all you know of her so coming ashore or being stranded. Describe the place where said accident happened, the manner and circumstances in and under which said vessel was stranded and the state of the weather and sea at that time.

6. Do you know of the shore on which said schooner was stranded? If so, describe the same, particularly state whether there are or are not reefs or rock or sand bar near the same and whether there is or is not a current more or less rapid and running in a uniform or varying course along or towards the same.

7. Was any aid offered or furnished to said schooner from the shore? If so, state by whom such aid was offered and whether any and what? Any attempt to board said schooner?

8. How long was it after the vessel was discovered before any person came from or went to her?

9. Was there or not a Bar outside of the schooner *Greek* and were any and what efforts made by her master and crew, or other, to find a safe passage over it?

10. Was there or not any damage to be apprehended in carrying the schooner over the bar at any time after she got under it and before she drove on shore?

11. Can a vessel lay in safety between this bar and the shore?

12. Did the Captain of said schooner seek any aid or advice for the purpose of relieving said vessel or of serving his own conduct, and any person or persons and who by name gave any advice or aid on the occasion to the captain?

13. How long was it before the crew of said schooner could land in safety upon the beach?

14. How long did said schooner remain within said bar before she drove on shore and what was her condition when she came on shore?

15. Was a survey completed? If so, how long after she came ashore, and by any person or persons and who by name and in what connection was she then found?

16. Did any person or persons and who by name advice the said schooner that is was necessary to sell said schooner for any and what cause?

17. Was said Schooner sold? If so, was said sale conducted fairly and with due regard to the intent of the concerned or otherwise were there many

persons present at said sale and did said schooner bring more or less than her just value in her then condition?

18. Would it or not have been capable of the captain to have attempted to get said schooner afloat again after her being driven on the beach? If so, how long would it, in all probability have required to have accomplished the work and what expense would it have occasioned and what would have been the chance of such?

19. Was there a wreck master or not at or near the place of the wreck and did he attend and render any aid or give any advice as to the coast or of the said schooner or was not such advice followed?

20. Did or did not the sand of the beach work up around the schooner at some and what time after her stranding?

21. Do you know whether any vessel or vessel were ever stranded at or in the neighborhood of the *Greek* when this schooner when on shore? If so, do you know whether any and how many of such other vessels were got off at any and what expense whether those which put afloat were more or less favorably stranded than the schooner *Greek*?[70]

Through the interrogative, courts hoped to determine fault, procedure taken, and the level of loss.

Most courts prohibited masters and crews from testifying due to their obvious bias in trying to prove their innocence. However, Alfred Conkling added that "in cases of collision and of salvage, the master and crew of a vessel, although interested, are nevertheless permitted to testify to facts which could not otherwise be proved."[71] In most shipwreck cases, those occurring beyond sight of land, the only evidence came from testimonies of the surviving crews.

The most common form of evidence concerning shipwreck cases was a protest. A protest was a formal declaration, made in a foreign port, which declared that the damage was not due to the crew's neglect. Mariners had to make protests within twenty-four hours of arrival at the nearest port. This limit helped expedite the case and prevented further damage.[72] Steel asserts that "if a ship ride out the storm, and arrive in safety at the port of destination, the captain must make regular protests, and must swear, in which some of the crew must join, that the goods were cast overboard for no other cause but the safety of the ship and the rest of the cargo."[73] Serious damage extended the protest to include excerpts from logbooks as well as statements from the crew and the senior surviving officer.[74]

The protest for the schooner *Hope* (1805) was a platform for determining the vessel's seaworthiness. On February 6, 1805, John Pickets, late master, stated before a notary public that on a voyage from Bilboa to Liverpool the vessel "foundered at sea in consequence of heavy gales of wind & rough & high seas & stormy weather." In front of a notary public the master, mate, and one seaman swore that the vessel was "totally & adequately manned & fitted, loaded with coca shells sailed fine."[75] The protest stated that the vessel was seaworthy when she left port and sustained damage only because of extreme weather.

In the case of *Thomas Miller against Robert Roscoe,* master, 1673, the courts reviewed a protest as evidence in Miller's petition for a survey. The *Good Hope,* bound from New Bern, North Carolina, to Fowey, England, with a load of tobacco, struck bottom four different times, as the vessel attempted to sail into New Inlet, North Carolina:

> Wee were fast on ground againe notwithstanding all our endeavours with Ancor & Cables and all the meanes wee could use shee cast thwart & Imediately there arose a violent storme or tempest of wind at Southwest or thereabout which caused the Sea to breake sheer over her & she beating soe violently that wee much feared shee would split in peeces. But wee tried the night with great labour & paines & with the help of food wee got her off In which time we received three or foure extraordinary knockes.. . . . wee found a great deale of water & that our vessel had received some harme by beating in which condition of leakiness Shee hath ever since Continued for which cause the aforesd master did resolve to put into some part or place in protest.[76]

Because of the repeated pounding, the vessel could no longer continue its voyage. In a deposition the captain claimed that the "Showles Tempest and Sea" were extraordinary and therefore allowed the vessel to deviate from its course legally and to find the nearest port for repairs. According to the surveyors, "her uppr worke and Riggin wee find Defective wch makes her if not repaired uncapable to performe a voyage soe long and full of Difficlty." Miller, however, claimed that Roscoe "sailed to places contrary to the will and design of Miller, and fallatiously protesting against the damage of the shoales incapacitating their vessel to continue its voyage."[77] The court found in favor of the defendant, indicating that the damage was a peril of the sea rather than something avoidable.

A protest almost two hundred years later incorporated the ship's log. The captain of the *Hudson* produced the log as proof of the events that led to the abandonment of the ship. Almost immediately the crew found the vessel leaky, which was exacerbated by continual heavy swells and squally weather through December. The log reads:

Dec. 17 Squalls of wind and rain and heavy seas, vessel laboring badly, shipped a number of heavy seas. One hundred and seventy days out.

Dec. 18 Strong gales, and hard squalls continuing with heavy sea running, shipped a number of heavy seas, . . . only one man able to do duty, . . . at 11 A.M. stove in rail, broke four stanchions.

Dec. 19 Violent gales and heavy seas continuing, carried away the bowsprit . . . and started the planks, so that the water poured in, in torrents, covered up the hole with canvas as well as we could, carried away the foremast ten feet above the deck, which fell on larboard side of deck, . . . carried away the mainmast, . . . shipped a heavy sea which carried away the boats, caboose, &c, . . . found the Brig settling deeper.

By December 21 the men of the *Hudson* had consulted one another, "and it was concluded to be necessary for the preservation of the Brig and our lives, to heave over part of the cargo, thru over, One hundred and eight pigs of block tin and forty bags of salt petre from the run." In doing so they came across a bad leak "near the counter." All this time they kept the pump going. The next day they threw over "eleven boxes of merchandise and thirty bags of salt petre." Two days later they threw over "forty nine boxes of merchandise, and twenty three bags of salt petre."

The log continued through January in much the same manner until recording that the brig *Volant* came upon the crew, at which time they abandoned the *Hudson*. The log demonstrated the crew's efforts to preserve the ship and that only after their attempts failed did they abandon ship. The protests for the *Good Hope* and the *Hudson* outlined the basic events, and both went to great lengths to attribute the weather and extraordinary circumstances as the reasons for shipwreck.[78]

During shipwreck crew members did all they could to survive. As described above, this often meant destroying or throwing out part of the cargo. When this occurred, the legal question of general average, in which a crew sacrificed part of a cargo or ship to save the remainder, came into play. Steel adds that "in order to make the act of throwing the goods overboard legal, the ship must be in distress, and the sacrificing a part must be necessary to preserve the rest."[79] For instance, several bales of cotton might be thrown overboard to lighten a vessel stranded on a sandbar, thus allowing the vessel to continue on to its port of destination. Under the laws of general average, the owners of the rescued goods paid the owners of the lost interest, in this case the owner of the bales of cotton, a proportionate share of the loss.

A Narrative of the Shipwreck and Unparalleled Sufferings of Mrs. Sarah Allen (1816), as well as other shipwreck accounts, directly addressed this issue when "the captain ordered all the heavy articles to be thrown overboard' in order to lighten the ship and decrease the chances of sinking.[80] This action demonstrated that mariners understood the legalities of loss and how to prove their innocence. Likewise if a "ship is voluntarily stranded to save the cargo, the loss of the ship becomes a general average; but where the ship is involuntarily stranded, and part of the cargo saved, and part lost, no general average is due." Cases concerning general average rarely went to court because insurers often settled through arbitration.[81]

In addition to general average, cases concerning shipwreck often appeared under the legal category of loss. Loss came in two different forms: total and partial. Total loss occurred when over 50 percent of the total value of property was lost, and less than 50 percent was considered partial loss, although Clarke considers partial loss as anything not amounting to a total loss. Clarke continues, "Shipwreck is in general a total loss. . . . A stranding is not, of itself, deemed a total loss . . . it is only when the stranding is followed by shipwreck, or in any other way renders the ship incapable of pursuing the voyage, or that the expense of repairs will exceed half her value, that the insured is entitled to abandon."[82] Stranded ships often refloated with the tides or were later tugged to safety; therefore these ships suffered only some damage rather than total loss.

Policies divided total loss into either actual total loss or constructive total loss. Actual total loss occurred when a ship and its cargo were destroyed or when a ship could no longer complete a voyage and the cargo or vessel was deemed unsalvageable. This applied to shipwreck in most cases, when a vessel was "said to be destroyed when it is so broken, disjointed, or otherwise injured, that it no longer exists in its original nature and essence."[83] Constructive total loss happened when over 50 percent of the vessel was damaged or destroyed and the assured opted to abandon it to the underwriters. This might also occur if a vessel became stranded but was not a total loss because the ship could continue its voyage through assistance or a fortunate accident. However, when the expense of repairs exceeded half a ship's value, the insured could abandon the vessel and cargo. The underwriters or insurers also had the option to accept or deny decisions by the insured to abandon. If the insured chose to accept this decision, they were subrogated (in which case they took control) to the assured's interest and therefore gained all the rights to salvage.[84]

In the case of the *Margaret*, which sailed from Boston in 1795, the master, John Hebden, applied for constructive total loss when, after experiencing severe storms, the vessel had not only a large hole near the bow but also "all the oakum out of both bilge seams so that she sinks every tide therefore its my opinion that is most advisable that the said ship ought to be put up at public auction to defray all charges. . . . the sooner it is done the better as she daily creates a great expense but not that alone for I don't believe she is worth repairing and would be attended with such an immense expense that I am afraid of her bottom falling out daily."[85] The cost of repairs outweighed the ship's worth, so the only option remaining was to sell or destroy the vessel in hopes of recouping any money.

Partial loss, also known as particular average, did not fall upon all insurers as did general average.[86] If a vessel sprang a leak that soaked several casks of dry goods, the owner of the dry goods alone accepted the loss. Likewise if a vessel ran aground and most of the cargo was destroyed, those with the luck to recover their goods did not have to make contributions to those who lost. As with all other types of damage, if masters were at fault, insurance no longer covered the loss.[87]

Many ships never returned. In those cases problems concerning general average and total loss did not apply. Typically if a ship failed to show up after a certain period, insurers assumed that it was a total loss. According to Blunt's *Shipmaster's Assistant,* "if a ship has been missing, and no intelligence received of her within a reasonable time after she sailed, it shall be presumed that she foundered at sea." Steel writes, "A practice prevailed among insurers that a ship shall be deemed lost, if not heard of in six months after her departure (or after the time of the last intelligence from her) for any port in Europe, and in twelve months if at a greater distance. If, under this usage, the insurer should pay the money, supposing the ship lost, when it really is not, he may, . . . recover it back in action."[88] Meanwhile, Clarke states that "in case a ship has not been heard of in four years after she sailed, the insurer may be sued as for a loss by sinking at sea."[89] The ability to collect on loss varied according to time and place, the nature of the shipwreck, and the agreed-upon contract.

～

The maritime industry made sure that sailors, owners, and masters understood who was responsible for what on a shipwreck. Manuals such as *Suggestions to Masters of Ships Approved by the Merchants Underwriters of New York* (1859) provided a detailed procedure for masters to follow when in distress:

1. Conforming to enclosed suggestions will obviate many problems concerning averages and insurance.
2. In every case the vessel must be repaired, if practicable, without gross expenditure exceeding ¾ value of the vessel.

3. If total repairs too expensive try temporary repairs.
4. If sails or spars cannot be replaced, without great expense, repair until suitable.
5. Do not unload cargo unless absolutely necessary, do not pay for it— it should be included in repair charges.
6. If cost is over ¾ then Masters can sell.
7. If wreck is off the United States, the Captain should keep control of the property, contact the owners, and contact a wrecking commission for advice.
8. If salvaged, have all goods and vessel appraised as they are brought in.
9. If destroyed, the master must collect all protests, accounts, and expenditures to determine remittance.
10. If cargo is jettisoned, throw the least valuable first and the most weighty.
11. Those who act or respond to disaster favorably will be advanced in character and reputation.[90]

Given the frequency of shipwrecks, each voyage represented a gamble. Sooner or later most ships wrecked, and insurers knew the risks. When shipwreck happened and the vessel was insured, the parties involved had two options, arbitration or litigation. Though they often chose the first, shipwreck cases still found their way to court. Despite minor changes over three centuries, shipwrecks continued to involve arguments concerning contract and fault. Insurers hoped to show deviation, unseaworthiness, or human error, while masters and crews claimed perils of the sea.

With the laws in place, shipwreck lost some of its terror as owners, crews, and insurers knew their rights and how best to receive compensation for their time and efforts. In legal matters neither side took into account the loss of human life, except where it concerned wages. The cost of the human element was not considered in maritime law or marine insurance until the nineteenth century with steamboat explosions along inland waters. Until then popular or sensationalized shipwreck narratives were a main avenue to bring such elements to light.

· 3 ·

God, Nature, and the Role
of Religion in Shipwreck

God rules by land and steers the course at sea / Both Winds and
Waves his great commands obey. He Spans the Heavens he levels
Hills with Dales / And Weighs all being with Unerring Scales. Main
Life on Shore with Seeming Safety Flies / But Death Still Stands
before the Seamans Eyes. Live then you Seamen Honest, Sober,
Just, / Courageous, Faithfull and in God your Trust.[1]

An 1834 collection of shipwreck accounts suggests that "nowhere more, than
in the dangers of the sea do we find the Hand of Providence."[2] The event
of shipwreck forced individuals to face the fragility of their own mortality,
and the narratives provided an excellent format for revealing the wonders of
God's abilities or for reaffirming the all-powerful forces of nature. Published
narratives portrayed shipwreck in a multitude of ways; in some accounts a
ship's loss was an irrevocable punishment for past sins, while in others human agency featured prominently in the struggle to survive. In general most
recognized the role of divine intervention, though many omitted a higher
being in place of a more rational understanding of events.

Religion transformed an ocean voyage into a person's spiritual journey
where shipwreck symbolized both God's wrath and his benevolence. Increase Mather stated in his 1684 *Essay for the Recording of Illustrious Providences* "that they who go down to the Sea in Ships, that do business in the
great waters, see the works of the Lord, and his wonders in the Deep. And
in special, they see wonders of Divine goodness in respect of eminent

Deliverances wrought by the hand of the most high, who stills the noise of the Seas, the noise of their waves."[3] Early American shipwreck literature is replete with accounts of sailors and passengers turning to God in moments of crisis and of offering thanksgiving for salvation.

Theologically shipwreck made sense as retribution for sin, a chance for redemption, or a reminder of God's power. As part of the larger deliverance genre, published narratives not only provided vivid accounts of shipwreck but also became outlets for promoting the Christian faith. Religion reconstructed the terrifying and random events into meaningful experiences for both participants and readers. Rather than impart a negative connotation based on death and destruction, the narratives were focused on faith and salvation by individuals' religious beliefs. In this way the accounts minimized fear while demonstrating, through God's intervention, that Americans were indeed "chosen ones" and worthy of redemption. Shipwreck therefore became a trial that transformed survivors spiritually and physically and delivered them into salvation.[4]

Early Americans understood shipwreck from different theological perspectives. Puritans, Anglicans, and deists interpreted shipwrecks in divergent ways that changed over time as individuals responded to cultural developments.[5] In general, while Puritans viewed God as an active agent in both catastrophe and providence, Anglicans removed divine punishment from shipwreck and storm while maintaining God's benevolence in salvation. Those who followed a deist understanding of faith excluded any spiritual interaction and instead relied on human ability as the principal cause of death or survival. Despite these differences, religious intercession, or the lack of it, gave meaning to shipwreck and modified it into an understandable event.

Unfortunately authors rarely stated their affiliations or denominations, making absolute classifications difficult. However, the narratives follow a general trend of increased secularization over time, while maintaining and overlapping older understandings of sin and redemption. For example, early narratives written in the seventeenth and eighteenth centuries demonstrated a personal relationship with God and emphasized sin and conversion. Other narratives from the same time period, however, minimized sin and, while giving thanks to God's benevolence, reflected a more distant and formal relationship with the deity. Focusing on reason and human ability, many late eighteenth-century narratives removed God almost completely. But by the nineteenth century, after the Revolution and stirrings of the Second Great Awakening, shipwreck accounts once again returned to an emphasis on special providences and a personal relationship to a higher being.

Early North American Religion

No examination of early American religious history can ignore the impact of Puritanism, and many shipwreck accounts suggest a strong Puritan influence. Puritans in New England settlements produced an important body of religious literature and set the tone of spiritual thought in British North America. However, their hegemony, even in this region, did not last long, and by the late seventeenth century Puritanism showed signs of fracturing. British rule during the Dominion of New England, internal schisms, as well as an increased presence of other denominations reduced the religious power of Puritan leaders; however, Puritan ideas of proper religious conduct remained influential in the colonies.[6]

Another major religious influence in British North America was Anglicanism. Anglicanism in the New World never proved to be an exact copy of the Church in England, and religious pluralism in the colonies decreased the Church of England's power. "Anglicans generally defended the role of reason in religion, the importance of free will, and their perception of God as both a rational deity and a model for moral perfection."[7] Free will, for Anglicans, did not mean democracy but instead stressed the need to keep one's place in the social order. Obedience to God's will was necessary but voluntary.[8] It is no surprise that Anglicans often accepted the eighteenth-century Enlightenment with its emphasis on reason and the inherent ability and goodness of each individual.

Although Puritanism and Anglicanism represent two major influences in the British New World, numerous others coexisted in North America. Rather than attempt to assign specific narratives to one of the myriad religious and philosophical attitudes, the remainder of this chapter demonstrates the general secularization that occurred over time. Despite a lack of specificity, religion was important to the narratives, and much information can be gleaned without making specific denominational classifications.

Shipwreck and Religion

Puritan leaders found in published narratives one means of demonstrating God's presence.[9] Shipwreck, when combined with the jeremiad, became an important format for reminding congregations of their covenant with God.[10] For example, Increase Mather prefaced *An Essay for the Recording of Illustrious Providences* (1684) with the following: "for God's Glory, and the good of Posterity it is necessary that utmost care shall be taken that all, and only Remarkable Providences be recorded and published." He continued that all such events that incurred "remarkable judgments upon noted sinners; eminent deliverances, and answers of prayer, are to be reckoned among illustrious providences."[11] Shipwreck was a favorite topic of Puritans and one that vividly demonstrated "illustrious providences."

Almost one hundred years later Joseph Bailey (1750) introduced his narrative with, "I conceive, my bounden duty toward the Supreme Being, to declare his wonderful Acts of Providence, and tender Mercies towards the most undeserving of Mankind; that he never leaves or forsakes them that sincerely humble themselves before him, and puts their trust in him through Jesus Christ."[12] The accounts provided a very public means for regaling God's omnipotence and allowed authors to share with a wide audience such wondrous events. As a part of the jeremiad literary type, these stories helped early colonists make the transition from being Europeans to being Americans through a formulized story that audiences understood.[13] As part of their covenant with God, colonists made public the intimate relationship between belief and redemption.

The jeremiad by the mid-seventeenth century was one of the few publications that supported a domestic market.[14] Even in the eighteenth century shipwreck played an important role in the jeremiads of sin and salvation. During a terrible storm Capt. Nathanael Peirce, aboard the *Portsmouth* (1756), advised the passengers to "endeavour to secure their eternal Happiness in the next, by looking unto Jesus Christ their merciful Redeemer for sincere Repentance of all their Sins, and Salvation thro' his Blood . . . and beg'd for the Continuance of their Reason till their appointed Time should come; and so humbly submitted themselves to his will and Pleasure." Peirce, the only survivor, attributed his good fortune to "trusting in the Merits and satisfaction of Jesus Christ for acceptance unto Salvation; and at the same time praying for a scarce submission to the divine will. . . . It pleased God that I should continue longer."[15] Peirce's passive attitude put both his life and eternal salvation solely in God's hands. Audiences understood that affliction came from sin that, if left unchecked, would only compound in severity. Evidently this format appealed to New England colonists.

Shipwreck in many early American narratives represented a test, punishment, or a means of conversion. Such definitions made sense to colonists and explained God's interventions as consistent and orderly.[16] Benjamin Bartholomew wrote a poem about his 1660 shipwreck in which he suggested that God did not bring about shipwrecks and storms randomly:

> Let us tel abrod his wonderous acts
> Lets Glorifie his Name for all his Facts
> Who bringeth loe and raiseth up againe
> God surly doth not these great things in Vaine
> He is expecting from us som Gret thing

And lookes more prayes we to his name should bring . . .
But when we hav our lives is safty had
We have forgote the vows that we have made
And now againe God has put us in Mind
How we oursevles by voues doe use to bind
And how oft those voues neglected have
And now again god brings us to the Grave.[17]

Bartholomew believed that God, through shipwreck, reminded Christians to remain pious and ever mindful of the Lord's glory. As a warning against backsliding, the published jeremiad revealed not only how sin led to affliction but also that God's grace could stop this slippery slope.

The prolonged trial of shipwreck provided Christians with an occasion for introspection and to reflect on previous transgressions. While sailing from Newbury to Marblehead in 1635, Anthony Thacher's family became shipwrecked during a hurricane, spurring reflections on their past actions. In conversation with his cousin Avery, Thacher stated that "what his [God's] Pleasure is wee know not. I feare wee have bin to unthankfull for fomer mercys."[18] Survivors and readers attempted to understand why shipwrecks occurred and to uncover the meaning behind such events. In doing so they often found themselves sinful or lacking faith.[19] In theory at least, Puritans constantly strove to justify conversion experiences through good behavior. Though they worked toward their own salvation, only through faith in God's grace could they achieve it.[20]

John Ryther devoted several pages of his 1674 sermon to shipwreck, where he asked, "But why doth God stay so long before he send deliverances and salvations?" In response Ryther stated that shipwreck presented a final opportunity, and that "if men will not pray, when sinking, when drowning, when dying, they will never pray." Rather God chooses when and where to send deliverances, and "if we had our mercies in our time, we should not see that beauty in them; for every thing is beautiful in its season; and God chuses the fittest seasons to send them, because he will put beauty upon them."[21] For Ryther, God used shipwreck as a last resort to persuade reluctant people to pray, and the moment was the most effective time to redeem sinners.

The trial of shipwreck often brought about humiliation and suffering that tested an individual's faith. The event became a moment of transformation, similar to a conversion experience in which God delivered those who persevered. "Providence separates the human from a community, reduces that person by means of suffering, trial, or isolation to an essence of belief or hope, and then restores the individual to the community as an exemplum of the hope of resurrection."[22] This message translated easily for many colonists, especially those with a Puritan faith.

Christian survivors justified their salvation through adherence to a social compact that placed community over the self. Thacher's narrative reflected a communal ideology as his family remained a "body politic," dying together rather than face death, or survival, individually.[23] According to Thacher's account, "there was a league of perpetual friendship between my cousin Avery and my self never to forsake each other to the Death, but to be partakers of each others misery or welfare."[24] "Likewise my Cozen, his Wife & his Children both of us bewailing each other in Our Lord and onely Saviour Jesus Christ . . . were contentedly resolved to dye together Lovingly as since our acquaintance we had Lived together friendly."[25] The narrative minimized potential isolation and excommunication from the church. Survival therefore returned people to the community and to the protection and care of the congregation.

In some Christian writings, the Atlantic voyage represented not only a transition from the Old World to the New but also the spiritual transformation of those who undertook the voyage. Richard Steere's poem of the *Adventure* (1683) expressed this spiritual journey in allegorical form. The voyage began well, with sunny skies and favorable winds, which the passengers and crew foolishly took for granted:

> We had bin Charm'd into a drowsie sleep
> Of calme Security, nor had we known
> the Excellence of PRESERVATION;
> We had been Dumb and silent to Express
> Affectedly the Voy'ges good success.

Soon a storm blew in and the vessel began to leak, which reminded its passengers of their precarious situation: "Whilst all the men and women then on board / With earnest Cryes did call upon the Lord." In response to their supplications, Steere claimed that it was "thus the Great God did Snatch from below" and allowed the vessel to remain afloat. However, once the winds abated, the crew and passengers failed to give proper thanks. Since they had not learned their lesson, God sent a second storm that prevented them from entering the harbor, and only after they "put no trust in Earthen powers" did the vessel make it safely into London.[26] God created storm and shipwreck as a reminder to remain humble, faithful, and repentant, and again following the format of the jeremiad; only when the crew fully submitted their wills to the deity did he provide salvation.

For the pious, the ocean journey bound sailors and passengers with God as they inspected themselves, faced personal sin, and offered thanksgiving for survival.[27] Every action had meaning that demonstrated the intimate relationship between a person's actions and God's will. Although the Puritans no longer ruled in Massachusetts after the Glorious Revolution of 1688, aspects of Puritan mentality survived their official demise well into the eighteenth century. For example, as late as 1788, when the *Nancy* ran into a storm off the Carolina coast, the crew prayed to God for assistance and were immediately rewarded:

> Nothing but God's almighty arm
> could save us in this dismal storm
> he still the winds and raging seas
> and rules and guides them as he please.
> In our distress we left our cry
> to God who reigns above the sky
> he answers us and sends relief
> When we are overwhlm'd with grief.[28]

A sermon presented by Andrew Brown (1793) at Halifax related the spiritual pilgrimage as he warned sailors to repent and give their will to God. He warned that in their last moments, "their past actions rush upon their memory, and conscience condemns them for every sin they have committed. Their eyes and hearts are lifted up to heaven, and they call upon the Lord if so be he will think upon them that they perish not." If an individual makes peace with God, then "the king of mercy listens to the supplication, rebukes the wind, and says unto the sea, peace, be still." Once a sailor redeemed himself, he may "go down to the sea in ships and do business in great waters in the calm and in the storm, knowing that God is your saviour, and that under his protection no lasting evil can befall you."[29] Not only did this message reach out to land-based audiences, but it did so through a symbol that had real meaning to those who plied the oceans for a living. Shipwreck could be a means of converting sailors, a notoriously irreligious and profane group.[30]

~

Favorable signs represented God's assistance and his continued covenant with those who stayed true. In 1750, during the height of a storm, Joseph Bailey assured his readers that "God was so wonderfully kind and merciful to preserve us all in this terrible Overthrow: We blessed God, and put up our earnest Prayer to Him in the best Manner we were capable." Bailey remained devout, declaring that "God will deliver us yet; he is All-Sufficient, if we put our Trust in him."[31] Supernatural intervention proved God's existence and the preservation of those who maintained their faith.

Puritan shipwreck narratives, despite the terrifying and horrible events, were promising and optimistic.[32] Rather than dwell on death and catastrophe, the narratives indicated that participants remained hopeful and stressed the joy of God's salvation. For example, although Anthony Thacher lost most of his family and all of his cousins, he continued his faith in God, looking toward the future: "What I shall doe or what Corse I shall take I know not, the Lord in his mercy derect me that I may so lead the new life which he hath given me as may be most to his owne glory."[33] Religion in the narratives imparted a positive outlook in which devastated survivors were secure in God's benevolence.

Following the jeremiad format, writers of many Christian narratives hoped not only to save readers but also to inspire audiences to "lead more sober and pious lives so that God might send prosperity to a virtuous nation."[34] Readers learned from Joseph Bailey's shipwreck that the survivors with the "utmost Sincerity of heart and Humility return[ed] humble and hearty thanks to Almighty God." In response God gave them "a due Sense of all the Mercies he had bestowed upon us; and that he would give us Grace to make a right Improvement thereof; that he might amend our Lives, and live to shew forth wonderful Acts of Providence, and Kindness to us the sinful Children of Men."[35] Ultimately the narratives were optimistic as they demonstrated the fortitude of New England Christians and stressed that the exceptional piety and strength of their people would benefit the entire community. Again, those who remained faithful to God would enjoy his favor and reap rewards of a higher benevolence.

Pious audiences read and listened to sermons regarding the fate of sinners and of a need for self-discipline. Perhaps as a warning, or in response to waning religious enthusiasm, a late eighteenth-century broadside entitled *A True and Particular Narrative of the Late Tremendous Tornado, or Hurricane, at Philadelphia and New-York, on Sabbath-Day, July 1, 1792* pointed out that this storm demonstrated God's wrath against those who failed to remain devout. On that day thirty individuals drowned while boating around New York harbor. According to the broadside, "It happened on the holy Sabbath, a day that our worthy and pious Forefathers revered as a time set apart for religious worship . . . and appointed Magistrates who feared God and dared to put their Statutes in execution." The remainder of the broadside, printed as a poem, warned:

> A solemn warning all may take,
> and fear his sacred laws to break:
> he shews he is a sov'reign God,

> who makes us feel his heavy rod
> You that do trample on his laws.
> Shall find he will espouse his Cause;
> he lays the proud and haughty low,
> and drives their counsels to and fro
> Contrast the scene and view with awe,
> The fate of those who broke the law;
> While those who met to worship God
> escap'd the anger of his rod.[36]

Those who profaned the Sabbath would surely meet their maker under less than favorable circumstances, while individuals who kept it holy experienced his benevolence. Though many met their demise that day, the true message remained one of morality and improvement.

These narratives exhibited God's intimate relationship with humans. Similar to nineteenth-century evangelical Christians described by the historian Philip Greven, early colonists often found "regeneration through denial of the self."[37] They demonstrated a person's ability to progress morally, but it ultimately rested on God to bring about salvation. In an allegorical sense, the shipwreck narratives paralleled the lives of Christians in which people worked toward transforming themselves and tried to subsume their will to God's so that he might deliver them back into the welcoming arms of the community, a community that sought to improve itself through continued belief and divine will.

Not all narratives rested on lessons of sin and salvation. Some authors minimized the presence of sin and the need for reflection. God remained almighty but exercised power with more restraint than did his purely "Puritan" counterpart. These tales insisted that humans contained some good and were not completely depraved when bereft of grace.[38] Conversion came about gradually, and individuals exercised their free will in accepting or rejecting God's blessing.

In these narratives shipwreck did not occur because of sin or God's wrath; instead they focused on God's benevolence and the need to give thanks for his kindness in the event of deliverance.[39] Aboard the *Sea Venture* (1610), the crew no longer held any hope of survival and were ready to perish, "but the goodnesse and sweet introduction of better hope, by our merciful God, given unto us. Sir George Summers, had discovered and cryed Land."[40] Such narratives forwent any lessons for sinners; nor did they suggest that divine retribution rather than past action might induce a wreck. Rather they indicated that God intervened only to provide assistance and to help those who remained faithful.

In 1707, while sailing from Lisbon to Virginia, a leaky vessel forced the crew into the ship's boat. Through the entire ordeal, the only mention of God in Captain Bilton's journal is a brief sentence: "It pleased God to Send us Fair Weather." The remaining aspects of his narrative instead detailed the sailing instructions, locational information, geography, and local flora and fauna. Reading more like a travel journal, Bilton's words gave little recognition to a higher being.[41]

Such narratives presented an almost Anglican emphasis and stressed orderly participation in public worship. For example, the *Nottingham Galley* (1710), from London, ran into trouble off the coast of Maine. When disaster struck, the master, "calling down all Hands spent a few minutes in the Cabbin in earnestly supplicating Mercy."[42] Prayer was a group event, and according to the accounts, thanksgiving took place through public demonstration rather than private reflection.

These narratives emphasized public ritual and performance while minimizing private introspection in the search for salvation.[43] Barnabas Downs's 1786 account of shipwreck, instead of stressing God's wrath and the need to redeem oneself, emphasized divine providence and benevolence. His preface suggested that audiences should relate all remarkable circumstances and that if "they have been deliverances from great and signal disasters, he will make this communication from a principle of gratitude to the Being who hath protected and preserved him." In doing so, the author would spread the word of God and "engage others to be thankful for his behalf; and a knowledge of the kindness of Heaven to him may lead others to trust in God, when they are brought into like distress and danger."[44] Such narratives disregarded the place of sin and instead looked to the individual's ability as a member of a godly society to obtain salvation. This was a public proclamation that Downs emphasized as necessary for continued survival.

This communal supplication reflected the belief that human ability directly affected the chance of rescue. When the survivors of the *Peggy* (1766) turned to cannibalism, Captain Harrison "offered to pray with the crew for an immediate relief, or an immediate eternity."[45] Harrison chose to make a public effort rather than resort to private prayers. With no indication of sin and fault, this group attempt was to bolster the crew's belief.

Some authors indicated that salvation came through a person's efforts rather than by the grace of God alone. Human ability, ritual, and public action led the struggle for perfection. Captain Harrison of the *Peggy* (1766), while floating helplessly and facing imminent starvation, prayed for salvation, though his attempts apparently fell short: "Our thanksgiving, however, to Providence, though profoundly sincere, were not offered in great form." He believed that their inadequate prayers led an unknown vessel to trick them. The ship came upon the desperate men and offered to bring them aboard; but the ship took flight and left the men of the *Peggy* to face starvation and cannibalism.[46] The suggestion is that perhaps if their efforts had been more sincere, the unknown vessel would have saved them from further despair.

Many denominations stressed that freedom of action meant freedom to sin. Therefore problems concerning proper behavior and attitudes took on increased importance in these narratives.[47] The *Providence Gazette* in 1763 recorded an instance of shipwreck that occurred due to the inappropriate actions of the captain: "A melancholy Instance this is of the bad Consequences of trusting a Vessel with an improper Commander. The Captain was a worthless drunken Fellow, and during two Days he was here, before the Accident happened, he never moored his Vessel, but lay at the single Anchor; and without parting his Cable . . . was upon the Rocks to the Eastward of the Bay."[48] Contemporaries might have determined that the captain used his free will to behave in a careless manner. Rather than a result of the captain's spiritual failings, shipwreck came from his negligence of the essentials of seamanship. The narrative also reflected an emphasis on how outward behavior reflected inner qualities.

The trend toward omitting divine intervention increased through the eighteenth and nineteenth centuries. For example, by 1780 Lieutenant Archer of the HMS *Phoenix* rarely mentioned God except for an occasional praise to providence for allowing people to escape certain death. At the end of the narrative he provided no thankfulness to God; instead he "remained his majesty's most true and faithful servant, and my dear mother's most dutiful son."[49] Emphasizing duty, late eighteenth-century narratives reflected influences of rationality, enlightenment, and reason, becoming ever more secular.

Many narratives therefore thanked specific individuals for their roles in rescue and recuperation. The charity of humans outweighed the benevolence of God in these accounts. Captain Harrison made a special point to thank Captain Thomas Evers of the *Susanna* for rescuing his starving crew and wrote, "before I proceed further, it is necessary to inform the reader of the person to whose benignity my people and I were indebted for our preservation."[50] He went on to thank Gov. Arthur Holdwordth, a friend of Captain Evers, and all those who provided assistance or sympathy to himself or any of his men.

Narratives of this genre often stressed human ability and agency as opposed to the passive perspective of earlier accounts. No longer inherently evil, human nature was recognized by authors as containing some good-ness that permitted the choice of a virtuous path. One such author, James Stanier Clarke, prefaced his 1805 collection of shipwreck narratives with, "I devoutly hope, that the Providential deliverance of Vessels from perilous sit-uations, may teach Seamen, and such of my fellow Creatures as are exposed to Danger or Distress, to emulate the Conduct of St. Paul; who thrice ship-wrecked, continually enforced this blessed precept, Against Hope, Believe in Hope!"[51] Human agency combined with God's assistance were both needed for salvation. Individuals could learn from published examples and freely decide to remain devout, or not.

Freedom of will did not release people from their duty but rather the opposite. They had the ability to choose to act in a virtuous and pious man-ner toward regeneration.[52] Barnabas Downs, reflecting upon his shipwreck and subsequent survival, added to his narrative, "But after all these distresses I am still among the living to praise God! Let my spared life be devoted to his service, and may I ever be mindful of his benefits!"[53] Downs took an active role in his decision to follow God, rather than wait passively for him to show them the way. Taking action diminished the terror of shipwreck and demonstrated the ability of individuals to save themselves, both physi-cally and spiritually. Shipwreck became a comprehensible event in which those who acted and remained true to God benefited and found the means to effect their own survival.

The narrative of the *Nottingham Galley* (1710) provides a unique example to contrast different perspectives of sin, fault, and redemption. The cap-tain, John Deane, gave "thanks to Divine Providence for their miraculous Deliverance from so imminent a Danger," and despite the crew's travails and almost certain death, Deane continued to believe in a "Wise and Good God."[54] He stressed that the crew sat in public worship as they went over "their Devotions," but in no instance did he refer to sin or redemption. He concluded his story with several pages devoted to thanking specific in-dividuals for their roles in deliverance rather than a statement of devotion to God.

In contrast, Deane's first mate, Christopher Langman, published an account in which sin and personal reflection were important for salvation. Langman's narrative blamed the captain's inept navigation and charged him with purposefully causing shipwreck in order to recoup the insurance. He stated that Deane "was cover'd with Shame and Confusion," labeling the captain as a sinful individual. Langman also thanked God repeatedly, while examining his own sins for hope of salvation. As the crew climbed on top of a large rock, Langman stated that he expected them to die but that he "return'd God Thanks for giving us more time to repent."[55] Sin remained central to Langman's account, while Deane provided no mention of personal introspection or redemption.

Differences also appeared in Deane's and Langman's personal relationships with God. Deane assumed a level of human agency, while Langman often begged for God's mercy, passively assuming that only God could save them. At the end of the narrative Langman added that the only reason he published this account was to "testify our Thankfulness to God for his Great Deliverance, and to give others Warning not to trust their Lives or Estates in the Hands of so wicked and brutish a Man."[56] Reflecting his theological background, Langman stressed the inherent evil in humans and the notion that the only true savior is God.

Not all narratives stressed the role of God in shipwreck and in survival. By the late eighteenth century several published accounts minimized a higher being in favor of fortitude, endurance, and capability. Deism was a movement that impacted Americans' understandings of the world around them. With the advent of deism in the eighteenth century, the image of God changed from an all-powerful being to "a governor of a mechanical universe."[57] In this view God acted as a "supreme architect who served as the original cause of uniform physical laws."[58] Deism acknowledged the presence of a higher being but one who acted in rational and reasonable ways and rarely interfered in human affairs or with the universe he had set in motion. Deism did not replace traditional religious thought in the shipwreck narratives but added a level of secularism not seen in earlier accounts.

Deism stressed free will and the inherent goodness of individuals, and it demanded that the self remain under control.[59] Reason, order, law, and freedom of expression and conscience outlined deism, with practical virtue and moral perfection constituting the highest form of worship.[60] Although deism minimized any direct tie between God and humans and deemphasized the need for God's intervention, this philosophical perspective respected and believed in a higher being.[61]

Into the nineteenth century the Enlightenment influenced these narratives, as seen when they stressed experience and reason as the basis of knowledge. Rather than merely spreading the word of God, these published accounts emphasized spreading truth and knowledge as necessary to help people survive. In 1804 Capt. David Woodard prefaced his narrative with the following: "It appeared interesting to myself, and to those friends who urged the publication. . . . And if it should be the cause of saving the lives of any of my fellow creatures, or of producing other narratives equally interesting and authentic, the object may be answered. As truth is the best guide to knowledge."[62] Judah Paddock hoped that his 1818 narrative "may render essential service to a deserving fellow citizen and greatly promote the cause of truth."[63] Authors of narratives did not concern themselves with thanksgiving or demonstrating special providences. Instead they provided useful knowledge for their audiences and promoted learning through their own and others' experiences.

Religion did have a limited place even in these narratives. It took the form of using human capability to understand and survive in God's universe and to take comfort in a higher being's rationality and goodness. Balancing reason with religion, William Vaughn, editor of Captain Woodard's 1804 narrative, wrote, "As there is a strong affinity between the powers of the mind and body to support each other under great conflicts, officers and men should so temper obedience and command to create confidence and union . . . for self-preservation. In these moments, when the impressions of religious feelings are always strongest, their sensations should be encouraged, from the tranquility of mind and consolations they produce, the hopes they encourage, and the exertions they create."[64]

The Enlightenment emphasized the empirical study of nature and demystified the cosmos. Shipwreck no longer occurred according to divine will; "science grounded the supernatural world in the material world," where individual intellect interpreted the events according to rational and natural laws.[65] For example, Arthur Cochlan, commander of the brig *Tyrrel* in 1759, used reason and past experience to survive while stranded in an open boat. From "the color and coldness of the water, he knew he was not far from land" and thus remained on a course that ultimately led to survival.[66] Rather than waiting for God to provide a sign for salvation, Cochlan used his abilities and intellect to bring about rescue. He understood the basic laws of nature, used empirical knowledge, and remained in control of his senses.

In several narratives crews and passengers eschewed introspection or the need to confront sin and fault. Instead authors presented an optimistic outlook that precluded any interest in determining punishment.[67] Such accounts typically ended with no special recognition of God but rather gave thanks to benevolent or competent individuals. Mate Purnell, the only survivor of the *Tyrrel* (1759), gave no sign of appreciation to a higher being but instead attested to several individuals who "treated him with the utmost tenderness and humanity . . . during which he lived comfortably, and gradually recovered his strength."[68] After their shipwreck survivors of the *Halsewell* (1786) wrote that "the benevolence and generosity of the master of the Crown Inn, at Blanford, deserves the highest praise."[69] Divine providence was rarely a recipient of the authors' gratitude, whereas human ability and humanitarian conduct took prominent roles.

By the mid-eighteenth century and even into the nineteenth century, the emphasis on rationality and empirical study secularized narratives.[70] Similar to murder narratives studied by the historian Karen Halttunen, shipwreck accounts became more realistic and provided great detail concerning the actions of various individuals.[71] Sailing from New York to Cork in 1800, the *Oswego* foundered on its outward leg. The master, Judah Paddock, provided minute details of each moment in the storm: "I put my hand on the tiller-head, and bore it hard to the rail. . . . When she began to gather head way, the helm righted with the wind a least two points on the starboard quarter, wanting not more than once her length coming round, heading off shore."[72] The account demonstrated the crew's knowledge and ability, while the technical details confirmed the story's veracity. This level of description was not seen in earlier accounts and reflected the growing emphasis on human ability. The narratives revealed how humans could save themselves, and detail was necessary to prove to audiences the means for survival.

Individuals demonstrated intelligence and rationality by relying on past experience. Having wrecked before, the chief mate of the *Oswego* (1800), "without hesitation, said it was his opinion that we should take the boat, and land; that he had once been shipwrecked in the West Indies, when choosing to stay by the wreck rather than to leave it, he very narrowly escaped death, and had then made up his mind, that, in a like situation, he would always leave the wreck the first opportunity." Using empirical knowledge, the chief mate made an excellent case for abandoning the vessel and heading for shore.[73] The inclusion of such information might help others in like situations, and taking time to dwell on past transgressions was not a sensible thing to do. Rather knowledge and experience influenced action with little recognition given to a higher being.

Deism emphasized a cosmic order and assigned no personal or providential meaning to events.[74] If "a miracle by definition constituted an infraction of the regular and predictable operations of physical reality," therefore if God interceded in any manner, structured order no longer existed and shipwreck became a chaotic and terrifying possibility.[75] Rather than placing their trust in a personal God, such individuals relied on natural law and order to regulate their experiences. Kerry Walters points out that for some, "reality was rational and hence capable of being understood by rational beings."[76] Enlightenment-infused common sense defined shipwreck as part of an ordered and reasonable universe.

As authors of narratives shifted their attention away from God's wrath, they began to emphasize humanity's conflict with nature. Benjamin Stout of the *Hercules* (1796) described a gale in which "the contentions of the sea and winds presented a scene of horrors, of which, perhaps, the annals of maritime history give us no example." Although he plied the sea for most of his life, "all I had ever heard of or read, gave me no adequate idea of those sublime effects which the violence and raging of the elements produced."[77] Nature could be calm and tranquil, but it could also be terrifying. The storm did not come about because of God's punishment; nor did God intervene. Such narratives situated humans against the forces of nature, where reason, intellect, and ability allowed sailors to weather storms successfully. And yet, as the scholar M. H. Abrams points out, the emphasis on the sublime resonated with theological implications: that "the beautiful elements in nature are the enduring expression of God's loving benevolence, while the vast and disordered in nature express his infinity, power, and awe."[78] These powerful images, though related to natural phenomena, echoed older traditions of an all-powerful being.

The movement toward increased secularism was not a unified linear progression. By the early nineteenth century many shipwreck narratives once again swung in favor of an evangelical perspective and a resurgence of the divine and special providences that assured Americans of God's favor.[79] By this time new evangelicals combined human agency with an enlightened understanding of a higher being.[80] Nineteenth-century popular religion stressed the ability of each person to find the grace of God without requiring years of learning or training. Moral perfection and reform encouraged individuals to improve themselves within a personal religious relationship. The narratives reflected the powerful presence of God but granted humans the ability to improve society on their own.[81] This progressive journey required individuals to reflect and idealize a more simple and pure lifestyle while looking forward with greater understanding and optimism.[82]

~

Beginning in the late eighteenth century, the religious revival known as the Second Great Awakening swept the United States. It led to the spectacular growth of several "American" denominations, including Baptists, Methodists, and Presbyterians. In general such individuals relied on the Bible, conversion experiences, social involvement, and the notion of Christ as a personal redeemer.[83] These groups came to the forefront of American history in the first Great Awakening of the 1730s and 1740s, as part of a "movement away from formal, outward, and established religion, to one more personal, inward, and heartfelt."[84]

With the Second Great Awakening came a resurgence of popular religious thought, which included that ordinary people, enlightened by Christ rather than reason, could be virtuous.[85] In the late eighteenth century virtue and morality increased in importance to confront fears of societal corruption and evil, problems frequently associated with the elite churches. Many believed that the new republican society needed a "virtuous" people.[86] For evangelical Christians, however, virtue increasingly meant piety rather than disinterested love of country and participation in the public sphere.

The Second Great Awakening came about "to convert lost sinners to faith in Christ and, through the reformed behavior of the converted, to improve society."[87] As ordinary individuals gained the capacity for virtue, other mechanisms came into play and allowed the populace to act independently rather than turn to the elite class for direction.[88] When Elisha Dexter, master of the *William and Joseph,* feared losing his ship in 1842, he reflected upon earlier actions: "As the Brig was going from under us, and I kneeling in prayer to God for protection and succor, the sinfulness struck me of my preserving this treasure (twenty-five silver dollars), now less value to me than a crust of bread, or a gill of water. It struck me as so heinous that I threw it into the deep."[89] Though it was not a sin to keep the silver dollars, in this moment of crisis Dexter clearly reflected upon his own greed. God did not cause the storm because Dexter kept the coins; nor did God save him because he threw the coins away. Rather, Dexter considered his past actions and consciously decided to follow a path toward moral perfection.

Yet divine intercession became a component of rescue, and only through atonement and reflection could this occur. Unlike rational deists who relied on human intelligence and natural laws, nineteenth-century evangelicals looked to a higher being for salvation. Because they remained faithful, God rewarded repentant sailors, who subsequently survived and had a chance to return home.

The narratives directly tied God with individuals in a personal relationship that emphasized divine involvement. God's interventions in shipwrecks and miracles were no longer perceived as random but instead demonstrated God's continued presence and protection. Even predating the Second Great Awakening, William Whitwell in his 1770 sermon stated that "storms and tempests are his usual methods of reproof and punishment to those who do business on the mighty waters."[90] Although an increase in the number of accounts of divine and special providences in the early nineteenth century reflected a renewal of religious thought, shipwreck remained part of a larger and rational plan. Humans were not left solely to God's whim, as seen in earlier narratives; they could change and work to improve themselves.

Another trend that appeared by the nineteenth century was an increased prominence of women in shipwreck narratives. At this time congregations often consisted primarily of women, and contemporary thought aligned female characteristics of piety and virtuousness with Christian behavior.[91] Women were portrayed as moral beings who provided stability in a period of chaos. Their growing presence in the churches, united with an increased emphasis on moral and social perfection, brought women into more public roles in shipwreck narratives. Women's spiritual role in nineteenth-century literature came not only from their "own extreme religiosity but also from the protective veneration it arouses in the other characters."[92] Indeed this sympathetic cloak enveloped female participants in shipwreck.

One of the more dramatic and descriptive narratives, written by a woman, is the *Narrative of the Shipwreck and Sufferings of Miss Ann Saunders* (1827). The narrative came about after her "late happy conversion" in which she hoped to relate the need for individuals to attend to their "immortal souls and in being prepared for death." She combined religion with reform to influence individuals toward improving self and society. When a storm struck their vessel, Ann Saunders and Mrs. Kendall, the captain's wife, immediately began to pray, "And, O my Supreme and Glorious Deliverer, who art a prayer hearing and a prayer answering God, how shall I acknowledge my thankfulness for the mercy shown me, and in what manner shall I adore thee?" Throughout the narrative the two women provided a stable moral center that focused on God's intervention and benevolence. Even after two ships abandoned the stranded survivors, Saunders continued in her faith that God acted reasonably and that his actions, or lack thereof, had significance. She added, "But, alas the Almighty, for his own wise and good purposes, saw fit once more, to disappoint us in our expectations of relief. . . . That they (such trials) are the means which a merciful Creator often makes use of to bring souls to the knowledge of Jesus."[93]

This tale took a terrifying direction when after being stranded at sea for days the crew turned to cannibalism. Even when forced by thirst to drink her fiancé's blood, Ann Saunders placed this terrible act in a religious context: "O, it was a chastening rod, that has been the means I trust of weaning me forever from all the vain enjoyments of this frail world. . . . I have been made to drink deep at the cup of affliction, never will I forget the unbounded mercy and goodness of God, in preserving my life, in raising me from the depths of wo." Even in cannibalism God took an active role in preserving life and preparing individuals for eternity. As with earlier narratives she underwent a transformation process that represented her continued moral progression.[94]

Because of her piety and religious conviction, Saunders believed that God made her physically stronger and able to endure the depravations of shipwreck, while those around her succumbed to death. Through her spirituality and "feminine identity" she found a sense of power.[95] The spirit of God in her revealed that "thy prayers are heard, fear not, for I am with thee."

DREADFUL SHIPWRECK.

Representation of the Crew of the Blonde Frigate in the act of rescuing six wretched Survivors from the Wreck of the Ship Francis Mary.

Engraving, *Narrative of the Shipwreck and Sufferings of Miss Ann Saunders*. Sabin 77169. Courtesy of Earl Gregg Swem Library, College of William and Mary.

Indeed her fortitude paid off, and the next morning His Majesty's ship the *Blonde* came to their relief.

After shipwreck Saunders used her remaining pages to extol God's benevolence and to warn others, especially sailors, to prepare their souls for death. Saunders reported that during the voyage members of the crew were "impiously blaspheming that God' and that now they must remember the promises they made on board, with "a recollection of his goodness I think must lead you to repentance." Religion, then, "not only purifies, but also fortifies the heart . . . he is enured to temperance and restraint, He has learned firmness and self-command." She ended with the words, "I have endeavoured to lay before you, some of the motives, to induce you to attend, without delay, to the concerns of your souls; and it is my sincerest prayer that you may all be encouraged to seek that grace."[96]

Reform was a part of moral and social perfection, necessary for the continued success of the new republic, and conversion remained central to American religion.[97] As part of the larger reform movement, Whitwell advised against cursing in his sermon: "We hope we shall hear no more cursing or profaneness, from your mouths; but that you will rather reprove those, whose tongues are 'full of deadly poison,' who, when they 'bless God, even the father, curse men who are made after the similitude of God.'"[98] Through such measures America would become once again a "city on a hill."

Early nineteenth-century shipwreck narratives retained strains of seventeenth- and eighteenth-century Christianity. All authors viewed God as an ever-present being and involved intimately with daily life. However, later accounts minimized any emphasis on sin and causation; instead they emphasized God's work during and after shipwrecks as a savior and a teacher. These stories returned to notions of thanksgiving and reflection rather than portraying purely rational retellings of the events.

∽

Several historians have suggested that religion at sea was secondary, probably arising only in times of need, and it obviously varied according to time and circumstance.[99] In support of this statement, the captain of the *Peggy* (1766) summed up how quickly sailors and crew turned to any sense of hope in a moment of crisis: "Distress generally inspires the human mind with lively sentiments of devotion, and those, who, perhaps, dispute or disregard the existence of a Deity at other times, are ready enough, in the day of adversity, to think every advantageous turn in their affairs a particular exertion of the Divine benignity."[100] When death seemed imminent, the most blasphemous sailor could become devoutly religious.

Furthermore some historians suggest that only when all hope was lost did sailors call upon God.[101] While the narratives can be used to support this statement, this oversimplifies the relationship between humans and religion. Many Christians, a large part of the colonial seafaring population, often turned to God at the first sign of danger, while others relied on human ability and intelligence for survival and rarely mentioned any higher deity. Not everyone remained pious, and some refused to turn to divine guidance even to the bitter end. They limited divine intercession or the need for special providences to overcome shipwreck. In many instances God was only a limited player in survival, taking a backseat to human ability.

Yet the narratives had to relate what happened to those who did not turn to a higher being. William Whitwell admonished the young in his sermon: "Once you thought there was time enough to repent of the follies of youth; and when you were reminded of the uncertainty of life, and certainty of death, and were urged to seek an interest in Christ, your language was, go your way for this time, at a more convenient season I will hear you of this matter."[102] Such language lent a sense of urgency to salvation and redemption. God at any moment could end a person's life and disrupt the security of family and community. This fear fed into broader trends that relied on emotion and faith.

Religion brought stability and order, and shipwreck narratives relayed them to audiences at home. "In the sea-deliverance narrative the terrifying and disorienting experience of a storm, of a shipwreck, or capture by pirates is thus brought under control by a creative act of the literary imagination."[103] Shipwreck narratives connected populations on land with those who went to sea, either as crew members or as passengers.[104] Religion as portrayed in these narratives "exhibited changing attitudes, and responded to the cultural developments"; essentially they provided stability in times of chaos.[105] When needed, God interceded on behalf of pious Christians, and at other times he allowed the crews and passengers to help themselves. In both cases the narratives provided the survivors and the audience with a means of understanding and ordering events around them within a religious context that had significance to all.

· 4 ·

THEY WORKED LIKE HORSES
BUT BEHAVED LIKE MEN

Accidents and escapes are worth recording, from the knowledge they
convey, and the examples they produce. They plainly show that hope,
perseverance, and subordination, should form the seamen's great creed
and duty; as they tend to banish despair, encourage confidence, and
secure preservation.[1]

The sea affords an excellent arena for understanding the concept of masculinity. Sailors often entered the maritime world at a young age, and they
quickly learned acceptable standards of behavior and created familial allegiances at sea.[2] The day-to-day living conditions indoctrinated new recruits
into the all-male society in which male-male relationships provided necessary support and brotherhood. On ships boys constructed second families,
replacing those left on land, and formed relationships that provided these
individuals with a sense of identity and belonging. Many friendships developed into lifelong associations that represented a form of kinship, becoming
brothers in arms.[3] Along the way "boys" became "men" as voyages transformed into tests of manhood. Physical and mental training inculcated a
heroic notion of masculinity that designated bravery, ability, and endurance
as true manliness.[4]

Romantic visions of hardy men sailing the open seas or of rowdy, vulgar
riffraff whoring and drinking at every port remain popular images of sailors.
By contrast, gentlemen captains and officers added a sense of dignity and
respect to life at sea. In shipwrecks these perceptions persevered to a large
degree, solidifying into a distinct definition of masculinity that incorporated

a level of status or class. Rather than promoting individualistic, emotional, or reckless behavior, the accounts remained conservative, insisting that men remain moderate, in self-control, sober, and honest. Essentially the stories stressed that maintaining traditional gender roles, as established by the upper classes, was the only way to survive.[5]

Audiences on land and at sea read the repeated lessons within these accounts that emphasized strength, moderation, and self-control. Reading these narratives, male audiences internalized a specific form of masculinity; they learned with whom to identify and the types of behavior to avoid. At moments of crisis, men revealed their true essence and either upheld masculine ideals or fell to the level of cowards. Prescriptive by nature, published accounts of shipwreck taught audiences the correct forms of behavior.

Not only did these accounts promote specific definitions of masculinity, but they also substantiated order and assured readers that social stability and hierarchy remained intact. Many of the stories demonstrated that captains or officers who failed to display proper masculine virtues and crews who failed to obey sealed the vessels' demise. To overcome the chaotic situations, survival depended on leadership and the preservation of social order. Of course, some level of hierarchy was necessary for the proper sailing of the ships, but the narratives took this idea a step further and related how those who remained brave, capable, and collected lived to tell their tales, while those who failed faced chaos and death. This reliance on continued social order added a level of status to gender definitions. The stories often posited the captains in opposition to the crews and in doing so not only strengthened gender expectations but also promoted a certain definition of masculinity.

Given the masculine nature of life at sea, it is not surprising to see a dominant male presence in shipwreck accounts. Men went to sea and sailed the ships, and predominately men experienced shipwrecks. This masculine emphasis is not to ignore women who sailed, but their place remained secondary in most published accounts. In addition the overwhelming ratio of men to women at sea makes it easy to see why shipwreck narratives revolved around male participation.

Men were a majority of the authors as well, creating a clear bias in published accounts. Captains and crew members wrote or dictated their stories, giving themselves the starring roles. Men survived shipwrecks more often than women did and therefore provided the only authoritative voices for narrating the stories. As a result the available material for shipwreck accounts offered a male perspective that supplied a masculine-defined meaning of gender.[6] Published narratives, in conjunction with other forms of popular literature such as songs and poetry, also projected a specific view of manliness that not only affected sailors but also "were projections for those not part of the trade."[7] Men on land and at sea understood and accepted similar definitions of masculinity. Sailors were not separate from land but continued to maintain ties to home, and therefore their understandings of masculinity and place should be situated within cultural and societal themes found on land.

By the late eighteenth century society "equated manhood with self-control, productivity, virtue, and independence."[8] During this time, as the middle classes emerged they began to emulate upper-class ideals—primarily the notions of refinement and manners.[9] Through this period images of culture, courage, and independence abounded, and by the nineteenth century they came together to create the "American Adam," an individual of "heroic innocence" and full of potential with innate capabilities to overcome future obstacles.[10]

Literature and other forms of representation influenced popular perceptions that reinforced ideals of male behavior.[11] Gender relations were never stable, and men had to reassert themselves continually to maintain control. As negative images of pirates and sailors emerged through the early modern era and into the nineteenth century, capable men had to refute these behavioral stereotypes. Rather, "hegemonic norms of manhood encouraged disorderly men to conform to a standard of manly conduct conducive to individual self-restraint, good citizenship, and public order."[12] In a time of mobility and social change the narratives' authors remained tied to a more structured understanding of society and reinforced a masculine definition that stigmatized the disorderly while they rewarded conformity.

In shipwreck narratives much effort went toward championing the brave and heroic and of regaling the deeds of extraordinary men. In this context men occupied several roles within the narratives: they were protectors, team players, leaders, and heroes—each confirming a specific masculine trait that showed strength, capability, confidence, and even altruism.[13] Although several meanings of masculinity could occur simultaneously, the accounts often related one based on continued preservation of class and status. While masculine behavior remained consistent in the narratives written from the seventeenth to the nineteenth centuries, some changes did occur. For example, over time portrayals of masculinity shifted from a reliance on outward qualities to stressing inner character.[14] At the core, however, was a masculine standard of moderation and self-control.[15]

As protectors, men placed family and wives in the most sheltered spaces on the ships, such as in a hold or an aft cabin. Though they often failed in saving women and children, their efforts allowed husbands and fathers to preserve their masculine reputations and to become tragic heroes. For example, in 1668 most of William Thacher's family (except his wife) drowned on a voyage from Newbury to Marblehead. The women, children, and a few

"Loss of the *Halsewell* East Indiaman" (London: R. Wilkinson, 1786).
Painted by James Northcote, Royal Academician. Courtesy of the
Trustees of the British Museum, AN943302001.

passengers huddled in the hold as they waited for the ship to break apart.
Thacher, taking a paternal stance, described them: "My Children bewailing
me and not pitying themselves, and myself bemoaning them poor souls
whom I occasioned to such an end in their tender years."[16] Thacher failed
at his role of protector and felt the loss deeply. Throughout his narrative
Thacher supplied great detail concerning the loss of innocent children that
surely created a sympathetic pull from any parent.

A century later Captain Pierce's account of his experience on the
Halsewell (1786) demonstrated increasing sentimentality. The captain realized that his two daughters would not survive the shipwreck. According to
the narrative, he returned to the passengers and officers. "The latter were
employed in affording consolation to the unfortunate ladies, and with unparalleled magnanimity, suffering their compassion for the amiable companions of their own danger. . . . At this moment what must have been
the feelings of a father—of such a father as Captain Pierce?" As the ship
fell apart, "Captain Pierce again seated himself between his two daughters,
struggling to suppress the parental tear which then started into his eye."[17]

The failure to protect produced a painful guilt, and in the eighteenth century men could be emotional, though not overly expressive, as sympathetic husbands and fathers.[18] Rather than a form of weakness, this sympathy was important as it portrayed a proper patriarchal order and duty to family.[19]

By the nineteenth century compassion and sympathy were important, but only to a limited extent if a man wished to remain within masculine parameters. The stigma of too much emotion persisted beyond this period, as Richard Henry Dana acknowledged: "An overstrained sense of manliness is the characteristic of sea-faring men. . . . any show of attention would look sisterly and unbecoming a man who has to face the rough and tumble of such a life." He added, "A thin-skinned man could not live an hour on shipboard."[20] Sailors kept emotion hidden or faced ridicule by their mates.

The published narratives indicated that one of the most important aspects of masculinity was to be a capable team member. Though predating factories, ships resembled such institutions where collective work and cooperation were necessary for proper functioning. The need for teamwork continued and increased during shipwrecks, when sailors and passengers worked together to man the pumps, cut down the masts, or prepare the lifeboats. Even after a shipwreck all hands had to work as a team to ensure survival. For example, on the *Sultanna* (1832) the men worked sixteen hours to remove goods from the ship onto shore. The author described their collective effort as "all hands hard at work on the rocks and in the surf all day. Some with very sore feet and legs cut to pieces by the rock and burnt with the sun."[21] Each man did all he could to secure the crew's survival, as only with everyone's participation could they persevere. As a side note, such actions also had legal ramifications, and a sailor who failed to assist in the salvage might lose his wages.

Sailing was dangerous, and the men relied on one another for their very lives. When the *Boston* (1828) caught on fire only six days out of Charleston, the crew and passengers worked together to save the vessel. "The passengers had exerted themselves to the utmost to assist us," said Captain Mackay. "The officers had with unwearied exertion, coolness and persevering activity done all that men could do. The ship's crew worked like horses and behaved like men."[22] Survival in the crisis situation necessitated such behavior from all men, regardless of rank or social standing. In addition reputation surely played a role, and survivors acted in appropriate ways to remain in good public standing. Public perceptions and reputation were important for continued social and fiscal success in early America, and so men worked hard to maintain their place in society.

To lead properly during shipwreck, a truly masculine male had to be moderate and steady in his actions. Captain Cobb of the *Kent* (1827), who possessed "an ability and decision of character that seemed to increase with the imminence of the danger," was one such figure.[23] According to Barnabas Downs, on the *General Arnold* (1778), Captain Magee provided an excellent example of leadership: "In the hour of difficulty and danger he was calm, hopeful, self-reliant. Without these qualities, the most experienced and energetic often fail. . . . None would have survived if our master's spirit had not been there to cheer them by his works, and encourage them by his example."[24] In every instance the captains who survived had innate character that allowed them to rise to the situations. They did not give in to emotion or fear but remained calm, cool, and collected.

In any crew someone had to assume leadership to ensure a vessel's proper functioning. Typically this role fell to the captain, with each sailor occupying a specific place under his guidance. In shipwreck a leader became even more important for survival, and quite often the captain or a high-ranking officer maintained his position. During crisis a leader not only held a post of authority but also had to tend to the social needs of survivors to keep them calm and optimistic.[25] After experiencing his famous mutiny, Captain Bligh achieved an amazing navigational feat by sailing thousands of miles in a small open boat, all the while being considered an excellent captain by his men. During his voyage Bligh went to extremes not only to keep his men physically alive but also to prevent them from succumbing to depression. According to his narrative, he created a log line. He knew that "the greatest art of all was to divert their attention from the almost hopeless situation in which they were placed, and to prevent despondency from taking possession of their minds."[26] He continued, "The log being daily and hourly hove gave them also some employment, and diverted their thoughts for the moment from their melancholy situation." Bligh realized the necessity of providing these diversions, and in doing so he became a model leader. He maintained authority but also tended to the physical and psychological needs of his men.[27]

Some men transcended expectations to become heroic figures. They not only worked as parts of teams but in addition went beyond the call of duty to save others. Though these men did not go to sea to become heroes, they found themselves thrust into the role.[28] Most men achieved a normative level of manliness by, for example, protecting the women and children; but individuals who risked their own lives to save others were heroes in the narratives.

Commended for his efforts in the wreck of the *Albion* in 1822, Captain Williams died when a large wave swept him overboard, "a circumstance which may be attributed to the very extraordinary exertions which he used, to the last moment, for the preservation of the lives of the unfortunate passengers and crew." Although Williams would not survive, the author clearly believed that he was a "true man," acting bravely and calmly in an effort to save others.[29] In another example, the captain of the *Phoenix* (1780) praised the efforts of his lieutenant: "Archer, we ought all to be much obliged to you for the safety of the ship, and perhaps of ourselves. Nothing but that instantaneous presence of mind and calmness saved her."[30] In another instance the log of the *Henry* (1845) recognized one sailor for his efforts. When all seemed lost and they were about to be thrown onto the rocks, "wee the ships officers render our thanks to Henry Benson [seaman] for doing all in his power to prevent it."[31] These men were singled out for their efforts and became central to the narratives. Readers surely recognized the heroic nature of these men and that specific behavior resulted in positive reinforcement.

Captains and officers were not the only ones with the capability of becoming heroes. Common sailors might take the lead, although their centrality to the stories was often only temporary. Their heroics, however, created a standard, something that encouraged men to be more "masculine"—to sacrifice themselves for the common good.[32] For example, the gunner on the *Renown* (1736) saved the crew from certain death and future hardships. As related by Chaplain Crespel aboard the *Renown*, "If it had not been for our gunner, our future situation would have been dreadful. He ran to the bread-room, and although the water had already made its way in, he threw a quantity of bread between decks. He thought also some muskets, a barrel of powder, and a sack of cartridges, would be useful to us in case we should escape this danger, he therefore caused all these things to be brought up. His precautions were not useless, and without the assistance of these articles I should never have been preserved to relate this."[33] The gunner had the presence of mind to think beyond immediate survival, and thanks to his abilities many of the crew survived.

Not all men, however, reacted to shipwreck in such an exemplary manner. The narratives labeled some men as cowards when they refused to help or when they exhibited effeminate characteristics of weakness and emotion. Most of these men ended up dead in the narratives. In published accounts such men were negative examples and quickly disappeared from the stories. For example, in 1726 a passenger, Nathaniel Gardner, made an already bad situation worse when he began to go mad. The only survivor, William Walling, stated that Gardner, after seeing two spirits in the shape of women, "pulled off his Coat and Jacket, and wrapt a Piece of an old Blanket about his Waste [and] Chest in Fashion of Indian Women." When asked why, he answered that "the Spirits told me that all those that wear Peticoats they won't get hurt, and all those that do not they will kill."[34] He later tried to kill himself, stating that the devil was on board and had threatened to take him away alive.

Such imagery informed the readers of the possible repercussions when an individual was unable or unwilling to respond in an appropriate manner. Panic in a crisis situation often led to widespread alarm, and as collective judgment and reasoning deteriorated, the chances for death increased. Thus bravery and strength not only had implications for displaying proper gendered behavior but also affected survival itself.[35] The narratives taught readers the necessity of being capable crew members and that failure to act might lead to death for all. In addition authors found a means to substantiate their own masculinity as well as to dishonor those who failed to respond appropriately.

And yet emotion did not necessarily indicate cowardice. After the men abandoned the *Peggy* in 1785, the author noticed "one of our oldest seamen, who at this moment was standing near me, turned his head aside to wipe away a tear; I could not refrain from sympathizing with him, my heart was already full."[36] The narratives did not contain criticism of this emotional behavior; instead the fear added to the stories' drama and sensationalism. During the shipwreck of the *Hercules* (1796), "the perpetual roaring of the elements echoing through the void, produced such an awful sensation in the minds of the most experienced of the seamen, that several of them appeared for some time in a state of stupefication." Despite their inability to function, most of these men retained their masculinity. Others on the vessel, however, did not fare so well, and their "shriekings and exclamations" served only to scare others.[37] Men who failed to overcome their fears were cowards whose emotions became signs of weakness, whereas those who regained control persevered.

Dishonesty was one failing of masculinity that did not appear in many shipwreck accounts but was an issue in some stories. To become a liar or thief in a time of crisis not only jeopardized lives but also threatened a person's reputation as a man. Fear that such accusations would destroy a reputation largely preempted negative behavior.[38] Reputation was very public, and the judgment of other men was the most effective tool for determining character. Both victims and survivors faced such rulings if a shipwrecked vessel returned to port. Well into the eighteenth century reputation and success relied on personal networks, and therefore reputation and trust were important for a masculine identity.[39]

Only one narrative overtly confronted the issue of reputation, and it is one of a handful to have two distinct versions in print. The captain John Deane wrote one version, and the other was by his first mate, Christopher

Langman. The *Nottingham Galley* struck a small island off the coast of Maine in 1710. All hands made it onto a tiny, isolated island, where the harsh weather conditions and lack of provisions soon led to death. Stranded for twenty-four days with little food or shelter, the crew turned on the dead for sustenance. Some men survived, including Langman and Deane, who published their accounts within a year of their rescue. Each author wrote his version fully aware of the other's publication.

The captain's brother, Jasper Deane, a survivor of the ordeal, published the first edition of the *Nottingham Galley*. In the postscript Jasper challenged Langman's version, although Langman's account had not yet gone to print: "We think it our Duty to the Truth, and our selves, to obviate a barbarous and scandalous Reflection, industriously spread abroad and level'd at our ruine, by some unworthy, malicious Persons (viz.) That we having ensur'd more than our Interest in the Ship Nottingham, agred and willfully lost her, first designing it in Ireland, and afterwards effecting it at Boon Island. Such a base and villanous Reflection, scarse merits the Trouble of an Answer, were not Truth and Reputation so much concern'd."[40] Jasper refuted Langman's assertions that Deane acted in a cowardly fashion and, most important, that he intentionally sank the ship. To the latter accusation Jasper stated, "And as for the other Part of the Charge, of willfully losing her at Boon Island, one wou'd wonder Malice itself cou'd invent or suggest any thing so ridiculous. . . . We presume Interest only can induce Men to such Villainies." Apparently the Deanes needed to insert this postscript as Langman's account, at least initially, found much support. Deane lamented, "How ridiculous is such a Supposition, and yet this is the Reproach we at present labour under, so far as to receive daily ignominious Scandals upon our Reputations, and injurious Affronts and Mobbings to our Faces."[41] John Deane's reputation was at stake, and the brothers were willing to do everything possible to preserve their public standing.

In this case the events of actual shipwreck were not in dispute; rather the quarrel centered on John Deane's behavior during crisis. Langman portrayed the captain as inept and called him a braggart and a fool who exaggerated events to make himself look the hero. In his account Langman began quite abruptly: "We having been Sufferers in this unfortunate Voyage, had reason to believe, from the Temper of our Captain, who treated us barbarously both by Sea and Land, that he would misrepresent the Matter, as we now find he has done in a late Pamphlet by him published." Striking at the heart of Deane's masculinity, Langman wrote, "The true Causes of our own and their Misfortunes, and how they might, humanely speaking, have been easily avoided, had Captain Dean been either an honest or able Commander."[42] Such statements attacked Deane's reputation and honor and surely threatened him as both a gentleman and a businessman.[43] To prevent the captain from further ruining their reputations, the three felt it necessary to publish their account and to minimize any damage he might do to another crew in the future.

Langman's account continued, "Then the Captain, who had been cursing and Swearing before, began to cry and howl for Fear of losing his life. . . . He cryed heartily, and begg'd the mate to do what he cou'd to save us, for he himself cou'd do nothing." Langman publicly challenged the captain's masculinity, portraying him as an emotional and effeminate male and, according to his version, physically out of control. By contrast, Deane asserted that this never happened. He wrote that instead we "call'd down all Hands to the Cabin, where we continu'd a few Minutes earnestly supplicating Mercy; but knowing Prayers without Endeavours are vain, I order'd all up again." In opposition to Langman's account, the captain insisted that he had remained calm and had done his part to assist the crew.[44]

Langman alleged that even in rescue the captain dishonored himself by behaving in an uncivil manner toward the rescuers: "and instead of being thankful to God for his own and our Deliverance, he returned with the Dog to his Vomit, and behav'd himself so brutishly, that his Friend Captain Purver was obliged to turn him out of his house."[45] In a society where outward characteristics, such as hospitality, were deemed to reflect a person's inner qualities, such comments could be extremely damaging. To be an honorable person was to exhibit proper social tact; likewise ungentlemanly individuals presented selfish and uncharitable qualities.[46]

Deane's account, first published by his brother, Jasper, introduced the differences of opinion in his 1711 edition. Jasper stated that he did not intend to write his narrative but that because of the "designs of others," he found it necessary lest "others less acquainted, prejudice the Truth with an imperfect Relation." He therefore published his narrative to expose Langman's "small Treatise to publick View and Censure." Modern collections of shipwreck narratives favor Deane's version, using his account rather than Langman's. Despite Langman's accusations, his account apparently did not appeal to audiences, and so only one edition exists. In the long run, Deane, with better resources and access to publishing, was able to print his narrative several times during the eighteenth century, which suggests that his narrative was the more popular and perhaps the more accepted version.[47]

Langman's account of the *Nottingham* is interesting in that it is one of few in which captains did not behave appropriately. Most narratives stressed that captains and officers remained cool and strong while the crews despaired. Published narratives reinforced a tie between masculinity and status, creating a primarily gentlemanly or upper-class definition. Audiences read how officers reacted in crisis situations as opposed to the actions of the crews and often found the crews' behaviors wanting.[48]

Social status in early America was not simple but depended on a number of factors, such as occupational prestige, income, education, religion, and family position.[49] To complicate matters further, wealth, status, and power overlapped while also operating independently of one another.[50] In addition such elements shifted over time and place.

Wealthy individuals in the American colonies modeled themselves after the elite in England by claiming to inherit long-standing traditions of deference and social hierarchy.[51] Deviations from this pattern emerged, however, as a belief in a natural order did not fit completely with the realities and mobility of the New World. Religious differences, new environmental situations, and an absence of individuals from the highest and lowest social ranks altered social development in the American colonies.[52] An abundance of land, not available in Britain, allowed many early colonists to become landowners and thus modified how they perceived social standing.[53]

Understandings of social order in the American colonies changed dramatically between initial colonization and independence. In early New England men of religion dominated colonial American society, though by the end of the seventeenth century status began shifting to those with economic wealth.[54] Indeed, "class was no stranger to Early America, but neither was Anglo-America thoroughly class dominated."[55] During the early seventeenth century land remained plentiful and society relatively equal, with no one person owning a majority of capital.

In the eighteenth century there were numerous changes in which class distinctions fluctuated. Paternalistic foundations diminished and sources of wealth moved from land to capital.[56] Families no longer provided every son with land, and children faced declining options in settled areas, forcing many into new occupations or to migrate into less settled frontiers. Working relations also changed in response to a reduction of available indentured servants, a prime labor source, especially in New England. As these transformations occurred, society fragmented, with wealth accumulating in the hands of a few while others negotiated a precarious status in a burgeoning commercial system.[57] Understandings of status shifted: the God-given hierarchy of the seventeenth century changed to one where the elite earned their position through hard work and innate capabilities. Their abilities provided the justification for them to govern the remainder of society.[58] Thus money and capital became synonymous with power, and the rich occupied seats of government and authority.

The creation of urban centers assisted in developing a wealthy class and conversely a large landless population.[59] As the colonies were settled and commercialization increased, social stratification intensified.⁶⁰ Communities were no longer ordered according to family structure. This period was one of increased mobility and changes in hierarchy as the American colonists reached out to the Atlantic and beyond, generating true urban, international ports.

Even during the American Revolution, with its rhetoric of equality and inalienable rights, society still maintained a hierarchy led by a dominant economic elite. Americans began defining themselves as opposed to "others" based on race and religion as well as money, hierarchy, and occupation.⁶¹ By the end of the eighteenth century, many port towns exhibited a broad social spectrum with a wealthy few and an expanding impoverished population. Those who took advantage of the market system rose in the social ranks, though many never found the means to prosper.⁶² The trend up to and through the early nineteenth century was a gradual widening between rich and poor.⁶³

Although men, and women, who went to sea took with them models of behavior learned from land, social order in a maritime context was not an exact copy of the life they left behind. The published narratives, however, reveal that general understandings of gender and class remained intact and seemed to solidify as danger increased. Readers learned to emulate the officers and captains, the elite of the ship. For example, the carpenter of the *Hercules* (1796) burst into tears when the captain reprimanded him for not operating the pumps: "The carpenter's miserable appearance . . . and the affecting tone of voice in which he delivered his apprehensions, considerably increased the terrors of the crew." The captain, in response, "thought it necessary to declare that he would perform his duty and stick to the ship until he was convinced from his own observation that all hope of saving her was at an end." The captain later threatened the carpenter, saying that unless "he made every exertion to encourage the people in their duty at the pumps, he should be immediately thrown into the sea." This threat had a profound effect on the carpenter, and he "exerted himself afterwards with a manly perseverance."⁶⁴ The captain offered a positive role model by demonstrating how a man of his standing should behave. The captain remained by his post and even offered to take over duties beneath his standing to save the ship. He proved his masculinity by shaming the carpenter who lacked self-control, thus aligning the carpenter with passion and emotion, characteristics often associated with effeminacy, while the captain remained calm and in control of his emotions.

Even in very early narratives captains sometimes failed, as related by the passenger Henry Norwood aboard the *Virginia Merchant* in 1649. The sailors were so terrified that they could not move, and in the moment of shipwreck they fell to their knees in prayer, "commending their souls at the last gasp." Then "the captain came out at the noise to rectify what was amiss; but seeing how the case stood, his courage failed." It was up to the mate to pull the crew and captain together and save the day.[65] If the mate had not become a powerful leader, the crew might have devolved into anarchy with no means of organized rescue. This case was an anomaly; only a few narratives portrayed captains or officers who lost control of themselves.

The key to masculinity rested in the necessary balance between moderation and excess. This meant that the ability to remain deliberate and in control was clearly a gentlemanly characteristic that did not take into account other forms of masculinity. For example, Simeon Crowell, a common seaman who went to sea in 1795, found his fellow sailors to be less than desirable. The crew included "the thief, lyar, drunkard, profane swearer and fornicator." He added that "by this crew I was derided (I suppose for my sobriety) and not being accustomed to their manner of life and conversation, could not make my self sociable with them."[66] Rather than give in to a variety of excesses, Crowell placed himself above the other crew members and retained a class standing higher than the rest. He also created a strong division between out-of-control lower classes and those who remained in control of their desires.

Although shipwreck was a moment of crisis, individuals, as described by the narratives, usually maintained their proper status. Fear that men were innately just like women—lustful, passionate, greedy, and unpredictable—meant that men had to be the opposite.[67] Gentlemen controlled the events, and the narratives devoted much time to articulating a masculine stereotype based on bravery and heroics. Over time such perceptions became normative, creating a standard to which subsequent readers aspired.[68] Although manliness was never a simple and static concept, shipwreck narratives emphasized a specific definition of masculinity, one that tied together civility, self-restraint, and strength. As related in H. M. Barker's *The Log Book; or Nautical Miscellany* (1826–27), for example, the characteristics of a nineteenth-century naval officer comprised "a high sense of honor and courage, with a friendliness of nature, and generosity of mind, that is conspicuous even to an enemy." In contrast, common sailors were "rough, hardy, and honest; regular in the points of their duty, disdaining all fatigue and danger when the service requires it. . . . There is a noble and true independence in the character of a seaman that frequently raises him above the ordinary difficulties of life."[69]

In addition to prescriptive literature concerning masculinity, most narratives related the need for continued social order and reasserted the differences between sailors and captains. Most authors tended to ignore any flexibility in defining masculinity; instead they promoted a definition that asserted a class bias and fed into knowing one's place in society. Numerous accounts suggested that sailors lacked refinement and morals and occupied a low level of social standing.

Among sailors there were different standards of masculinity that did not require genteel behavior. For example, in cases of shipwreck common sailors often became intoxicated. Some did this to quicken the possibility of death, others to deal with stress and fear. Of course, drinking had several implications for masculinity. From a positive viewpoint, it could create brotherhood and an opportunity for showing honor and trust between men. On the negative side, it could test self-control and lead to a loss of rationality. Drunkenness allowed individuals to lose reason and the characteristics appropriate to the male gender; therefore to be a drunkard was to exhibit feminine qualities and a loss of honor.[70]

Intoxicated sailors on the *General Arnold* (1778) from Boston refused to follow their officers and continued to drink rather than help save the ship. Not only did these men refuse to work as a team, but they also exhibited "unmanly" qualities and were the first to despair.[71] On the *Peggy* (1765) the crew broke open the supply of liquor and remained intoxicated up to the time of their rescue, according to the captain's narrative: after several days afloat, the crew "made very free with both [wine and brandy]. . . . I could neither be sorry nor surprised at this motion.—What gave me concern was, the continual excess to which they drank—and the continued course of execration on blasphemy, which was occasioned by that excess." The *Providence Gazette* and several other publications, such as the *London Magazine,* added, "During all this time the poor wretches were drunk, and a sense of their condition seemed to evaporate in execration and blasphemy." The newspaper made a clear distinction between the captain and the crew: "While they were continually heating wine in the steerage, the Captain subsisted upon the dirty water at the bottom of the case . . . with a few drops of Turlington's Balsam."[72] The captain removed himself from the crew and became the sole voice of reason. Not only did he refuse the alcohol, but later in the narrative he was said to be the only one who did not cannibalize his servant. Rather than give into physical desires and lose control, the captain remained above such impulses.

The captain went on, portraying the behavior of the first mate after rescue: "The next day my inconsiderate mate, Mr. Archibald Nicolson, who had so long wallowed, as I may say, in every mire of excess, having reduced himself, by a continued intoxication, to such a state, that no proper sustenance would stay on his stomach, fell a martyr to his inebriety."[73] Such narratives demonstrated that moderate behavior was beneficial for survival and that those who failed often died. Indeed since the captain of the *Peggy* persevered, it was his reward to write the story and to portray his first mate in such a light. Knowing that someone else would live to tell the tale made reputation and slander effective tools for controlling conduct.[74]

On ships each man had a specific place and duty, and each man knew his fellows' ranks. At sea status and power usually followed a typical hierarchy, with masters having absolute power. Below him were the mate, the boatswain, the quartermaster, fully trained or able seamen, and at the lowest level ordinary sailors and various "boys." The proper functioning of ships necessitated a strict hierarchy, though there was no one type of class relationship at sea. Depending on sources studied, order might vary from ship to ship.[75] Rank, knowledge, watch, and pay all had roles in determining a ship's hierarchy.[76] Status came about by a variety of means that differed from ship to ship, according to time and place. Promotion was fluid, based on age and experience, and though one could move up, the path might lead down as well.[77] Everyone knew the others' ranks and the duties assigned to them. In a highly visible world, sailors who were forced to do a job below their ability were degraded; likewise claiming status higher than one's experience produced resentment because the crew had to fill in for a less able person.[78]

Some captains gained their position through wealth and influence, while others achieved their rank through years of experience. In many instances little social difference existed between owners and crew members, and quite often captains' personal backgrounds were not much different from those of the crew. A captain's status came from "personality, age, and skill," with power derived from custom and necessity rather than economic status before the law.[79] As the eighteenth century progressed, wealth consolidated in the hands of the few and some captains, taking advantage of increased colonial shipping, became quite prosperous, thus widening a gap between masters and sailors.[80] A demonstration of this difference can be found in a description of a parade honoring George Washington in which sea captains held a prominent place, behind only merchants, professionals, and various government officials; sailors came second to last in the parade—ahead of common laborers.[81]

Shipwreck narratives portray a conservative stereotype concerning order and class and as a result reflect how society perceived authority and status. The narratives support a continuation of an older social order. They suggest that when a vessel met with catastrophe the crew generally clung to traditional roles and hierarchies in their efforts to save the ship and themselves. The captain, mate, cook, sailor, and cabin boy understood that each had a part in survival and that each must do his duty to persevere. Shipwreck did not mean total chaos. The narratives reassured readers and potential participants that even within this event order and stability persevered.

In general captains exercised supreme authority over everyone and everything on their vessels. A captain's primary directive was to "prosecute the voyage," and all his actions were directed to this end. It was his responsibility to divide the men into watches, proportion food, take sightings, and determine courses—in essence to make sure everything ran accordingly.[82] By law (1848) a captain had the "right to compel prompt obedience to his orders" and "could subject the offender to corporeal punishment." But the law also stated that this punishment be "moderate, just, and proportionate."[83] His authority was not absolute, and although captains resorted to brutality or the threat of it, to maintain order the most successful captains exercised control judiciously, knowing that sailors refused to tolerate such extreme measures.[84]

Status aboard ships was manifest in the physical spaces and material goods afforded to those of higher rank. Furthermore "space was inseparable from the authority it displayed and the relationships it enclosed."[85] Captains (and usually officers) lived in the best cabins in the ships' sterns, while more ordinary sailors occupied large, open areas in the ships' bows. A captain was often the only person on board to have his own private cabin, and he received better food and comfort.

Edward Ward, writing in the eighteenth century, provided a vivid, if somewhat sarcastic, view of captains. According to Ward, a sea captain was "a Leviathan, or rather a kind of Sea God, whom the poor Tars worship as the Indians do the Devil, more thro' fear, than affection; that he's more a Devil, than the Devil himself." He remained hidden, "for such a Prostitution of presence, he thinks, weakens his authority, and makes his worship less reverenc'd by the Ship's Crew. It is impudence for any to approach him within the length of a Boat-hook."[86] Ward's sarcasm aside, he did point out the rigid differences between captain and crew.

Because it was a captain's duty to make sure a ship made it safely to port and that merchants and owners received maximum profits, a competent captain asserted all available power to ensure a safe and prosperous voyage. He had to remain calm and in control of himself and his crew. Captain Magee on the *General Arnold* (1778), of Boston, ran into rough seas: "under such circumstances, the stoutest heart might quail. Captain Magee was heard to list only one word of complaint—he never despaired—he cheered and encouraged his men to persevere."[87] In hoping to preserve future voyages, William Vaughn stated that patience and perseverance were necessary to overcome all obstacles. However, there was no one means to do so. Rather, "it is not always possible to prescribe rules of conduct in most cases that must, in general, form their own rules; but a great deal may be done by management and good conduct."[88] Such men possessed natural strength and ability that allowed them to overcome shipwreck, and perhaps live another day. The narratives substantiated an upper-class image that tied one specific form of masculinity to self-control and status.

During shipwrecks it was critical that leaders organize and command the scared and confused (that is, the crews).[89] Emergencies required immediate action and reaction. "It is necessary, therefore, that all matters relating to the navigation of the ship, and to the preservation of good order on board, should be under the supreme direction of a single person."[90] To take this further, the narratives warned against captains wavering or listening to lesser individuals. The leaders must remain strong and in command or chaos and death became ever increasing possibilities.

Despite the captains' authority and strict regulations, sailors asserted their power when necessary. Common mechanisms included protests, walking out, desertion, and mutiny.[91] In the early eighteenth century John Cremer related that when he was unhappy or dissatisfied at sea he often changed ships, quit a voyage, or at least made the motion to, in which cases the captains either addressed his concerns or let him leave. At the end of these voyage he was paid and "set free" to wander until he was out of money and then had to find another berth.[92]

Sailors had several options for creating better situations. Word of mouth let mariners know of "good" captains and ships, contracts provided legal assistance against owners who denied pay, or they could work as a collective body that proved, as it did on land, that a mob possessed great power.[93] Often to gain better wages, to improve conditions, or to counter an overly brutal captain sailors simply refused to sail. Such actions limited captains' "absolute" authority, permitting sailors a modicum of power and agency in their daily lives.[94]

One example of a crew taking matters of punishment into their own hands, bypassing the captain's authority, came from the *Peggy* (1785). The crew "got the cook laid on the windlass, and were giving him a most severe cobbing with a flat piece of his own firewood." The cook ordinarily used freshwater to boil greens but instead had boiled them in saltwater, "which rendered them so intolerably tough, that they were not fit for use." The sailors found offense in this and exacted the above punishment. "As soon as the captain had reached forward, he was much exasperated with them for their precipitate conduct, in punishing without his knowledge and permission."[95] Life aboard ships was not easy, and sailors expected whatever few perks were available. If slighted they took matters into their own hands and reacted in a collective manner that often saw results.

Within the shipwreck narratives, sailors often argued against captains to leave the ships at first danger. William Vaughn in 1804 stated that sailors "should be impressed with the danger and folly of deserting ships upon the first alarm." Quite often, Vaughn warned, survivors might face greater risk in small, exposed boats. "As [a] seaman should never abandon Hope—it should be his motto as well as his sheet-anchor. He should be strongly impressed with the idea, that the buoyancy of a ship in itself, in all cases, will keep her long afloat when leaky."[96] Within his warning Vaughn hoped to minimize chaos and to prevent undue injury or damage. Someone, the captain if possible, must organize and lead panicked crew and passengers.

Although narratives, advice books, and common knowledge relayed the importance of following orders, not all seamen did so. During shipwreck a crew could, and sometimes did, question a captain's decisions. Captain Riley of the *Oswego* (1800) had to convince his crew to stay aboard the ship rather than abandon her. Not satisfied, the crew came forward with a bargain, that if the captain allowed them to cut the masts, "they would stay still till morning." After much arguing the crew, afraid that the ship would sink during the night, insisted on going ashore.[97] The *Tyrrel* (1786), sailing from Sandy Hook to Antigua, began to leak, and according to the chief mate, the "captain was now earnestly entreated to put for New York, or to steer for the capes of Virginia." The next day the captain agreed to sail for North Carolina.[98] Good commanders often listened to crew members but did not necessarily give up power. They understood their fragile position and that if they ignored crews' fears, all authority might fail. Moderate behavior and a need to balance force with understanding made a strong leader. On the *Oswego*, in cutting down the masts the second mate "raised himself up very deliberately and said, 'It is all d——d nonsense, we will go ashore.'" The captain, who realized the tenuous situation, later wrote, "As grating as that expression was, prudence forbade me making a reply or noticing it."[99] Narratives demonstrated that good captains balanced power and understanding.

A popular conception associated with shipwreck involved the notion of the noble captain going down with his ship. Though an admirable sentiment, and one that gave great drama to any account, shipwreck narratives rarely supported its occurrence. Captains and officers authored a majority of published accounts, indicating that they survived. Of the narratives used in this study, captains or officers authored almost a third, with passengers writing another quarter of published accounts.[100] Captains and officers might "pull rank" and regard their place in the lifeboats as necessary to navigate the crafts to safety. Officers and subalterns frequently gained access to lifeboats, shelter, or food ahead of common seamen, thus increasing their chances for survival. On the rocks near Seacombe, the *Halsewell* (1785) struck ground with little hope of rescue. "It was agreed that the boats could not then be of any use, but it was proposed that the officers should be confidentially requested, in case an opportunity presented itself, of making it serviceable, to reserve the long boat for the ladies and themselves, and this precaution was accordingly taken."[101] The narrative failed to mention saving the sailors or the soldiers' wives, though the narrative indicated that they were on board. According to the narratives, status had its rewards, although only up to a point, when death became the ultimate leveler.

Narratives were replete with examples showing the advantages of status during shipwreck. In 1796, while sailing to Bengal, the captain of the *Hercules* had to contemplate abandoning ship. The captain prepared the longboat, but afraid that the crew might sail away, he "directed the second mate and three seamen to take possession of her; at the same time giving them arms and express orders to shoot the first man who attempted to board her without permission."[102] The crew of the *Margaret* (1810) faced a similar situation when they foundered on their way from Naples to Marblehead. When disaster struck, several individuals (including the captain) jumped into the longboat. The thirteen individuals in the longboat remained close to the ship, promising not to leave those still stranded on the vessel. However, they kept at a distance to prevent remaining crew members from swimming to the longboat and possibly capsizing it. After several days the longboat became separated and was eventually rescued. Nothing more was ever heard of the *Margaret* and those left on the wreck.[103]

This is not to say that all captains jumped immediately into lifeboats. Many captains and officers worried about their reputations when, and if, they returned home. Lieutenant Archer of the *Hercules* initially offered to run a line to shore to enable the crew's escape when he realized, "This won't do for me, to be the first man out of the ship, and the first lieutenant; we may get to England again, and people may think I paid a great deal of attention to myself, and did not care for any body else." Instead, he proclaimed, "I'll see every man, sick and well, out of her before me."[104] Captain Cobb of the *Kent* (1827) too declared "in his immovable resolution to be the last, if possible, to quit his ship."[105] A gentlemanly reputation was important for success in a commercial environment, and quitting a ship before others might demonstrate a lack of concern for the owners' cargo and vessel. Men needed to "preserve and earn the trust of other men" so that they might one day sail other ships.[106] This level of assurance in the narratives possibly pertained to legal matters, as by law a captain had to show that a wreck did not occur due to negligence and that he did all he could to save the vessel and cargo.[107]

After wrecking, as survivors reacted to the aftermath of crisis, traditional hierarchy could fail. With immediate danger past, individuals could begin to rethink events and turn to the obstacles ahead. In some instances the captains' and officers' authority decreased and even failed, though usually only temporarily. Despite the possibility of mutiny, in most instances crews presented only minor challenges.

After abandoning ship, the remaining crew members of the *Betsy* (1756) found themselves in a small lifeboat with few provisions. On the fourth day they saw a sloop, but it failed to see them, throwing two sailors into a deep depression. According to Captain Aubin, these men refused to help or even to bail water. Both he and the first mate tried to reason with them but turned to more drastic tactics, when they threatened "to kill them instantly with the top-mast, which we used to steer by, and to kill ourselves afterwards, to put a period to our misery. The menace made some impression on them, and resumed his employment of bailing as before."[108] Aubin had to negotiate with the sailors but found that only with the threat of violence did they react. Using force to maintain authority was one means for captains and officers to remain in control.

William Bligh, after the infamous *Bounty* mutiny, sailed several thousand miles from Tofoa to Timor in a small open boat with those who remained loyal. While in the boat Bligh managed to maintain authority, though at times it seemed that a second mutiny might occur. According to Bligh, "On this occasion, fatigue and weakness so far got the better of their sense of duty; one person in particular, went so far to tell me . . . that he was as good a man as myself. . . . I determined to either preserve my command or die in the attempt; in seizing a cutlass, I ordered him to lay hold of another and defend himself; on which he called out that I was going to kill him, and immediately made concessions."[109] When desperate and far from land sailors often took survival into their own hands; however, once an authority figure appeared, old hierarchies fell into place. Again, the accounts related lessons of leadership and of maintaining control. Chaos within the narratives, while a threat, rarely became a reality.

Yet in some narratives deference to a large degree remained unquestioned. The men of the *Kent* (1827), while waiting for rescue, found a box of oranges, and though exhausted, hungry, and "beginning to experience the pain of intolerable thirst, [they] refused to partake of the grateful beverage, until they had afforded a share of it to their officers."[110] Sailors often allowed officers into lifeboats or gave them special consideration with food and other necessities. To some extent this served their own purposes as officers might be the only ones with navigational skills or have knowledge of approaching coastlines. Although crews no longer legally had to follow their captains after shipwrecks, they often resorted to the established chain of command.

Conversely some captains had difficulty controlling crews, primarily when sailors lost respect for their abilities. Capt. Nathaniel Uring (1726) experienced such a problem. When shipwrecked off modern-day Honduras, most of his crew decided to go on their own, without regard to their injured captain. Uring stated that, "there being no Remedy but to comply with them, or be left there to starve, I consented to go." They attempted to take a canoe out past the breakers and paddle their way to the nearest settlement. Once in the canoe, Uring again took control and coordinated efforts to steer the canoe over a high surf. However, the waves proved too much. "The sea rose so high, and broke so terribly, they [the sailors] were frighted and confounded, and stared like Men amaz'd without obeying my orders." They made it back to shore only by the captain's quick thinking, and once they were again safe on land, the men swore that they would never get back into the canoe. So they returned to the beach, where Uring once again had problems of authority and the sailors attempted several times to abandon him.[111]

In occasions of shipwreck crews who lost trust in their captains' abilities instead looked to their own survival. For example, the captain of the *Oswego* ordered his crew to remain with the ship, but they insisted on leaving. The captain tried to reason with them "upon the impropriety of that measure [leaving the ship], when the only reply I heard, was, 'we are in duty bound to take care of ourselves, and not stay here and drown.'" The captain lost this round, and the crew climbed into various boats and headed for shore.[112]

Common sailors, according to the narratives, often experienced shipwreck in a variety of ways, many of which differed from the officers' conduct. Some lost control of their emotions, while others rose to meet the new demands; a few took advantage of their situation, and yet many continued as if nothing had happened. These men sometimes gave into fear, drinking and refusing to work for the ships' common good. Rather than follow the captains' orders, many wallowed in self-pity or formed their own courses for survival.

A common factor regarding a loss of order came from the sailors' inclination to drink. Aboard the *General Arnold* (1778) the crew attempted to cut down the masts in hope of keeping the ship upright. However, some sailors refused to do their duties and instead became intoxicated. In the bitter cold and with no hope for survival, "the authority of the officers had ceased—each one sought, as best as he could, his own safety." Several sailors became drunk and, "to keep their feet from freezing, had filled their boots with rum, and they were first to yield to dispair."[113] The narratives provided behavioral lessons, including the need to avoid intoxication, and warned that those who yielded to such passions would fail and die.

Losing control, especially when intoxicated, often meant death. While adrift in a small boat Joseph Bailey, master of the *Alida and Catherine* (1749) of New York, remained collected and encouraged others to fast and protect limited provisions. After several days in this condition they spied a ship, and "our people fell to and eat and drank heartily, not considering that though we saw the vessel, she might not see us, or at least might not discover our Distress, and so pass by."[114] The captain maintained the ideal quality of moderation and strength, not giving in to his hunger and self-preservation. In effect he as the leader kept his responsibility to the common good rather than thinking only about himself.

In a similar light, the survivors of shipwreck aboard the *General Arnold* did not regard the safety of all; rather, "there was such a crowd upon the quarter deck we could not stand up without treading upon one another." The author stated that as soon as he recovered his footing, he "trampled upon others in my turn; for the immediate regard which every man had to his own life prevented him from attending to the distress of others."[115] These accounts suggest that the stereotype of masculine ideals, set forth earlier in this chapter, did not always prevail. In cases of shipwreck, survival often took precedence over maintaining masculine and social expectations. Yet the narratives taught that when these norms failed, a person could expect death.

Images of masculinity, as portrayed in the narratives, promoted an ideal that kept men in line, preserved social order, and placed the public good over the private.[116] Individualism had its place, but in cases of shipwreck it was limited by the greater need for survival. Although the narratives supported the maintenance of status and authority and the overall persistence of order in crisis situations, the ideal was never complete.

One area of masculinity and status that rarely entered the main course of events in shipwreck narratives was the place of African American sailors. Much as did women, these individuals appeared only momentarily. Black sailors and slaves became central figures only through their extraordinary efforts or deeds. These were acceptable, but only temporarily, because their actions did not subvert traditional hierarchy. Instead they acted for the moment and then disappeared, allowing the accounts' focus to remain on white males. Despite their marginality, black individuals surfaced, or were at least mentioned, in thirteen of the narratives studied.

In most aspects of maritime trade, free and enslaved blacks comprised an important component.[117] Going to sea allowed a sense of freedom and identity unavailable on land, but by no means did it provide equality for such men. Instead they often acted in supporting roles, such as in positions as cooks or stewards, rather than as able seamen, as substantiated by the narratives.[118] In fact the narratives allowed blacks no sense of identity except as useful labor.

Of the shipwreck narratives studied, five listed blacks as slaves and one as a servant. Three narratives had black crew members, with one mentioned specifically as a steward. In eight accounts most or all of the blacks on board died, with only two narratives suggesting that black individuals made it back safely. Reflecting black men's class, most narratives failed to provide them with names, and those mentioned were identified only by their first names.

The narratives generally portrayed blacks as physically strong or loyal. In the aftermath of the wreck of the *Hercules* off the coast of Caffraria (1796), the survivors realized that despite the presence of natives, their only hope was to navigate through a heavy surf. Having given up hope, a black crew member showed them the way: "At length one of the crew, who was a black, plunged into the waves, and by exertions which seemed more than human, gained and seated himself on the raft." He struggled to gain the raft but was turned over several times. "Still he buffeted the waves, and gained the raft, until at length suffering two hours of fatigue, which, until then, the captain could not possibly imagine human nature could survive, he drifted on land."[119] In seeing this individual arrive safely, several other crew members jumped into the sea and also made it to shore. The narrative never provided the man's name, and he appeared in the account only when his efforts helped save the white crew members.

There were two black men on board the *Oswego*, "Sam of Philadelphia" and "Jack of Hudson." Both individuals proved themselves worthy in terms of physical endurance and loyalty. Sam became a momentary hero when the survivors attempted to retrieve goods from the ship. "Black Sam, who after two or three hard efforts, succeeded in getting through the breakers, but his strength was so much exhausted that he sunk." The others jumped in and seized hold of Sam and found no difficulty in returning, as the first surf hove them all up together. "He was entirely helpless and apparently almost gone: we laid him on the rocks, face down, and by moderately rolling and moving him he was made to discharge much water from his mouth."[120] Sam then disappeared from the story.

The other black individual, Jack, appeared only during the overland trek, where he proved his loyalty to his master and mistress. As the survivors loaded their packs to cross the wilds of Africa, Judah Paddock decided that he could not carry two gown patterns he had brought from Ireland for his wife. Upon hearing this, Jack "rushed forward, and got hold of the pieces saying, 'Master, my mistress shall wear these gowns yet.' I told him he had already too much to carry, and that his mistress would never see those patterns. 'She shall, master, depend on it,' replied Jack, 'they are too pretty to leave here.'—and he packed them up." For Jack's reward Paddock later sold him to an Arab master and never mentioned him again.[121] Much like Sam, Jack proved his ability through strength and loyalty to the ship (and master). He exhibited nonthreatening attributes that perhaps comforted audiences, reassuring them that such individuals remained subordinate and did not subvert social hierarchy in times of crisis.

A few black individuals wrote their own accounts of life at sea in the eighteenth century; these included Briton Hammon (1770), Olaudah Equiano (1789), Jahn Marrant (1785), Venure Smith (1798), and Boston King (1798).[122] Equiano's shipwreck account was unusual in that he took an active role. He "congratulates himself for being the main reason for the saving of ship and crew, thereby showing a black man as a human, able and a capable citizen."[123] During shipwreck Equiano blamed the captain for sailing too far to the west, risking the boat in shallow waters. He further related that white crew members did little to preserve their lives; indeed "they soon got so drunk that they were not able, but lay about the deck like swine." The only individuals who proved of any worth were three black men and a "Dutch creole sailor" who acted like gentlemen while the rest failed to uphold their manly duties.[124] Equiano was an exception to the rule and demonstrated that personal initiative could have positive results, even if it meant subverting accepted hierarchies.

Some historians argue that through such narratives blacks began to define themselves within a larger market economy; in balancing freedom and slavery, "mariners became conduits for an emerging sense of transnational blackness."[125] Although by the nineteenth century some blacks did well at sea, few ever achieved full independence. Most went to sea only part-time, when sailing was profitable, but they always met with limited opportunities.[126] The narratives supported the continued presence of blacks in maritime ventures but kept their role peripheral and within the traditional order. They were allowed a place in the stories because they did not threaten status or hierarchy but instead proved themselves able members who understood their status.

~

Above all, narratives reassured readers that gender and racial expectations remained solid. Men, both common sailors and officers, acted appropriately even when all else seemed beyond control. The accounts minimized catastrophe and imparted a positive outlook for the spectator-reader. Rather than develop separately, larger trends concerning class and authority involved the maritime world. In urban centers in the American colonial and early republic eras ports were developed, and there merchants, sea captains, and sailors worked and lived. How society ordered itself affected how mariners at all levels situated themselves within a social hierarchy. Generally transient and owning only what they carried, many sailors occupied the lowest levels, though some, especially officers and captains, made substantial fortunes from lives on the sea.

Although shipwrecks occurred at sea, sailors' perceptions and beliefs reflected religious, cultural, and political experiences learned on land. However, the maritime world did not re-create an exact copy of social order or cultural expectations. At sea men were no longer constrained by society's watchful gaze and so were afforded some relaxation of male gender roles. Many sailors "had their own ideas about the social relations of work at sea. The organization, pace and the process of work became the focus on an often fierce struggle for control."[127] The narratives minimized this "struggle" but did allow for some movement regarding power and authority. Common sailors could and did act in their individual best interests, but by the end of the narratives traditional forms of hierarchy and status remerged. Those at sea were located within a social environment with a less rigid gender order but one that still looked home for definition.

· 5 ·

TO HONOR THEIR WORTH, BEAUTY, AND ACCOMPLISHMENTS

That sage hit it best undoubtedly, who compar'd a Ship to a Woman. Not for that both are of the female gender; not for that she's very apt to be leaky; nor for that her pump-dale smells strongest when she has the soundest bottom, but chiefly because her rigging, and fitting forth, is always worth double her carcass.[1]

According to traditional scholarship, women rarely went to sea. Nineteenth-century concepts of separate spheres supposedly kept women tied to home and family while men explored the vast oceans. Romantic views of wives waiting anxiously for returning husbands and issues of a proper middle-class behavior distorted historians' depictions of women's place in the maritime world.[2] From such representations, women's greatest contributions in relation to maritime activities were support on land and the ability to maintain hearth and home.[3]

Despite such perceptions women did go to sea, though only a few worked as sailors. Those who sailed were usually captains' or officers' wives, while others sailed as passengers. Unfortunately crew lists rarely included women, keeping their identities hidden and participation silent. Even when physically absent, women symbolically came aboard when men sailed with gifts, food, and clothing that loved ones had made. Sailors stowed these items in special areas, hidden from shipmates, as if women's presents were as private as the sphere of women. Historical evidence gleaned from letters and diaries reveals that these items were important and occupied a cherished place in the sailors' lives. Although male solidarity existed on ships, men still looked with fondness toward land and the women they left behind.[4]

Women did go sea, however, and by the nineteenth century the concept of separate spheres actually worked to keep women on board. Wives could maintain hearth and home on ships, bringing the private sphere to sea.[5] At sea women had various jobs, most within appropriate gender roles. On larger ships with passengers, women acted as hostesses, making sure that food, drink, and entertainment were available. Such women became civilizing influences in their efforts to reform sailors' drunkenness, cursing, and ubiquitous whoring.[6] With children on board, women worked as nannies, nurses, teachers, and companions, essentially taking over all spiritual and educational duties.[7] Additionally women often took charge of the pantries; but with galleys forward in the bows, wives found it imprudent to be in the men's quarters. Women instead made recipes or mixtures in the pantries and then sent the food forward for cooking. They could cook on the aft stoves, but these were small and difficult to use. Such constraints physically hampered wives' abilities to perform traditional duties, requiring innovative means to achieve basic tasks. In women's absence captains often assigned such "women's work" to cooks and stewards. These individuals often occupied a lower status on ships and reflected broader understandings of gender, as well as racial, differences.[8]

Beyond traditional female duties, some women also learned the art of navigation. In several instances women took control of the ships when their captain-husbands died, being the only ones able to bring the ships into port.[9] Such actions conformed to society on land when widows took over businesses after their husbands' deaths. Women sometimes participated in the ships' daily chores, helping to prepare the sails or to work on smaller projects. Most women, however, kept themselves busy with sewing, cleaning, and writing. Ironically women could not sew on Sundays as it represented work, while men were allowed to sew because sewing was not "work" to them.[10] Following societal expectations, women remained productive but not self-sustaining, maintaining a code of female dependency.[11]

Captains tried to retain some semblance of normal family life when their wives and families came aboard. A captain's place on a ship was lonely because his status required distance from the crew, so a wife provided companionship.[12] Ship life forced private life into a public sphere, and a ship offered little room for creating a home. Societal expectations demanded that women remain secluded, but with privacy at a minimum, such aspirations often fell short. Depending on the vessel's size, the captain's cabin often served as a separate space for conducting the ship's daily business. Additionally officers might share the aft cabins, forcing wives to interact with these gentlemen on a daily basis, further reducing privacy.[13] Social ranking and propriety separated women from much of the crew, allowing them to venture into only a few acceptable areas.

Women at sea tried to create a domestic atmosphere but had to adjust to meet new and challenging constraints.[14] The private and the public regimes, both dominated by patriarchal relations, were not isolated but overlapped or blurred into one another.[15] The sea provided some opportunities for women to be "manly" and take control, but never permanently and only when circumstances absolutely required it. As seen in the larger world of maritime history, women at sea lived in an ambiguous state: somewhat private but not public, constrained to be wives and mothers within their floating houses, but existing in a social world. These "sister sailors" influenced the masculine sea, leaving signs of their presence that are only now beginning to resurface.

The published shipwreck narratives provide an additional lens to understand gender and the role of women at sea. As prescriptive literature, shipwreck narratives reinforced the dominant worldview; they helped people understand and organize their society by strengthening accepted ideologies.[16] As women rarely wrote the narratives, historians must understand femininity through a male perspective. Shipwreck narratives did not promote new ideas; rather they reflected accepted perceptions of an already established order.[17] The stories did not attempt to instill a new form of gender definition but rather maintained a conservative stance that reinforced established forms of behavior. For example, James Clarke, in his 1821 collection of narratives, felt that shipwreck accounts were to "inculcate the lesson of Resignation and Perseverance; to point out the Resources which Shipwrecked or distressed Mariners had discovered. . . . to form a work, which yielding not in point to the horrors and unnatural Incidents of the Modern Novel, might engage even the female Mind, without poisoning its Principles, or Tainting its Purity."[18] Unlike fictional novels, widely condemned for their immoral influence, shipwreck narratives provided something useful and appropriate for the female mind. They did not promote female independence and instead reinforced women's place as wives, mothers, sisters, and daughters.

Understandings of female gender shifted between the seventeenth and nineteenth centuries. In the seventeenth century Eve's weakness in the Garden of Eden indicated that men needed to contain women's physical and emotional deficiencies and control their excesses. The ideal woman strove to rein in her emotional and immoral self by being hardworking, pious, quiet, and submissive. More so than men, women were considered dangerous, associated with nature (and therefore more primitive), and unable to reason or remain stable.[19] Essentially female obedience and modesty were necessary to maintain order in the home and community; to do or be otherwise threatened social order.

In the early eighteenth century self-control remained important, though literature suggested that women continued to be more passionate than men.[20] By this time advice literature guided female readers to conform to an emerging genteel model. Writers emphasized manners and behavior, and gender expectations incorporated refinement as the New World civilized and expanded in a larger cosmopolitan Atlantic world. Women's image shifted significantly when the negative portrayal of the seventeenth century shifted to a more positive understanding of women that stressed their compassion, virtue, and piety. No longer considered inherently sinful as a result of Eve's fall, women were seen as stronger and morally superior because of their gender.[21]

By the nineteenth century women's supportive roles expanded to incorporate images of uplift and reform.[22] Women had a duty to gain a better education and to strive for a more active role at home as well as in the public sphere; they should become acceptable helpmates and to raise upcoming generations properly.[23] After the American Revolution their roles as helpmates became necessary for the nation's continued success. They became the "guardians of virtue." No longer needing men to control them, women were instead considered necessary to control male corruption.[24]

In the nineteenth century the perception of a female moral foundation expanded to incorporate the concept of separate spheres. The home became a haven where men could retreat from the degenerate world. Societal expectations further removed middle- and upper-class women from participating in household production and placed them in charge of the families' moral upbringings.[25] While piety and industry remained important female characteristics, and despite their moral superiority, their biological fate kept them subordinate and dependent on men.[26]

Of the twenty shipwreck narratives that mention women, about half suggest that all or some of them perished at sea.[27] In most instances circumstances prohibited any chance of removing women, and their only hope for survival rested on the vessel remaining afloat. Rather than assisting women and children, men seemed to have the attitude that it was literally "every man for himself."[28] The presence of women in shipwrecks added to the stories' drama and tragedy. Despite their moral foundation and the role of male protectors, many women did not survive shipwrecks. Their small chance of survival is surprising as popular conceptions held that women and children went into lifeboats before crews and officers.

The historical emphasis on the preferential preservation of women and children came about in the mid-nineteenth century as greater numbers of women went aboard ships. Women and their families going to sea possibly found this concept reassuring, believing that sailors and passengers might protect them in times of crisis.[29] For example, in 1825, while evacuating the *Kent*, "one of the officers asked major Macgregor in what order the officers should abandon ship." The major replied that they should leave by "funeral order." Colonel Fearon agreed and stated, "Most undoubtedly the juniors first—but see that any man is cut down who presumes to enter the boats before the means of escape are presented to the women and children."[30] This sentiment proved rare among printed narratives and was practiced only when time allowed. Instead most shipwreck narratives suggested that the crews acted for themselves, choosing life over honor. Without time or a readily available means of securing women's safety, men opted to save their own skins. The narratives rarely indicated the women's deaths were avoidable, and little attention was given to the possibility of their rescue.

On a practical level women at sea faced a poor chance of survival in shipwrecks compared to common sailors. Women were less familiar with the ships, usually traveling as passengers in the company of male relatives. Ann Saunders wrote in her 1827 narrative, "The whole of the ship's stern was stove in! this was only the beginning of a scene of horrid calamities! Doubly horrible to me, (as the reader must suppose) who had never before witnessed any thing so awful."[31] Her statement implied that she rarely went to sea and had never experienced the rigors of storm and shipwreck. Physically weaker than men, women had less endurance to hold onto railings or to keep their footing on rolling, pitching ships with waves crashing over them. In addition their dress affected their ability to move and swim when petticoats inhibited women's movements.[32] Wearing a long, wet skirt was not conducive to moving about on a tossing ship. Add a scared, screaming child, who might cling to one leg, and the chance of moving decreased dramatically.

Of the one hundred narratives examined, twenty refer to at least one female but only ten go beyond mentioning the vague "female passenger." It is not surprising that most narratives that included women appeared in the late eighteenth century or early nineteenth century, reflecting a time when women increasingly went to sea.[33] Women provided a sympathetic focus that increased the horror and sensationalism inherent in popular literature. For example, after being shipwrecked and when attempting an overland trek across Florida, the only female passenger, Mrs. Sarah Allen, who was on the verge of death, lamented that her life was over and she would surely remain there forever: "My unhappy companions could only answer me with tears and moans. . . . it is a consolation to the unhappy to see themselves the objects of compassion. The captain took my hands between his, and pressed them with the utmost tenderness. . . . No, my dear friend (said he) I will not abandon you." The captain went on with words of encouragement and suggested that the men go in search of refreshments to help her persist.[34] Mrs. Allen's presence added to the narrative's interest as the men heroically did all they could to protect her. Her inability to continue situated the men around her in a protective role and supplied a means for the men to redeem a level of control and authority. In addition a woman struggling to survive in the wild surely affected the sentimental or romantic reader and added to the narrative's overall appeal. The presence of such ladies, all virtuous Christians, added another layer to the narratives that "meant visualizing the titillating prospect of a test of female delicacy under the threat of physical dissolution."[35]

Audiences often did not realize women were on board until accounts of shipwreck began. Even then many narratives failed to give names, instead referring to "a female passenger" or "the women." Even in their deaths many women remained anonymous, as on the French East Indiaman *Prince* (1752), where the author "saw one of the ladies fall off the mast with fatigue, and perish; she was too far distant to save." That bit of information is all we know about her. A lieutenant related that two other women, who were female cousins of a passenger, were on board the *Prince*; despite efforts to save them, these women perished in the water. Although we do not know their names, the author pointed out the extraordinary efforts put forth by the sailors to save these women. According to the author, these women were stripped and placed in hen coops so that a few sailors could swim with them. The sailors grew tired, however, and the hen coops sank.[36]

Even when women did survive, they might remain nameless. The "Dutch-Merchant's Wife" is the only name given to one poor woman even though she and only one sailor lived to tell their tale.[37] Although her husband died early in the narrative, the text continued to label her in reference to a male figure. The stories suggested that these women remained outsiders, coming onto ships only because they were passengers or had male relatives on board. We know almost nothing about them except for a few vague references to their relationship to men. According to the account, the Dutch-Merchant's Wife "was of great fortune, a gentlewoman of many worthy accomplishments, and exceeding Beautiful."[38] Even though she was one of only two survivors and from a well-to-do family, the author thought it unimportant to relate her name (or perhaps tried to protect her reputation).

Special efforts were made in the narratives to differentiate female servants, slaves, and sailors' and soldiers' wives from the "ladies." For example, the *Kent* (1827) carried families of soldiers, including forty-three women. When the vessel caught fire, chaos ruled the deck, with men, women, and children running around, some "in a state of absolute nakedness." According to the author, the soldiers' wives and children prayed and read scriptures with the "ladies." The soldiers' wives were not mentioned further, but the author added that the young ladies were "enabled, with wonderful self-possession, to offer to others those spiritual consolations."[39] The separation between ladies and soldiers' wives continued when the first boat lowered contained "all the ladies, and as many of the soldiers' wives as it could safely contain."[40]

The narratives suggest that only with available time and space to place all women in boats did both upper- and lower-class women survive and that upper-class women were given preference to any possible means of safety. According to the account of the *Halsewell* (1786), it was proposed that if "the opportunity presented itself, to reserve the long boat for the ladies and themselves [the officers], and this precaution was accordingly taken."[41] The narrative failed to mention the soldiers' wives or black women who were also on board. On the hired transport *Harpooner* (1818), 385 men, women, and children accompanied several regiments and the crew on their way to Quebec. The vessel went aground that year and eventually came apart due to rough seas and weather. The "suddenness of the sea rushing in" between decks killed many women and children instantly, and only 177 people survived. The narrative neglected to mention how many of these were women except that the "daughter of Surgeon Armstrong" and "the wife of a sergeant" survived shipwreck.[42] Neither of them was given a name, and each was recognized only in relation to a male family member.

Despite the class difference, gender permitted certain allowances. On the *Kent,* while waiting for the hull to give way, the ladies and officers were sitting in the protected roundhouse when three black women and two soldiers' wives entered, even "though the sailors, who had demanded entrance to get a light, had been opposed and kept out by the officers."[43] These women, although from the lower classes, gained access ahead of common sailors. However, even in a crisis, status remained fundamental. These lower-class women came into the roundhouse late in the narrative, and this is the only information we have about them. The lower-class women were not allowed immediate entrance but came in only as the situation worsened. The narrative minimized their role while emphasizing that the "ladies" remained calm and pious throughout the ordeal. The unnamed women appeared only because of their gender, but their status failed to provide a focal point for sympathy. Emphasis instead remained on the upper-class ladies and the tragedy of their demise.

Defining women by family or in relation to male figures implied that they were not of the ship's company, keeping the vessel a male-dominated realm. Not only was it rare to have women on board, but in addition they rarely actively participated in the shipwreck events. A survivor from the *Albion* thought it so unusual for a woman to assist in saving a ship that he wrote, "it is an interesting fact, that Miss Powell, an amiable young lady, who was on board, was desirous to be allowed to take her turn [at the pumps]."[44] Of course they refused the young lady's offer. Without her help any chance for life remained with the men alone. The narratives suggested that women in shipwreck situations relied on men to save them, adhering to historical implications of female dependency and the need for men in survival.

Supporting women's marginalization, the narratives situated most women in relationship to the men on board. Such writing subordinated women and "helped position the women of the new nation as domestic dependents and disenfranchised citizens even as the developing economy and expanding public sphere were providing potential new places for men and women alike."[45] For example, the narrator identified all the female passengers on the *Halsewell* (1786) in association with males: "The passengers were Miss Eliza Pierce, and Miss Mary Anne Pierce, daughters of the commander; Miss Amy Paul, and Miss Mary Paul, daughters of Mr. Paul of Somersetshire, and relations to captain Pierce; Miss Elizabeth Blackburne, daughter of the captain, etc."[46] These labels not only identified women through men but also designated them as upper-class or gentlewomen, thus adding an element of status. All of the women were single, and therefore their place on the ship must be justified and their honor intact for the story to have sentimental meaning. Later in the narrative other women appeared, but since they lacked proper social standing, we learn little about them. The narrative described them as merely soldiers' wives and "three black women." Readers learned next to nothing about them, except that they died.

As daughters, nieces, and sisters, women had male family members to protect them in these moments of crisis. For example, a young lady on the *Boston,* Ms. Boag, died in her brother's arms while in a lifeboat. "This amiable young lady's firmness of conduct at the first alarm of fire, and during the whole scene, is worthy of the highest praise. To the divine will of her God she submitted without a murmur, and at 11 o'clock on Wednesday, she died in the arms of her brother, in the boat, thanking him in the most affectionate manner for his kindness, giving her blessing to us all." Although she died, she did not die alone surrounded by strangers. Ms. Boag had her brother, whose presence reinforced his masculinity and her dependency.[47]

"*Halsewell* East Indiaman." Painted by Robt. Smirke/Aquatinto
by F. Jukes/Engraved by Robt. Pollard. (London: R. Pollard, 1786).
Courtesy of the Trustees of the British Museum, AN1057864001.

Women on the *Halsewell* had their father to care for them. The author
wrote, "Captain Pierce was seated on a chair . . . between his two daughters,
whom he pressed alternately to his affectionate bosom."[48] The captain opted
to stay by their side and offer what protection he might. He too perished
with the ship. Although these women did have male protectors, none of
them survived—at least physically. The author went to great lengths to extol
their virtues and to make sure their reputations as gentlewomen persisted
beyond the grave.

The presence of women directly affected representations of males, and
the narratives situated these men as protectors. In doing so the narratives
reiterated the submissive and passive role of women. For example, on the
Halsewell the captain expressed fear for his "beloved daughters," hoping to
find a way he might save them. Later, describing when all was hopeless,
the narrative continued, "Amidst their own misfortunes, the sufferings of
the females filled their minds with the acutest anguish; every returning sea
increased their apprehensions for the safety of their amiable and helpless
companions."[49] In most narratives the women waited in protected areas of
the ships while the men determined the best course to save their "amiable

and helpless companions." Readers must surely have anticipated finding out whether the women died or found a means of rescue.

Fear and anguish associated with losing family members remained a central theme throughout the narratives. The *Kent* (1827) carried forty-three women and sixty-six children; most belonged with the forty-nine soldiers on board. Several of the men took on the added weight of their children but could stay in the water only a short time. These men "perished in their endeavours to save them." Others realized their inability to save both women and children and made a choice: "Another individual, who was reduced to the frightful alternative of losing his wife, or his children, hastily decided in favor of his duty to the former. His wife was accordingly saved, but his four children, alas! were left to perish."[50] The men were the ones who chose between life and death, not only for themselves but for their loved ones as well. The burden of being a father and a husband weighed heavily on the men, and audiences at home understood the magnitude of this responsibility.

Historically the family unit was important for community. Families needed to persist in order for society to remain stable. Part of this sympathy in relation to family revolved around the accepted male responsibility to shelter, clothe, and feed loved ones.[51] "Sympathy promotes a deeply felt psychic investment in proprietary power over, and in control, of objects of love."[52] Readers empathized with the survivors, experiencing through print the pain of losing a loved one. Audiences could relate to the difficult choices these men made in determining who survived and who did not.

On another level, death destroyed the family structure, and the need to sacrifice women during shipwreck revealed the fragility of such a system. The family remained the paramount unit, more important than an individual. For example, after her husband killed himself to spare her from being the next chosen to be eaten, the Dutch-Merchant's Wife "swounded and almost dyed with grief, and beg'd to be her own executioner."[53] She refused to eat her husband's corpse, choosing loyalty to her husband and death over life.

While protection usually came from relatives, men outside the family units also offered various levels of support. On the *Halsewell* a passenger, Mr. Meriton, "observing that the ladies appeared parched and exhausted, fetched a basket of oranges from some part of the round-house, with which he prevailed on some of them to refresh themselves." Mr. Meriton provided sustenance and comfort to the ladies and attempted to alleviate the hopelessness of their ordeal. George Carpinger, seaman, spared the above-mentioned Dutch-Merchant's Wife from execution. Carpinger did his utmost to keep her from harm and "used all the consolation he could, by words, or device, to comfort the despairing Lady till at length she was prevailed to hearken to him, and give her promise to spare all violence on her self, and waite her better fortune." As a side note, Carpinger was well rewarded for his efforts: "And considering the care and kindness of Carpinger, the lady seems much to favour hime, and when time of mourning is over, will undoubtedly make him Happy in her embraces."[54] Perhaps not all efforts were merely altruistic.

When women appeared in the narratives, they became the stories' moral centers. Acting as spiritual guides, women released the men from having to worry about their souls. This way women did take active roles in their survival, but always within the acceptable constraints of femininity. For women's efforts the narratives portrayed them as honorable, firm, heroic, skilled, beautiful, and virtuous—positive role models for readers. These women remained focused on proper female concerns, religion and family, and therefore never threatened traditional understandings of social place.

Women, as moral beings, prevented shipwrecks from being moral as well as physical disasters.[55] The shipwreck narrative of the *Kent* (1827) provided useful detail of how women in crisis centered disaster around a spiritual foundation. The author related that "several of the soldiers' wives and children, who had fled for temporary shelter into the after-cabins on the upper deck, were engaged in praying and in reading the scriptures with the ladies." These women "enabled, with wonderful self-possession, to offer to others those spiritual consolations, which a firm and intelligent trust in the Redeemer of the world appeared at this awful hour to impart to their own breasts."[56] The ladies in this narrative revealed an inner superiority. Their strength was not physical but manifested as spiritual fortitude, above and beyond that of their male counterparts.

As the narratives regaled the few women who comprised a moral foundation, the authors once again imparted a class distinction between the "amiable ladies" and the soldiers' wives. Only the ladies exhibited the moral attributes worthy of mention. "The dignified deportment of two young ladies in particular, formed a specimen of natural strength of mind, finely modified by Christian feeling, that failed not to attract the notice and admiration of every one who had an opportunity of witnessing it." Although death seemed inevitable, "one of the ladies above referred to, calmly sinking down on her knees, and clasping her hands together said, 'Even so come, Lord Jesus,' and immediately proposing to read a portion of the scriptures to those around her." Her sister, yet another fine young lady, selected several "appropriate psalms, which were accordingly read, with intervals of prayer, by those ladies alternately to the assembled females."[57] As with men in the published narratives, there was a marked social distinction between those who remained in control of themselves and of their spirituality and those who did not. Middle- or upper-class women displayed an inherent ability to remain calm in the face of danger and upheld proper comportment in the middle of chaotic situations. These women created a strong image that demonstrated the narratives' use as prescriptive literature.

Proper women waited for men to save them while praying to God for salvation. Women did not have to be physically strong because they excelled in emotional and moral strength. When the *Halsewell* finally broke apart, taking all of the women with her, the author wrote, "Thus, perished the *Halsewell*, and with her, worth, honor, skill, beauty, and accomplishments!"[58] On the *Kent*, while the women climbed into the lifeboats, the narrator commended them for "the fortitude which never fails to characterize and adorn their sex on occasion of overwhelming trial, [they] were placed, without a murmur, into the boat."[59] Their strength did not come from being physically able to handle the pumps or cut down the masts. Rather the women demonstrated their abilities through inner fortitude.

Occasionally women did act in uncharacteristic ways. In the nineteenth century women began to write their own narratives. For example, Ann Saunders wrote a version of her shipwreck experience aboard the *Francis Mary* (1827; sometimes spelled *Frances Mary*). Two accounts exist; Ann Saunders and Captain Kendall each wrote a version, showing how gender altered the story's overall tone. In both narratives, full of human suffering and cannibalism, Saunders played a major, indeed bloodcurdling, role.

According to Captain Kendall's account, the *Francis Mary* (1826) hit rough seas that crippled the ship, leaving it to the mercy of the tides. For several days the crew struggled against starvation. On February 22 the survivors turned to cannibalism when John Wilson, seaman, died. They "cut him up in quarters, washed them overboard, and hung them up on pins." By March 5 several individuals had perished, including James Frier, cook, whose betrothed, Ann Saunders, was on board as a female passenger and servant to Mrs. Kendall. After Frier's death Saunders claimed the right to his blood. She fought with the mate. "The heroine got the better of her adversary, and then allowed him to drink one cup to her two." Finally on March 7 the *Blonde* rescued them from eventual starvation. Upon boarding the *Francis Mary*, Lieutenant Gambier noticed that they had meat, at which time the survivors admitted that it was human.[60]

Rather than dwell on the morbidity of the situation, Kendall's narrative instead turned to regaling the two women, perhaps in an effort to make his narrative more appealing to female audiences. The captain wrote that his "wife, who underwent all the most horrid sufferings which the human understanding can imagine, bore them much better than could possibly have been expected." She endured not only emotionally but physically as well: "She is now, although much emaciated, a respectable, good-looking woman, about twenty-five years old." Given that she was once posited as a gentlewoman, he complicated her image but did not tarnish it completely. Rather he used her actions to demonstrate the depths to which the survivors had sunk in order to survive: "What must have been the extremity of want to which she was driven, when she ate the brains of one of the apprentices, saying it was the most delicious thing she ever tasted; and it is still more melancholy to relate, that the person, whose brains she was thus forced by hunger to eat, had been three times wrecked before. . . . and then became food for his remaining shipmates!"[61] The perception is one of continued composure and refinement. She remained a gentlewoman to the end, which was proper for a woman of her ranking.

The captain, however, painted Ann Saunders in a much different light. While she too exhibited an internal fortitude, Ann transformed into something on the verge of losing control and possessed no form of sophistication: "Ann Saunders, the other female, had more strength in her calamity than most of the men. She performed the duty of cutting up and cleaning the dead bodies, keeping two knives for the purpose . . . and when the breath was announced to have flown, she would sharpen her knives, bleed the deceased in the neck, drink his blood, and cut him up."[62] Saunders was not the traditionally submissive woman waiting for men to act, and yet she was still portrayed as at least a quasi-proper woman. She was not trying to subvert authority but was working in a proper arena for women, that of food preparation.

The captain's account distinguished differences between the two women based on status and class. While Mrs. Kendall, his wife, remained a gentlewoman, Ann Saunders became a harpy, on the verge of losing control. This image appeared primarily in Kendall's narrative when he stated that Ann "shrieked a loud yell, then snatching a cup . . . cut her late intended husband's throat and drank his blood!"[63] She fought with the mate for this right and continued to do so until rescued. Although she did not threaten authority, she overstepped boundaries of subordination and acted in ways that the captain deemed unbefitting a proper female, providing a sinister impression of women in crisis.

Ann Saunders's account of the event was much different. Her narrative focused on religion and the need for people to attend to their immortal souls. She began with a short summary of her background that placed her somewhere in the lower classes. Saunders worked for "respectable families in the neighborhood," and at age eighteen she became acquainted with Mrs. Kendall (the wife of Capt. John Kendall), who persuaded her to accompany her on the *Francis Mary*. Thanks to the entreaties of this "lady of pious and amiable disposition" and of Saunders's fiancé, James Frier, Saunders found herself aboard the *Francis Mary*. Little of note occurred on the outbound trip, but the return voyage supplied Saunders with her story of sympathy and drama.

Early on Saunders outlined the importance of the family unit with her concern for the women and children affected by this shipwreck: "many of the seamen were married men, and had left in Europe numerous families dependent on them for support—Alas! poor mortals, little did they probably think, when they bid their loving companions and their tender little ones the last adieu, that it was to be a final one, and that they were to behold their faces no more, forever, in this frail world!"[64] Shipwrecks affected more than just the men on board. Wives, mothers, and children at home often lost the families' only breadwinners, and many subsequently went on poor relief. Saunders's pleas probably affected readers, the very people often left behind, in reminding them of shipwrecks' disastrous consequences. She also created a framework that presented family and loved ones as central to the story.

On the way home the vessel encountered a series of incapacitating storms. Saunders stated that throughout this time, "Mrs. Kendall and myself were on our knees, on the quarter deck, as earnestly engaged in prayer to the Almighty God that he would in his tender mercy spare our lives."[65] As with many published accounts, the women became the narrative's moral center, as they alone prayed to God while the men consulted with one another. The women looked to spiritual affairs while the men controlled more secular concerns.

As with Kendall's version, on February 22 John Wilson died and his body was processed for consumption. After much lamenting Saunders finally described the death of her fiancé. She had not given consent to marriage until well into the voyage, and they planned to marry upon reaching port. At this point she directly pleaded to female readers, "Judge then, my Christian female readers (for it is you that can best judge) what must have been my feelings"—that as she watched him die, she chose to preserve herself and to "plead my claim to the greater portion of his precious blood, as it oozed half congealed from the wound inflicted on his lifeless body!!! Oh, this was a bitter cup indeed!"[66] Not bound by marital obligations, as was the devoted Dutch-Merchant's Wife, Saunders looked to the individual rather than family, and self-preservation instead of sacrificing her life for others.

Saunders's account continued to parallel the captain's regarding general events, but she refocused her actions from being a harpy to being a more respectable or spiritual image. She omitted the struggle with the steward for the blood and instead exhorted readers to remember God's mercy and to be prepared for death. Through her undivided trust in God, she remained physically and emotionally stronger than the other survivors, to the extent that it fell to her to proportion the food.

Throughout the narrative Saunders remained true to God. She was a proper female who supported the survivors in their moral direction: "I exerted the feeble powers which God in mercy had left me, to exhort them to have recourse to Heaven, to alleviate their misery, and to trust in Him."[67] Her account was much more intimate and emotional than the captain's, and she continued to detail the women's sufferings and the spiritual crisis of shipwreck until the *Blonde* rescued them and Saunders returned to her family. Even after rescue, for nineteen additional pages, her narrative warned individuals to remain pious, virtuous, prepared for death, and to always be proper Christians.

Saunders's narrative was exciting for its in-depth portrayal of shipwreck, especially as experienced by a woman, and was much more emotional than those written by men. Unlike male-authored accounts, hers omitted the practical details of sailing a ship; she instead focused on the emotional turmoil that she and Mrs. Kendall underwent. Despite cannibalism these women remained respectable and honored. Indeed they both persisted in a quasi-proper sphere. Mrs. Kendall remained a good wife and mother, and only under extreme conditions did she descend to cannibalism; even then she did it with grace and gentility. Saunders kept everyone alive by preparing the food. Although the food of choice was nontraditional, a middle- or lower-class woman would know how to process meat.

Only in an exceptional circumstance, far from land and with no alternatives for survival, could such female behavior be tolerated or even honored. Being at sea permitted some relaxation of gender roles, but assigned positions still persisted. Women's behavior reflected "strategies of the weak," by becoming what the authors thought as desirable and pleasing to audiences.[68] Although their efforts were secondary to those of males, women could take control of events and preserve others to live another day.

Since they were no longer constrained by society's watchful gaze, being at sea afforded some relaxation of gender roles for both men and women. They located themselves within a social environment with a less rigid gender order, but one that still looked home for definition. Although shipwreck was a moment of crisis, women usually maintained their proper gender roles as dependents and with men their saviors. Shipwreck did not question the traditional but reinforced the necessity of proper deportment. Following traditional roles, these women were quiet, submissive, and pious. They could be heroines through their suffering.[69] They attained their greatness by focusing on others and offering the ultimate sacrifice of their lives as they comforted fellow passengers.

Although being at sea provided some with the ability to expand gender roles, this chance was exceptional and occurred only in extreme circumstances. Women did not fare well in shipwreck narratives. Their subordinate social rank prevented them from obtaining access to the power necessary for survival. Women in shipwreck lived and died in an ambiguous sphere that was somewhat private but not public; they were constrained to be wives and mothers and yet were able to assert their strength and fortitude. Above all, shipwreck narratives reassured readers that gender expectations remained solid and that both men and women acted appropriately even when all else seemed beyond control.

. 6 .

CHAOS AND CANNIBALISM
ON THE HIGH SEAS

Disaster situations allowed participants a level of flexibility with regard to behavior, when they were no longer bound by conventional social constraints. And yet disasters rarely led to total disruption; rather after an initial period of confusion the victims sought any means available to reestablish social order. Even after shipwrecks, when sailors could legally choose their own courses for survival, order remained relatively intact. In most cases some level of deference persisted and any inversion existed only temporarily. Mutiny or mutinous conduct did occur after shipwrecks, but the narratives minimized this behavior, blaming it on drunkenness, exhaustion, or fear. Even when it became necessary for victims to eat one another for sustenance, traditional social hierarchy remained the ultimate determinant for survival.

This chapter focuses on the chaotic nature of shipwreck situations and examines particularly two extreme results: cannibalism and mutiny. While there were numerous accounts of cannibalism in shipwreck narratives, cannibalism was by no means isolated to situations at sea. For example, nineteenth-century settlers headed to California or Oregon territory sometimes ate fellow travelers to withstand long winters. Throughout the nineteenth and twentieth centuries, postwar famines forced civilians and military personnel to resort to this act. More recently an Uruguayan rugby team ate their teammates after a 1972 plane crash in the Andes.[1] Much like shipwreck accounts, these incidents suggest that cannibalism did not occur randomly but followed a general outline where eating the dead was a last resort to maintain the living. These were not individuals without a sense of morality or humanity; they used cannibalism to minimize death rates and to preserve those still alive.

Despite the "practical" situations of cannibalism, the act itself continues to represent one of the more terrifying experiences that humans can endure. Europeans for centuries made cannibalism a defining element of uncivilized savages, occurring only in the farthest corners of the world. Explorers to Africa and the New World encountered evidence of ritual cannibalism, with some eating human flesh as an act of vengeance or to absorb another's power.[2] In this context cannibalistic acts were not arbitrary; they served a purpose in particular societies. Although cannibalism was rarely random, that did little to lessen Europeans' revulsion to it, and it became a means to situate foreign individuals in opposition to "civilized" Christian behavior.[3] Language barriers and cultural differences often prevented the observers from fully understanding the events before them, and frequently an isolated incident or anecdote increased in magnitude with each retelling.

What set shipwreck victims apart from "savage" cannibals was the way in which they consumed their victims. Savages were often portrayed as having no ethical concerns, and accounts suggest that they ate human limbs, hearts, or organs with gusto and even looked forward to such fare.[4] European accounts show cannibals as willing participants in an ungodly act. And yet Europeans made sure to situate ritual cannibalism in remote areas of the world, far away from well-structured urban centers of western civilization, and therefore far away from proper society. The shipwreck narratives followed this pattern and placed cannibalism at a distance, "veiled in fancy and exoticism."[5] Because of this distancing, even Europeans who participated in cannibalism did not threaten society, and the act lost some of its terrifying power.

Cannibalism, at first glance, might be viewed as the "most disturbing act that can be performed on the human body."[6] Cannibalism occurs "when conditions become such that the traditions, rules, and laws that regulate normal day-to-day existence are no longer effective. These cases freed people from constraints instilled by their resident culture, and existed only when . . . severe and prolonged disasters drove them to the edge of starvation." At those times cannibalism became a viable option.[7] In addition shipwreck narratives suggested that even in extreme situations of starvation, traditions related to status, gender, and race often remained in place. Although shipwreck compromised acceptable behavior and stressed the laws that defined civilization, social order never perished. Cannibalism therefore was not random but was a rational decision made by its participants.[8]

Starvation cannibalism was always a last resort, and survivors turned to it only when all other options had expired. In the first days of shipwreck, hunger moved from a distraction to an obsession. The body used stored fat first, followed by a reduction of muscle tissue and internal organs, with some individuals losing between 20 percent and 50 percent of their body weight. The body destroyed dispensable organs in favor of vital ones, beginning a process of decay and disintegration that ultimately led to death.[9] A person could live twenty to thirty days without food if in good physical condition.[10] However, most sailors were already malnourished and exhausted, two factors that affected a person's ability to withstand hunger. As the body continued to decline, the pulse rate and blood pressure dropped; the person felt cold and apathetic, and chances for mental illness increased.[11]

Much of our understanding of how the body reacts to deprivation came from a study during World War II. The Civilian Public Service enlisted conscientious objectors during the war to "scientifically isolate and study the effects of hunger."[12] The experiment involved starving thirty-six men for one year in a controlled environment. The men were placed on a restricted "starvation" diet and then slowly given ever increasing amounts of food. Designed to mirror famine conditions in postwar Europe, the purpose of the study was to find the best method for relief feeding in war's aftermath.

The findings from this experiment are interesting for the parallels to shipwreck survivors. During the early stages the participants' physical and mental abilities deteriorated and they developed a lack of morale. As they lost weight, the men found sitting uncomfortable and continually felt cold. Once the starvation period ended, researchers discovered that the human body was capable of recovering quickly and that humans had evolved to handle periods of starvation.[13] Victims of shipwreck underwent the same deterioration and reported similar complaints of being uncomfortable and cold. Most survivors recovered their physical health quickly after their ordeal, though some took a lifetime to recover fully.

Although a person could survive several weeks without food, the body can last only a few days without water, and individuals can become delirious in as little as four days.[14] The first signs of severe dehydration were a cracked and ulcerated tongue and mouth. Many drank whatever was available, the most common being blood and urine. Some survival accounts suggested that objects placed in the mouth, such as pennies or buttons, helped stimulate saliva production, thus alleviating thirst. Many sources, including the narratives, warned against drinking saltwater; anyone who did became delirious and died an "active, noisy death."[15] For example, several crew members aboard the *Francis Mary* (1827) succumbed due to a lack of water, and "those who perished drank their own urine and salt water. They became foolish, and crawled upon their hands round the deck when they could, and died, generally, raving mad!"[16] Rather than providing some level of hydration, these actions actually accelerated the loss of water. Modern survival guides follow such cautions and warn that urine and saltwater are never good substitutes and that drinking saltwater was the most common cause of death, second only to exposure. If a shipwreck victim must use urine in some capacity, authorities suggest that urine is best used to cool clothing through evaporation rather than taken internally.[17]

By the time of the *Francis Mary*'s sinking in 1827, nineteenth-century readers knew well of cannibalism's association with shipwreck. The innate repulsiveness of cannibalism, while objectionable to refined audiences, also made the stories appealing to read. They fed into what Karen Halttunen calls "a popular voyeuristic taste for scenarios of death."[18] Throughout the seventeenth, eighteenth, and nineteenth centuries, popular accounts of shipwreck appeared in most major newspapers, and many involved tales of cannibalism. A short list of nineteenth-century shipwrecks whose survivors reported its occurrence includes the following: *Nauticus* (1807); *George* (1822); *Francis Mary* (1826); *Granicus* (1828); *Dalusia* (1833); *Lucy* (1834); *Francis Spaight* (1835); *Elizabeth Rashleigh* (1835); *Caledonia* (1836); *Home* (1836); *Hannah* (1836); and *Earl Moria* (1838).[19] In addition to those listed, this study adds the following ships: *De Ruyter* (1683); *Enterprise* (1793); *Virginia Merchant* (1649); *Nottingham* (1710); *Peggy* (1765); *Tyrrel* (1759); *Acorn* (1809); *Medusa* (1816); and *Essex* (1820). In addition many nineteenth-century authors, such as Edgar Allan Poe and Herman Melville, included accounts of cannibalism in literature and in fictional accounts. Given its wide literary distribution, cannibalism was no stranger to American audiences.

In 1827 Ann Saunders wrote in response to her shipwreck experience, "alas, how often in my childhood have I read accounts of seafaring people, and others, having been driven to the awful alternative of either starving, or to satisfy the cravings of nature, subsisting on human flesh. . . . accounts generally discredited by those who have not been placed in a similar situation."[20] Her statement indicates that although audiences read about such events, until physically placed in the situation, readers could not fully fathom the level of desperation it took to eat human flesh.

The narratives suggested that when people died of dehydration or exposure, the first rarely were cannibalized. Frequently the living threw the initial few bodies overboard, and only when conditions worsened did survivors contemplate cannibalism. Shipwrecked sailors and passengers utilized every possible food source before turning to human flesh. Although there is no one scenario, the path to cannibalism generally followed a sequence of actions.[21] Individuals first looked to normal foodstuffs, drinking wine, using up stores, and even eating moldy or rotten food. Once these resources were finished, they moved on to animals not normally used as food, such as dogs, cats, and rats. For example, off Bermuda in 1649 the *Virginia Merchant* ran into trouble, leaving the survivors stranded in a drifting boat. After several days the need for food became apparent, and "the infinite number of rats that all the voyage had been our plague, we now were glad to make our prey and feed on." These common pests became a choice selection, and "a well grown rat was sold for sixteen shillings as a market rate." Over time the price went up and even twenty shillings would not buy a rat for a pregnant woman.[22] Animals with a social bond such as dogs or cats fared a little better and became food only after survivors explored other alternatives.

Once shipwreck victims exhausted these options, hunger compelled them to find any available protein, such as that found in leather, candles, and oil. Finally, with nothing else to eat, human flesh provided the only means for survival. Mark D. Dornstreich and George E. B. Morren calculated that a 60-kiligram (132 pounds) man could provide each of sixty adult eaters with about 102.6 grams (3.6 ounces) of protein per day, assuming the group ate a man per day. One man per day would fulfill the group's protein requirement.[23] Cannibals, whether ritualistic or from starvation, tended not to kill more than was needed and often preserved fresh meat to postpone the need to kill again. Shipwreck victims proportioned available protein to maximize available resources.

Survivors usually ate the dead or dying first, but when no such bodies were available they "dispatched" some to save the others. Accounts suggested that shipwreck victims followed a rough pattern: they generally ate those of another race, then strangers, then friends, and finally kin. Young men without families often went before older individuals, men before women and children, passengers before crew members, and crews before officers and captains.[24] To be an "other" in any shape, way, or form singled out a person ahead of the remaining passengers and crew. For example, on the *Francis Mary* (1826) the order of death (though natural in these instances) followed such an outline. After several days the men began to die, and the order in which they expired is interesting: "James Clark, seaman; J. Moore; Henry Davis, a Welsh boy; Alex. Kelly, seaman; John Jones, apprentice boy; James Frier, cook; Daniel Jones, a boy."[25] Not surprisingly, all of the officers survived.

Even on land cannibalism followed a rational pattern. The Donner party incident of 1846–47 represents one of the most famous cases of cannibalism in American history. Of eighty-seven people stranded in the Sierra Nevada mountain range, forty died, of which thirty-five deaths were related directly to exposure and starvation. The party was made up of several families as well as some single men on their way to Oregon territory. They endured a series of setbacks that delayed their mountain crossing and entered the mountains already exhausted and hungry. When the snow became too deep, the settlers stopped to build shelters; approximately five months later, in April, the last survivor left. Throughout this extended ordeal age, sex, and size of kin group determined who survived and who did not.[26]

Once trapped in the mountains the Donner party split into three different camps or cabin areas: the Breens and Keesburg cabin; the Murphy and Eddy camp; and the Graves and Reed camp.[27] The archaeological record indicates that the inhabitants of the Murphy cabin site went through a process of eating similar to that of shipwreck victims, in which they ate animals, leather, and other sources of protein before turning to cannibalism. Faunal remains included bear and mule, both expected from historical documentation.[28] By January they had no meat and looked for any available protein. Patrick Breen's diary suggests that by this time few families had anything but hides to subsist on.[29] The stranded settlers ate bits of rug, leather, and any other edible items. Archaeologists found fragments of human bone as well, but they were too small to determine if cannibalized.

Mortality demographics from the Donner party indicate that males died at a higher rate than females. Although both men and women participated in foraging for food and fuel, men often performed more intense physical labor such as clearing trails, hunting, and building shelters. By the time they reached the cabins, many men were physically and psychologically exhausted. Indeed all who died in the first few weeks were men. This first phase suggests that death came from exposure, initial levels of exhaustion, and an inability to replenish much-needed nutrients. From December 15 to January 5 fourteen males and no females died; however, after a brief period when no one died, death came again and affected men and women evenly. While the first episode represents exhaustion, only after starvation leveled the playing field did both men and women perish.[30]

The shipwreck narratives often related a similar scenario with few women dying early. Such individuals were not part of the crews and probably did little to help with the overall maintenance or sailing of the vessels, and so they expended little additional energy. Only when starvation acted as the ultimate equalizer did women succumb "naturally." Post–World War II data suggest that females are better adapted to surviving starvation. Despite being considered the "weaker sex," women statistically fared better, surviving where many men did not, and areas with higher levels of famine had a higher male than female mortality rate.[31] Physically women have greater stores of subcutaneous fat and a smaller body size, and they are able to withstand longer starvation periods.[32]

The notion of "choosing lots" provided a dramatic theme in stories concerning cannibalism. One of the earliest recorded incidents of drawing lots dated to 1641, in Nicholas Tulpius's *Observationem Medicarum,* where seven Englishmen, lost at sea, drew lots to preserve the rest.[33] In choosing lots the survivors demonstrated that all put their lives at stake and all shared the same risks. Each narrative stated explicitly the need for lots and that this method was fair and unbiased, at least most of the time. Rather than a random act of violence, choosing lots made the selection process and the act of cannibalism less threatening. The method is similar to one used in marine insurance: the concept of general average, where some cargo is sacrificed to save the rest. As a result shipwreck victims situated the act within a framework understood by all parties involved.[34]

A common justification used in many narratives was that it was "better for some to have survived by sacrificing one or more lives."[35] The women aboard the *Virginia Merchant* (1649) were "to endeavour their own preservation by converting her [a woman who recently expired of natural causes] dead carcass into food, as they did to good effect."[36] Instead of dwelling purely on the situation's morbidity, the narratives detailed the process of selection to justify who went first. Survivors often asserted that the first victims died natural deaths and that only when necessary did they turn to drawing lots to decide whom to kill.[37]

Though variations existed, a common method for choosing individuals began with the first round of determining the intended victim. One person held a series of sticks (or something similar that could be hidden in a hand or hat) with one different from the others. A second person, unable to see the lot selected, called out a random name that then corresponded with the lot chosen. A similar process was described in Sir John Barrow's *Mutiny and Piratical Seizure of HMS* Bounty to determine who received which portion of food: "One person turns his back on the object that is to be divided; another then points separately to the portions, at each of them asking out loud, 'who shall have this?' to which the first answers by naming somebody." This technique supposedly ensured fairness because the person drawing lots and the person calling out the names did not see one another; therefore the two could not pass signals. After selecting a victim, a second round then began to choose the person to kill the intended. Using this process, or a similar one, survivors justified killing when everyone had an equal stake. Rarely did courts bring charges against a crew that employed a random, impartial method of choosing victims.[38] All took a chance and all faced the same odds. Rather than murder, courts viewed the method of choosing lots as defendable in the eyes of the law.

To add further drama, men were not the only ones who participated in drawing lots. A few shipwreck narratives included women and families in this process. One of the more tragic accounts occurred on the *De Ruyter*

(1684), carrying a merchant, his wife, and their two children. On its way from the West Indies to Rotterdam, the ship encountered calm seas for several weeks, straining already limited food supplies. The merchant's children died naturally and after much deliberation were the first individuals eaten, although they provided only a small amount of food. After depleting this source, the crew "consented by Lot or otherwise to destroy some one in the number to save the rest." In this decision a dispute arose as to whether the merchant's wife should be exempted "from the fatall lot." Some said she should be included, while others felt she had paid her dues with the deaths of her children. In the end they included her and the "lot fell on the woman for Death, and on her husband for Executioner." The husband refused to let his wife die, and he "resolved never to be her Executioner, who that been so loving and just a Wife to me, but in her stead are resolved my self the sacrifice," at which point he drew out a gun and shot himself.[39] The account indicated that foul play may have had a part in the decision. The woman was the only noncrew member and probably did little to assist in the ship's daily functions. Therefore the crew might have seen her as a useless, additional mouth and not necessary for survival. This supposition played out in a second round of lots when the poor woman again became the selected victim.

Before the merchant killed himself to save his wife, George Carpinger, a sailor, and his supporters promised the merchant that they would protect his wife. When the woman became the chosen one a second time, those who supported her fought the faction who wanted her killed. In the end four men died, which conveniently provided enough food for their present needs. The tides and wind eventually carried the ship off the Plymouth coast, but due to ice they could not make it to shore. By that time only four people survived: Carpinger, the wife, and two sailors who were too weak to leave their cabins. Somehow Carpinger and the wife found enough energy to make it across the dangerous ice to safety, but the two sailors died before help could arrive.[40]

Stories of choosing lots periodically suggested foul play. The typical pattern of strangers before friends, unrelated before kin, and passengers before crew happened too often to be purely coincidental. This selection process is probably one reason that captains and officers often survived while foreigners and slaves rarely made it home.[41] During this process those with authority remained in power and had the ability to manipulate or control circumstances. Although this pattern applied to most shipwrecks, in a few accounts captains or officers went before common sailors. Rather than indicating fairness, this inversion might instead represent crews' attempts to rid themselves of unpopular leaders.

On land the Donner party faced a similar situation when a small group, "The Forlorn Hope," in an attempt to escape the mountains, found themselves desperate to find any form of sustenance. In mid-December five women and ten men attempted to make it out of the mountains. It took them thirty-three days to reach the first signs of civilization. Of the ten men only two made it out alive, and all five women survived.

One of the group, Patrick Dolan, brought up the issue of casting lots, but the remainder refused to comply.[42] This instance was the only mention of choosing lots in the Donner party saga. Ironically a few days later Dolan was the third to die but the first to be consumed. Although the Donner party refused to choose lots, they did follow a pattern similar to that found in shipwreck narratives. Rather than kill one of their own they began to plot against two outsiders and "proposed that they should kill the two Indian boys, Lewis and Salvadore." The boys escaped, temporarily, and took off on their own. About a week later the party came across the two boys, on the edge of death. According to J. Quinn Thornton, both were shot in the head.[43]

This same party continued to persevere, but conventional social lines blurred when Mr. Foster proposed to "kill Mrs. McCutcheon, alleging that she was but a nuisance, and could not keep up." When others refused to assist, he then "proposed that they should kill Mary Graves and Mrs. Fosdick, as they had no children." Again the Donner party followed patterns similar to those discussed in shipwrecks, where less valuable members were often selected over those who had skills necessary for survival or had families to support. Luckily for these women, the remainder of the party threatened to kill Mr. Foster if he attempted to take anyone's life.[44] The arguments within "The Forlorn Hope" paralleled cultural values seen at sea. Issues of usefulness often allowed one to survive longer, as did the presence of loved ones and dependents. Eventually the desperate settlers decided to sacrifice one for the benefit of the others but also that this person was "supposed to have less claims to life than the others." Fortunately for the survivors, some died naturally and saved them from having to select one of their own.[45]

One of the better-known narratives of shipwreck and cannibalism occurred on the *Peggy* (1765) as she sailed from the Azores to New York. After encountering a storm, the vessel drifted helplessly for days without sails and masts. When the provisions ran out, the sailors "fell upon the wine and brandy" to appease growing hunger pangs. After four days they devoured the remaining pigeons and a cat, of which the sailors respectfully apportioned the head for the captain. When these were gone, the crew "supported their existence by living on oil, candles, and leather."[46]

Two weeks later the crew came to the captain, as a body, and declared that "they could hold out no longer, that their tobacco was exhausted; they had eaten all the leather belonging to the pumps, even the buttons off their jackets," and that it was necessary "to sacrifice one of themselves for the preservation of the rest." Captain Harrison stated, "They expected my concurrence to the measure," but "with all my authority, I [commanded them] to relinquish the idea of committing such an atrocious crime." They replied that they intended to go ahead and "they would oblige me to take my chance as well as another man, since the general misfortune had leveled all distinction of persons." The crew immediately chose lots and, not surprisingly, it fell to "a negro, who was on board and belonged to Captain Harrison."[47]

Even the author saw through this charade and challenged that the "lot had been consulted only for the sake of form, and that the wretched black was proscribed, the moment the sailors first formed their resolution." To make matters worse, the crew bypassed the privilege of last rights and "instantly sacrificed him." James Stanier Clarke's 1821 version added that "the captain could only regret his want of power to protect him, and saw him the next morning dragged into the steerage where he was almost immediately shot through the head."[48] There is no mention of another lot to see who might dispatch the poor victim or that any saw this as murder. Perhaps this action had more to do with the slave's social standing as a piece of property rather than as a person who deserved due process.[49]

In a unique twist to social hierarchy the men of the *Essex* made a difficult decision in casting lots. On November 20, 1820, the whale ship *Essex* was destroyed by a whale, forcing twenty men into three small boats. By January 14 the second mate's boat was out of supplies, and a week later the captain's boat and the second mate's boat shared the remains of Charles Shorter.[50] Over the next few days three more men died and each was consumed. On January 26 the two boats separated.[51]

On the captain's boat the four remaining men decided to cast lots. The first lot fell to the cabin boy and nephew to Captain Pollard. The boy was not only the youngest and the least skilled but was also related to the captain. Once the boy was selected, Captain Pollard exclaimed, "My lad, my lad, *if you don't like your lot,* I'll shoot the first man that touches you." The young boy responded, "*I like it as well as any other.*" They drew lots again to see who would shoot him, and he was immediately dispatched.[52] In this instance usefulness and hierarchy within the ship won over familial or social ties from land. On February 11 Brazilla Ray expired and was the last man to be consumed. Twelve days later the survivors, Captain Pollard and Charles Ramsdale, were rescued by the *Dauphin*.[53]

Unlike the men of the *Essex*, who remained well within established boundaries, the crew of the *Peggy* lost control, and all sense of social order seemed to disappear temporarily. The men paid for their rash behavior, however, when "one of the crew tore out his [the slave's] liver and devoured it, without having the patience to dress it by broiling, or in any other manner. He was soon after taken ill, and died the following day, and with all the symptoms of madness."[54] This man became a monster when he lost control of himself, and he deserved no better than the savages they encountered on land. The others, perhaps in response to the sailor's death, decided to cook the rest of the victim's flesh; they took stock of the man's actions and modified their behavior. They made a large fire in which they intended "to fry his entrails for Supper." Clarke added that "they continued busy the principal part of the night with their feast, & did not retire until two in the morning."[55]

For several days, while the crew members "were stewing and frying some steaks, as they called the slices which they cut from the poor Negro," the captain began to fear for his life. His fears increased when he discovered that they next intended to choose lots for the captain. When the crew announced a second round, Captain Harrison gave "his consent, fearing lest the enraged sailors might have recourse to the lot without him." If Harrison participated, he might be able to control the lots and ensure a level of impartiality, and to minimize the possibility that the crew would choose him as the next victim. With Harrison drawing names, the choice fell upon a popular crew member, a foremastman. Despite the shock, the man resigned himself to his fate and stated, "My dear friends, all I have to beg of you is dispatch me as soon as you did the negro." He turned to the man who had performed the first execution and asked him to perform the second. He then asked to have an hour to prepare for death. Giving in to compassion, the crew decided to wait until eleven o'clock the following morning. During the night the poor man was seized by a violent fever and fell into a state of delirium. In spite of this, in anticipation of a meal, the crew made ready a large fire at ten o'clock. But luckily for the man, about that time the crew sighted a sail coming toward the *Peggy*.[56]

The narrative had one last dramatic moment when the excited men burst into the captain's cabin to tell him the good news. The captain, starved and already paranoid, assumed that they instead came to kill him rather than dispatch the well-liked foremast man. In a last attempt to preserve his life Harrison picked up a pistol, but before he could take aim the crew gave him the good news. The captain later wrote that it was with "the utmost exertion of my strength that I desired them to use every expedition in making a signal of distress."[57] Once again the crew followed their captain, and the hope of rescue restored order.

A similar progression of whom was eaten was found on land as well. The first recorded date of cannibalism in the Donner party camps was February 26, after three months in the mountains, when Patrick Breen wrote in his journal that Mrs. Murphy "would commence on Milt and eat him." At that time Breen did not think she had but was aware of such threats four days earlier by other members.[58] Over the next few months thirty-five members of the Donner party died, in addition to two Indian employees; at least seventeen of the dead became sustenance for the survivors. Unfortunately exact dates of death and of cannibalism are difficult to recover, as is the exact number of those cannibalized. In some instances records fail to give a name or date or may have been written about the act in passing several days or weeks later. The identification of who ate human flesh is further complicated by movement between cabins or camps.[59]

The most surprising victim was Jacob Donner; rescuers supposedly found him as a meal for his own children. He had died early, around December 15, but rescuers mentioned his body late in the ordeal. This was one of the few instances of a family possibly eating one of their own, although this is not certain, as most references gloss over or fail to mention who specifically ate whom.[60] The most violent episodes of cannibalism within the Donner party saga occurred when "The Forlorn Hope" tried to escape in December. It took this group thirty-three days to find rescue, and in the process they lost almost half of their numbers. Two of ten men and all five women survived.[61]

Although most accounts stressed that survivors refrained from eating loved ones or family, Ann Saunders, aboard the *Francis Mary*, chose to consume one of her "own" rather than keep sentimental attachments. Throughout early February the ship experienced a series of gales that left it incapacitated. By the 12th James Clarke, seaman, died of famine, and ten days later a second sailor died. Those remaining cut the body into slices, washed them in the water, and let them dry in the sun. The captain's report added that they "cut him up in quarters, washed them overboard, and hung them up on pins."[62] Over the next two weeks five sailors, two cabin boys, and the cook expired. The survivors ate the heart and liver of one sailor but omitted details concerning consumption of the rest.[63]

Most horrifying to Ann Saunders was the death of the cook, James Frier, her fiancé.[64] The survivors were in the habit of slitting the deceased's throat to drink the blood before it congealed, and Frier was no exception. She claimed that it was god's will that she drink her fiancé's blood.[65] Apparently,

Ann performed such work on all the deceased except for Daniel Jones, a boy, whom they threw overboard, "his blood being bitter."[66] She processed the bodies, including that of her fiancé, making efficient use of available sustenance and perhaps delaying the need to choose lots.

Similar to the narrative of the *Francis Mary*, the story of the Donner party gained some of its drama from the inclusion of women and children and the horror of subsisting off of loved ones. As part of "The Forlorn Hope," Mrs. Fosdick, the day after her husband died, watched two companions "cut out the heart and liver, and severed the arms and legs of her departed husband." She refused to partake of the flesh, however, being "unable to endure the horrible sight of seeing latterly devoured the heart that had fondly and ardently loved her until it had ceased to throb."[67] The survivors knew of such possibilities. Mr. Graves, on death's door, pleaded with his daughters to "use every means possible to survive." Although they claimed that they "would never touch the loathsome food," the girls turned to cannibalism to survive. In his last breath Graves "urged that his flesh be used to prolong the lives of his companions."[68] Two days later the survivors, still stuck in the "camp of death," followed his advice.

Although the previous accounts stressed a level of order and that survivors tended to remain within conventional moral or ethical standards, the tale of the *Medusa* presents a very different story of shipwreck. On June 17, 1816, the *Medusa* left the Island of Aix for Senegal. The authors, J. B. Savigny, the surgeon, and Alexander Corréard, an engineer and geographer, related a tale of murder and anarchy. On July 2 the *Medusa* hit a reef, forcing her passengers to abandon the frigate. The captain and most of the gentlemen found passage on a variety of other ships that sailed in convoy with the *Medusa*. According to Savigny and Corréard, this left "one hundred and twenty soldiers, including the officers of the army, twenty-nine sailors and passengers, and one woman" to throw their lot to the raft, a poorly constructed "vessel" that measured approximately twenty meters in length and seven in breadth. With so many on the raft, the survivors stood to their waist in water, exposed to all elements.[69]

Although those in the boats promised to tow the raft, it was soon cut loose, and "the whole line was thrown into disorder, and no measures were taken to remedy it; it is probable, that if one of the first officers had set the example, order would have been restored; but everyone was left to himself."[70] In their despair the soldiers and sailors drank the wine on board and soon lost all reason. It was these men who became "deaf to the voice of reason" and "openly expressed their intention to rid themselves of the officers" and destroy the raft.[71] This episode began a long struggle between rational officers and passengers on one side and insane sailors and soldiers on the other. Many died needlessly because of the violence, but those who died increased the chances that others might live.

During the night of July 6 the mutineers threw over most of their drinking supply, two barrels of water and one of wine, leaving them with only one cask of wine.[72] It had now been three days since they had eaten. Some turned to cannibalism when the soldiers "seized upon the dead bodies with which the raft was covered, cutting them up by slices, which some even instantly devoured." Seeing that this revived them, the survivors proposed to dry the flesh in an effort to preserve it and make it more palatable. However, many of the officers abstained from flesh and subsisted on shoulder belts, cartouche boxes, linen, leather, and any other means available to them.[73]

By July 11 only twenty-seven remained, and the survivors debated about giving precious wine to twelve individuals on the brink of death. The injured might consume most of the wine before they died and would therefore waste the precious sustenance. Putting them on half rations was tantamount to death, so they expedited matters and threw them overboard. The survivors continued on for several days, subsisting on a little wine, bits of human flesh, leather, and urine. The measures worked; fifteen remained when rescued by the brig *Argus* six days later.[74]

Accounts typically glossed over the actual process of eating people, though the narratives suggested some trends. For example, on the *Peggy* survivors threw out the heads, hands, and feet—anything distinctively "human"—and survivors generally preferred specific body parts such as brains and livers.[75] For example, sailors and passengers on the *Francis Mary* in 1827 used only the heart and liver of the second man to die. More specifically, the captain's wife commented that the seaman's brain "was the most delicious thing she had ever tasted."[76] Her statement may have a ring of truth, as according to various sources, human flesh tastes like pork, only sweeter.[77]

On the whale ship *Essex* (1820) the men did not turn to cannibalism immediately as they floated helplessly in the middle of the Pacific Ocean; they resisted the urge for several weeks. On board the first mate's boat Isaac Cole began to decline, and despite everyone's help he passed away on February 8. They prepared to throw the body over but realized that they were close to casting lots and that they might do better by processing an already dead body.[78]

The men "separated the limbs from his [Isaac Cole's] body, and cut all the flesh from the bones; after which, we opened the body, took out the heart, and then closed it again—sewed it up as decently as we could, and committed it to the sea."[79] They immediately ate the heart and a few pieces of flesh but let the rest dry. By the next day the flesh had turned green, so they roasted the bits of meat to preserve it and were able to feed on the meat for almost a week. Two days after they finished their food supply, the *Indian* rescued all three men from the second mate's boat.[80]

The Donner party exhibited similar eating patterns. Rescuers found the "mutilated body of a friend, having nearly all the flesh torn away . . . the head and face remaining entire." They recorded that Jacob Donner had his head cut off and that "his limbs and arms, had been severed from the body, which was cut open—the heart and liver being taken out."[81] In general the bodies were processed away from living areas. Rather than severing entire legs or arms, survivors typically cut away flesh or utilized internal organs. Such pieces leave little in the archaeological record, and therefore it is not surprising to have few archaeological examples of cannibalism.

Whether people were stranded at sea or on land, cannibalism served as a last, desperate means of survival.[82] Although cannibalism among "savages" denoted barbarism and dehumanized the society that performed it, cannibalism associated with shipwreck narratives instead showed the human ability to adapt and survive. John Leach in *Survival Psychology* states that if the process is rationalized or justified, cannibalism "can be accommodated with little or no psychological ramifications."[83] It is clear from the shipwreck narratives that order was necessary in this extreme situation. Rather than align themselves as savages, survivors cannibalized their peers within understood parameters of social hierarchy. In addition choosing lots was important not only from a social standpoint but from a legal standpoint as well. The supposed impartiality of lots meant that risk was distributed evenly and that each took the same chance. No longer murder, survival cannibalism represented a logical means to preserve the greatest number of individuals.

Mutiny also threatened order but was rarely successful in subverting it completely. Desertion, protests, and strikes while operating within traditional hierarchies recognized the continued authority of captains and officers. Sailors used a variety of means to limit a captain's ability or to declare their discontent regarding life aboard ship. In some instances, however, sailors took their complaints to an extreme and challenged all forms of authority. Though mutiny was often associated with the navy, it occurred on all types of ships, all over the globe, in calm seas and in storms, and yet mutiny did not devolve into anarchy—hierarchies shifted but some level of authority remained intact.

In actual moments of shipwreck, mutiny rarely occurred. Mariners scrambled to stay alive rather than worry about a lack of food, low wages, and limited liberty. In the aftermaths, however, with survivors stranded on sinking ships or on deserted islands, discontent could turn into action. Such movements did not occur lightly. Mutiny was a last, desperate measure open to sailors, who knew that it was considered a crime at sea punishable by death.[84]

Rather than subverting traditional society, mutiny was in response to a specific problem in which a captain had failed to do his job properly, at least in the eyes of the sailors. Sailors often looked to the short term, using mutiny to alleviate problems regarding daily life at sea, which meant that the outcome should then improve living conditions.[85] Dissatisfaction and discontent alone were not enough to incite mutiny. It usually required a situation that seemed hopeless with no redress in sight.[86] Shipwreck intensified physical and psychological stress; when combined with a lack of food, it is amazing that mutiny did not occur more often at such times. In shipwreck situations cabin fever and hallucinations often set in, and survivors compensated by withdrawing from one another. On a ship or tiny island, however, private space was impossible and contact unavoidable, intensifying tension and discomfort. Decreased control of the situation and of the self lowered toleration dramatically, increasing the possibility of conflict.[87] For example, after several days on a cold, barren rock the men of the *Nottingham Galley* (1710) no longer behaved like a crew. The captain noted that "instead of obeying my commands, as they had universally and cheerfully done before, I now found even prayers and entreaties vain and fruitless; nothing was not to be heard but brutal quarrels, with horrid oaths and imprecations."[88] These sailors found themselves in a desperate situation in which authority and order degraded into a state of anarchy.

Seamen often cited brutality as a cause for mutiny, and indeed several cases detailed the violence of captains. However, violence alone did not incite mutiny; only when the punishment seemed unfair or arbitrary did sailors stand against it.[89] Even before shipwreck, the crew of the *Nottingham Galley* was on the verge of mutiny. The first mate felt that the captain's "barbarous Treatment of our Men, had disable'd several of 'em, and two of our best Sailors were so unmercifully beat by him, because they oppos'd his Design . . . that they were not able to work in a Month." Later the mate accused the captain of taking up a perriwig block, "with which he came behind the Mate, and struck him three blows to the Head, upon which he fell down and lay as dead for several Minutes."[90] Although the crew worked in a violent world, the captain's brutality, as related by the mate, implied a man out of control acting in unfair or arbitrary ways. Rather than seeing the violence as reasonable, the crew felt that it was not acceptable. In turn, these accusations assaulted the captain's reputation and affected his

status within society. He did not behave as a man of his standing or authority should.

The presence of agitators also brought mutiny into action.[91] In such
situations one or several individuals led and organized those who wavered
or who might not otherwise rise against authority. Captain Uring found out
that his men planned on taking over the ship and had made a round-robin,
which by the time of discovery contained signatures of most of the crew.
A round-robin is a piece of paper on which the signatures form a circle;
therefore no name stands at the top of the list and no one person can stand
accused as the leader. Upon learning about their intention, he ordered all
men on deck and demanded the keys to their chests. He began with the
gunner, "whom I knew to be a seditious Fellow, which I suspected to be
the chief Conspirator." He stated that the gunner laughed and said that the
captain was mistaken, but Uring "gave him two or three such Strokes with
a Stick I had prepared for that purpose." According to Uring, "The Seamen
upon the main Deck were all silent while I was correcting this Fellow, till
one bolder than the rest, and Consort to him, began to open and speak some
seditious Words." A sailor, not involved, said he knew where the conspira-
tors had hidden the paper, and he turned it over to Uring. More than half
the company had signed it, including those Uring had previously punished.
"Some others, whom I looked upon to be the honestest Men I had, and
who had been the most serviceable in the Voyage, had signed it also: To
these I said, that above all Men, I little expected that they would have been
Mutineers; and let them know what they had done would be deemed Piracy,
which was a hanging matter, . . . but that I believed they were persuaded
into it against their Inclinations. I bid them be very diligent for the future,
and I would take no farther Notice of it."[92] The narrative implicated only
a few agitators rather than the whole crew. This was not anarchy or a total
reversal of hierarchy, and quite often there was no punishment once order
was restored. Captains indicated that a failure to punish did not necessarily
mean weakness; rather it was a necessity to keep men loyal and able to
work.[93]

As stated, the most common causes for mutiny were lack of respect for
the captain or officers and for their failing to promote a sense of security.
Without respect for authority, common sailors found their own means for
survival. Although Capt. Nathaniel Uring lay injured on a desolate coast-
line, his crew refused to wait for his recovery. Shipwrecked off Central
America, the crew decided to trek overland to the Plantane River. The captain begged them to stay and warned them of the dangers of going overland. They remained unconvinced, and in his narrative the captain stated,
"The Obstinacy of these People shewed me very plainly, what wretched

ungovernable Creatures Men are, when there is no Power nor Laws to restrain them; not the least Pity or Compassion was found amongst them; for now they were become their own Masters."[94] The men showed little respect for their captain, much to his dismay, and chose their own path for survival. Despite these potential problems, when captains once again proved themselves capable, order was reestablished.[95] Indeed, Uring found temporary authority when the men tried to go to sea. They attempted to take a canoe out past the breakers and paddle their way to the nearest settlement. Once in the canoe, Uring again took control by coordinating efforts to steer the canoe over a high surf. However, the waves proved too much, and they returned to the beach, where Uring once again had problems of authority and the sailors attempted several times to abandon him.[96]

In the aftermaths of shipwrecks some crews did turn on the captains and officers in an effort to assert their desired courses for survival. Working collectively was common for sailors, and this group mentality might expand into mutiny, although only if a captain seemed deficient in leadership. Order, not initiative, was essential in shipwreck situations. Those who took matters into their own hands usually paid with their lives. Although questioning the masters or slighting superior officers was a form of subverting hierarchy, such measures rarely went beyond legal limitations. Instead of imparting a negative connotation, through such means sailors exacted a level of independence within the daily monotony of sailing that perhaps moderated the level of crisis, obviating the need to mutiny or to take matters further.[97]

Yet stories persist of total anarchy and continue to frame our understandings of shipwreck and chaos. The account of the *Medusa* was a tale of chaos in which little status persisted. After wrecking on dangerous reefs, the *Medusa* was abandoned on July 2, 1816. During the first night approximately 20 of almost 150 died, though exact numbers are hard to determine. Many individuals lay dead on the raft, were stuck between timbers, or were too tired to stand. Numbers continued to decline, and during the following day many more became delirious and threw themselves overboard.[98]

Those who remained fell into two camps: rational officers; and uncontrollable sailors and soldiers. Out of despair, the sailors and soldiers knocked holes in the wine casks, drank the wine, and became inebriated. In an attempt to maintain a level of authority, the officers tried to control the drinking, but their actions only incited a rebellion. The soldiers, many actually criminals taken from various jails, were "Spanish, Italians, Portuguese, and Negroes, as well as Frenchmen." But it was a large "Asiatic" who presented the most danger. He yelled, "Get rid of the officers!" and came at them "waving a boarding ax above his head." He then began to knock apart the raft while his fellow soldiers drew closer to the officers clustered in the raft's middle. The mutineers temporarily retreated when they met the officers' swords. What had been a small skirmish became an all-out war with officers and passengers fighting the soldiers and sailors, and they "cut and slashed their way through the ragged lines into which the mutineers had drawn themselves."[99] The wine and lack of food had led the soldiers and sailors to follow social hierarchies no longer. These men later paid the price with their lives.

By the next morning only sixty individuals were left.[100] The survivors quickly devolved into small groups that consistently shifted their allegiance. "The castaways were divided by nationality, by color, by caste, by age, by occupation, by experience and, most dangerously of all, by the marks of the branding iron which indicated whence many of the soldiers had been recruited—the jails of France."[101] Those who threatened order did not come from society's highest levels; the violence came from those who might benefit from change. On the fifth day all allegiances broke down. "Negroes among the soldiers became Negroes first and soldiers a long way second." They suggested that their "nearness to Africa gave them a supposed advantage that enabled them to concoct a plan by which they would survive at the expense of others." In addition they sided with the Italians and Spaniards to rid themselves of the French officers, but the officers once again managed to repulse any attacks. By the end of the day only thirty remained.[102]

They continued with only a little wine and bits of human flesh until July 11. Those who could denied the weakest any sustenance and executed 12 of the weakest. Their bodies were thrown overboard. Only fifteen remained alive, and among those rescued were only one soldier and one sailor.

Conservative by nature, the accounts revealed a sense of social order that readers and participants recognized as necessary. Despite the language of egalitarianism and independence, respect for rank and place remained important.[103] The narratives detailed the importance of knowing one's place in society, whether this was a part of God's design or from natural order. Such conduct extended to shipwreck and often meant the difference between life and death. Continued order was necessary not only for survival but also to prove oneself as rational and civilized. To subvert authority or to act outside of traditional social structures threatened continued existence. Published shipwreck accounts reassured audiences that even in mutiny order remained intact.

During shipwrecks captains and crews needed each other to stay alive. Although someone with navigation skills proved necessary, especially when in an open boat, this knowledge did not always translate into survival.[104] Captains required sailors to man longboats, cut down trees, or perform necessary manual labor. Good captains learned to balance authority with understanding.[105] Especially on ships where social standing might not differ widely between officers and crew members, authority depended on malleable features of respect and experience.[106] Mutiny rarely occurred in the shipwreck narratives and then only when crews lost respect for captains and officers. Mutiny was not meant to be a long-term solution but rather was a short-term means to ensure survival. Once the survivors felt that authority was in the right hands, the crews again fell into place and followed orders as necessary.

Traditional power relations were extended to cannibalism by those who ate versus those who were eaten. Captains and officers often were the last to go, bettering their chances for coming home. Directly tied to status by way of race, religion, position, and gender, the order of cannibalism provided an accurate reflection of social order. Drawing lots represented the "original model for all risk in insurance; it corresponds to the sacrificial premium we all make so that others (or ourselves) are compensated in the event of disaster."[107] Even in such moments hierarchy remained stable, even if it did waiver somewhat. The narratives demonstrated a "triumph over the forbidden" and fed into a growing sense of sensibility in American taste.[108]

The narratives, whether printed in England or in America, bespoke an Anglo-American, upper- and middle-class, Protestant ideal.[109] As an Atlantic tradition, the narratives supported a nationalistic image of perseverance and triumph. Americans, even black Americans, proved superior in their capabilities to adapt and survive. The narratives supported a conservative response: that hierarchy, moderation, and remaining within acceptable boundaries were necessary for survival. Perhaps this is why the French *Medusa* tale was so popular with Anglo-American readers. In general, rather than promoting a negative portrayal of crisis, shipwreck narratives imparted positive images in which status and order remained safe and intact. Although shipwreck was a potentially threatening situation, those who experienced it were able to maintain social order and to preserve the accompanying elements of class, gender, and race.

Cannibalism blurred lines of civility and savagery. In participating in the "savage" practice of cannibalism, Christian men and women reflected attributes placed on barbaric natives. However, the narratives did much to place these individuals in an orderly context that allowed shipwreck victims to retain a level of propriety. Choosing lots or eating those already dead minimized the act of cannibalism to one of general average. And yet, as in the case of the *Peggy*, Capt. David Harrison was criticized for his supposedly civilized airs because he did not support the pickling of the victim. Instead he "had failed to distinguish true barbarity from civilized Christian, behavior." Rather than preserve what food remained and therefore reduce the need to kill others, Harrison stated his disgust in using the meat as such.[110] In such instances who acted responsibly and who were the savages?

While hierarchies might collapse, they were rebuilt as quickly as they fell apart. Once salvation came into sight the crew again found hope and perhaps the need to return to "civilized' manners. For example, when the *Susanna* appeared on the horizon, the crew of the *Peggy* again followed Harrison's orders: "My poor men found my orders now so essential to their own preservation, that I was obeyed with all imaginable alacrity." With provisions from the *Susanna* the starving sailors began to recuperate. The only exception was the mate who had remained drunk for the entire ordeal and had "fallen a martyr to his inebriety."[111]

Even at the lowest moment, cannibalism, the shipwreck narratives continued a message of order.[112] Those who survived maintained traditional lines of hierarchy despite having eaten human flesh. Choosing lots justified their actions to courts and to audiences at home, situating survivors within acceptable boundaries of behavior. Mutineers found pardon for their behavior as well when captains or officers no longer were acting as respectable leaders. Legally they did not have to follow their masters but went to great lengths in their accounts to show that they had little choice but to subvert authority. In either case, cannibalism or mutiny, the narratives reinforced social order but demonstrated its flexibility under the most chaotic of circumstances.

· 7 ·

PORTUGUESE NARRATIVES

A Comparative Perspective

This enterprise they undertake so unmindful of their consciences, and of what they are beholden to God, that where they should be most devout, which is in the worst dangers wherein they find themselves, there they are most negligent and careless, committing a thousand different sins whereby they provoke the wrath of the Lord to descend upon them. . . . And withal, He is so merciful that He never strikes so harshly but that He recalls his ancient mercy, for the amendment of the guilty and as an example to those who would mock him.[1]

Printed Portuguese narratives, though written almost a century or more earlier than the English and American accounts, provide a useful comparative model for understanding the major themes of shipwreck narratives: gender, status, and religion. In addition Portuguese narratives express a different national and religious identity from English and American publications. They allow us to discern what was distinctive about Protestant Anglo-American stories by contrasting them with Iberian Roman-Catholic narratives of shipwreck. As is the case with shipwreck narratives published in America or England, few historians have studied or collected Iberian accounts. The most prominent collection of Iberian narratives comes from an eighteenth-century collection by Bernardo Gomez de Brito, and those tales comprise the comparative body for this chapter.

The Portuguese accounts concern the *carreira da India,* the voyage between Lisbon and Goa. They were written during a time of Iberian expansion in the sixteenth and seventeenth centuries. Though the Portuguese reveled in their conquests, they remained powerful for only a brief period.

Their Asian empire soon began to crumble and decay, as did the ships they sailed. The treacherous winds, waves, and reefs of Africa exacted a huge price on those willing to make the journey. Comparing shipwreck to a ship of state, James Duffy states, "As shipwreck became commonplace it was possible to visualize in the destruction of a bulging ship of cargo the approaching collapse of the Portuguese empire—like the ship, overbuilt, poorly defended, and fraught with greed and dissention."[2] Competing nations, especially the Dutch and English, supplanted Portuguese holdings, and by 1660 the Portuguese no longer held primacy in the *carreira da India*.

The Portuguese shipwreck narratives were set up along a format similar to those published in America and England. These narratives recorded a voyage from its inception, through shipwreck, to the eventual return of survivors. Each account related the physical, psychological, and moral trials of shipwrecked individuals and their struggles to overcome all obstacles. The Portuguese narratives, however, were much longer than American and English accounts and expended a great deal of space discussing the overland trek across Africa. The Portuguese vessels often shipwrecked along the southeast coast of Africa, and survivors marched north to "civilization" in hopes of meeting with Portuguese ships. This trek typically required several weeks of marching to reach safety, and along the way survivors succumbed to hostile natives, starvation, and exhaustion.

The survivors who endured the march across Africa told their harrowing stories to eager audiences. Much like English and American shipwreck narratives, Portuguese accounts were originally published in a cheap format, as string literature (*literature de cordel*) available to the masses. Although numerous Portuguese vessels never made it home, only a few shipwreck narratives from the sixteenth and seventeenth centuries survive to this day. In the eighteenth century Bernardo Gomez de Brito collected twelve stories and combined them in two volumes known as the *Histório Trágica-Marítima*. Six more were subsequently collected by an unknown editor and published as a third volume to the set.

It is difficult to identify the narratives' original authors because many remained anonymous or were identified only to the story. For example, a survivor of the *São João*, Alvaro Fernandes, gave his account to someone who then printed the story. Many of the eighteen narratives appeared for the first time in the *Histório Trágica-Marítima*, while Gomez de Brito copied others from earlier publications.[3] Therefore the stories represent two periods of interpretation, one at the time of writing and one almost two hundred years later.[4]

Unlike the Anglo-American stories, the Portuguese narratives cite greed, laziness, and duplicity as reasons for shipwreck. Those who survived were able to do so despite their personal failings. The literature "exposes and promotes breaches in the expansionist mentality and in the textural culture associated with that mentality.[5] This statement raises an interesting point that complicates the interpretation of published shipwreck narratives. At a time when the Portuguese Empire was thriving, it paid a heavy price for that success. And yet although the subject matter indicated failure, it also emphasized triumph.[6] These accounts maintained a positive outlook. Despite catastrophe, the Portuguese citizens persevered and overcame all obstacles put in their way, by both nature and their immoral countrymen.

Soon after the sea route to Asia opened, enormous vessels, filled to the brim with precious cargo, brought untold riches to Portugal's empire. The demand for spices in Europe doubled in the late sixteenth century, raising both profits and prices. During this time Portuguese ships carried annually between 40,000 and 50,000 quintals, or 2,056,200 to 2,570,250 kilograms of cargo.[7] On the outbound voyage, ships often carried silver pieces of eight to buy spices and silks, copper for cannons, lead, various European manufactured goods, and of course soldiers. In return, the Indiamen brought back pepper, spices, indigo, silks, and porcelain, with pepper being the largest commodity.[8]

By the mid-sixteenth century the empire had become one of maintenance rather than expansion. With the ascension of Phillip II of Spain (1556), the Estado da India faced new problems of Dutch and English intrusion. In 1620 the Dutch imported roughly 10,000 tons of goods to Europe while Portuguese vessels carried only 2,000 to 3,000 tons.[9] In the 1660s England's presence became so powerful that Portugal surrendered territory to buy English protection. In doing so the Portuguese lost much of their trade to Dutch, English, and Muslim traders.[10]

The Portuguese had overextended their resources and as a result were unable to protect, hold, or maintain their empire.[11] Communication between the Far East and Lisbon was difficult at best, and it often took years for correspondence to make the round trip. In a government where viceroys changed every three years, orders often failed to arrive in time and were subsequently never carried out. Despite the problems of men, power, and communication, the *carreira da India* did circumvent old Muslim-held routes and allowed Asian goods to enter European markets.[12]

The establishment of the India trade ushered in a new era of merchant shipping in which ships were built larger and sailed greater distances than ever before. The dangerous trip to the Indies might take six to eight months, and each leg had to overcome monsoonal winds and the dangerous weather and currents off the Cape of Good Hope.[13] To preserve space and increase profits, captains and merchants reduced food supplies, so passengers and crew often went hungry, which only grew worse during long trips when water became foul and food supplies rotted. With poor diets, bad hygiene, and the presence of various diseases, it is no wonder that many never made it to a safe harbor. Often one-third to one-half of a ship's passengers and crew might perish before arriving in the Indies.[14]

To make matters worse, repeated success for the *carreira da India* rested on commercial profits. On return voyages owners, captains, merchants, and sailors often overloaded these vessels and made little effort toward stowing goods properly. Indeed most wrecks occurred on the homeward journey when decks were loaded to their fullest.[15] Greed especially appeared throughout the narratives as a major cause for the downfall of empire. For example, the crew of the *São João Baptista* prepared for battle against two Dutch ships but did so only with much difficulty, as she was overburdened. Because of their lack of "sufficient gunpowder and armament for fighting," they were forced to surrender to the Dutch.[16] The desire for profits had disastrous results for the individuals sailing on Portuguese Indiamen. Of sixty ships employed in the *carreira da India* between 1580 and 1640, more than half sank or were wrecked during their service.[17]

In addition to being overloaded, many *nãos* were in bad shape. Rather than make room for spare parts (or even proper parts), crews put any extra space toward additional cargo. According to the narrator of the *Aguia,* the ship suffered great damage during a storm: "with the heavy pitching and tossing of the ship, thirty-five of the knees were sprung by their throats, and there were twisted more than forty tree-nails ... and there were broken eighteen strengthening pieces which clamp the knees. All this damage added to the rottenness of the ship."[18] The *São Gonçalo* also met disaster and could not complete its voyage due to the stress from careening that weakened its overall structure.[19]

By the mid-seventeenth century Portugal lost nearly all its holdings in Asia and was no longer a major maritime power. Maladministration by Portuguese officials resulted in overloaded and poorly built ships. The inability of the Portuguese to compete with English and Dutch merchants helped lead to the empire's decline. By the late seventeenth century the Portuguese no longer controlled the high seas and could only look back on better times.

Despite these failings, the ships did sail and did function as any other vessels of their time. It was essential that order be maintained on ships if crews hoped to make port safely, and this need increased during storms and shipwrecks. Similar to English and American narratives, Portuguese accounts suggested that status and power remained intact but allowed for temporary relaxation. The Portuguese accounts provided the same sense of order as English and American narratives and also strove to reassure readers that some semblance of society remained despite the tragic experience of shipwreck.

In general, Portuguese narratives revealed that status and power persisted along traditional lines and that only when all hope was lost did authority crumble under the weight of a stressful situation. The concept of order in these narratives was much more fluid, and the conventional hierarchies often failed in the face of extenuating circumstances. Unlike the English and American accounts, however, the Portuguese narratives quickly pointed out the failings of officers, crews, and passengers, and in the aftermath certain individuals chose to preserve their lives by overstepping hierarchical boundaries.

Despite such cracks, a leader typically appeared and saved the day. On a voyage of discovery the captain generally served as supreme authority on a vessel, though if a commander in chief (*capitán general*) was present, the captain became second in command. *Capitáns* often came from nobility, but some did have nautical experience.[20] This last point is important as these men typically felt little allegiance to the ships and crews and were often the first to abandon ship.

Portuguese Indiamen carried a broad spectrum of society. Nobles, captains, officers, and passengers as well as sailors, servants, and slaves all came aboard, and each occupied a distinct space. When shipwreck threatened loss of life, these men worked together in a collective body, but in the aftermath nobles and officers attempted to maintain their status and place and to keep others in a subordinate position. Much as in English and American narratives, hierarchy in Portuguese accounts remained relatively intact, though common sailors often found means to destabilize the traditional framework. This collapse was never permanent, and officers and gentlemen reestablished their place and a sense of order.

In Portuguese accounts, as in English and American narratives, gentlemen and officers worked alongside seamen during shipwrecks in an effort to preserve the ships. To use an example, the narrator of the American ship *Boston* claimed, "The passengers had exerted themselves to the utmost to assist us. The officers had with unwearied exertion, coolness and persevering activity done all that men could do."[21] Paralleling such efforts, the narrator of the Portuguese vessel *Santo Alberto* stated that "the captain, the gentlemen, and the soldiers worked with great speed and diligence in some places, and the master with the seamen in others."[22] Their combined efforts included manning the pumps and clearing the decks of excess cargo—anything necessary to save the ship. "In the melee of the last moments the Portuguese social structure collapsed into a classless society having only a morality based on survival." No matter his nationality, each man did what was necessary to keep the ship afloat, even if it meant doing work beneath one's status.[23]

In times of shipwreck, judicious captains listened to others as means of deciding on the best course for survival. Numerous English and American accounts demonstrated the need to listen to others, and Portuguese narratives echoed this theme. For example, Francisco Barreto of the *Garça* "called a council comprising the pilot, master, boatswain, assistant-pilot, and the other ship's officers" to state "what they thought about the condition the ship was in, and what they ought to do about it."[24] Although he ordered them to do this, Captain Barreto did not enforce his personal authority but instead delegated power to various ship's officers.

Captains and officers remained gentlemen and performed their duties to the utmost of their ability. English and American narratives suggest that such men remained in control of themselves, as did Captain Magee of the *General Arnold.* When in 1778 he and others on the ship ran into rough seas, he "never despaired . . . [instead] he cheered and encouraged his men to persevere."[25] Such men possessed innate characteristics that allowed them to persevere and overcome the chaos of shipwreck.

Masculine parameters merged with class issues in Portuguese narratives. When all hope was lost, Capt. Francisco Barreto "inspired all his companions with new spirits and gave them new strength, so that they could carry on and press forward despite the hardships they endured."[26] Jorge d'Albuquerque of the *Santo Antonio,* "seeing us all so affected, and with such good reason, although he himself felt the same way, he began to encourage us with brave words, and gave orders to some people how they should try to find some way to save the ship, while the others they should kneel and pray."[27] The captains' and officers' superior behavior provided models for readers to emulate. The narratives suggested that the nobility, in general, remained calm and collected and provided the means for others to persevere. By this means the authors created a heroic image for the Portuguese that developed and strengthened a sense of superior national identity.[28]

Sometimes, however, captains and officers maintained control only through force of arms, killing those who threatened to subvert order. In the American and English narratives this never happened at a moment of shipwreck. Only in the aftermath did this possibility arise, and even in such instances it came about only temporarily and officers and captains soon regained control. Indeed few of the published narratives described the need for violence.

Portuguese narratives, in contrast, explicitly demonstrated a call for force. In several accounts gentlemen took control by wielding swords to keep the sailors, soldiers, and passengers at bay. The captain of the *São Paulo,* when it became necessary to lower the lifeboat, "stood by the side with a drawn sword in his hand, preventing anyone from getting into the skiff until all the women and the children had safely disembarked ashore."[29] The captain of the *São João Baptista* went so far as to kill an insolent offender who wanted to leave all the children and women behind. The captain refused to do so, but in response the master declared that he and several sailors were ready to abandon these passengers. When the captain "realized all the trouble, sorrow, and loss which would be caused by such evil counsel, he determined to kill him (the master)."[30]

On Portuguese ships the use of violence extended to keeping lower-status individuals out of various life rafts or boats. The sailors of the *São Paulo* had good reason to be wary of their captain. After the vessel wrecked and the survivors made it to shore, they built a small skiff in which the captain, with the women, several of his cronies, and the padres, took off to leave the remainder onshore. The captain claimed that there was not enough room for everyone on board and that the others should march south, where they would meet up and build a second vessel. Several individuals swam out to the skiff but were "repulsed with many blows of the hand and strokes of the flat of the sword when they reached them, throwing them back into the sea together with some others who were already hanging on."[31] Only the captain's duplicity allowed him to remain in charge, and he never fully controlled movement within the narrative. But status had its rewards, and those with authority remained in control despite the ever-present threat from the lower sorts.

The crew of the *São Thomé* experienced a similar problem when the captain, officers, women, and gentlemen took off in the vessel's only lifeboat. Still, the overloaded boat could not hold everyone. At that time the officers began to throw "selected' individuals into the ocean. "These were lifted into the air and thrown overboard, where they were swallowed by the cruel waves and never reappeared." The officers threw several men overboard as well as a number of slaves, leaving ninety-eight persons to reach the shore alive.[32]

Unlike the American and English narratives, which stressed a virtuous community, the Portuguese accounts were quick to point out moral failings of others. Greed, cowardice, and laziness were often cited as reasons for shipwreck. Sometimes in opposition and at times parallel to the heroic imagery, these weaknesses represented the same Portuguese national identity. When the *Aguia* began to sink, the officers of her traveling companion, the *Garça*, did not want to provide assistance. Instead, "neither the pilot nor the master nor the other officers were willing to obey this order of the captain." They reasoned that there was no hope of her being saved and that it was a "lesser evil to lose one ship than two. . . . And taking advantage of their majority opinion, they disregarded the captain's order and continued on their voyage to Portugal."[33] Although the captain remained a man of honor, his officers lacked a sense of duty to the ship and felt no shame in abandoning the crew and passengers. Officers instead chose to save their own lives and subsequently lived to see another day.[34] This is not to say that captains and officers in Anglo-American narratives did not abandon ship before others, because they did. The English and American narratives, however, justified such moves as a necessity. They declared that someone must survive to navigate or lead the survivors to safety.

Overall, though the reaction to shipwreck manifested itself in slightly different ways among American, English, and Portuguese accounts, they ended with the same results. In English and American accounts, lower-class men often despaired and were the first to lose control. In such situations it was "every man for himself." In several accounts sailors drank and became insane, and eventually many died. By situating the sailors in a negative light, the narratives taught readers not to follow such a course of action but rather to remain in control in order to survive.

In Portuguese accounts this loss of control came in the form of a threat to hierarchy by the able-bodied sailors. When the crew and passengers of the *Santo Antonio* lost hope, sailors decided that rather than "prolonging the agony they would scuttle the ship, so as to go to the bottom more quickly and thus end their lives and their sufferings together." Jorge d'Albuquerque discovered this plot and prevented the men from carrying it out. Despite the sailors' best efforts, d'Albuquerque reestablished order and authority.[35]

Sailors on the *São Paulo* "pillaged chests, robbed cabins, and tied up bundles, bales, fardles, and packages" rather than help with preparations to disembark.[36] They found an opportunity to take advantage of shipwreck and looted the valuable cargo. Sailors who received low pay and bad treatment rarely felt the need to sacrifice themselves for the good of nobles and officers who offered them only contempt and brutality.[37] During shipwreck common sailors were the first to jump ship without making any effort to save the ship or give preference to women and children. Without a personal investment in the vessel or passengers they had no desire to risk their lives.

On land power struggles among the Portuguese continued and often intensified. On the first night ashore the captain, priest, pilot, master, and "some of the most prudent and sensible persons" from the *São Paulo* held a meeting to decide their best course of action. However, the "common people" had a different plan and divided into gangs, "thinking that their betters wished to make off in the skiff and abandon them." According to the narrative, "Some of them said that they would no longer recognize the captain; and thus these seamen were the cause of all these disputes and mutinies, some of them saying that we should kill the women and children and make our way along the land." Tension increased until Father Manuel Álvares called everyone together under the necessity of maintaining a Christian brotherhood.[38] During that first night the sailors had an opportunity to take over, but unable to organize themselves, they failed to become a true threat. Yet they were ready to abandon hierarchy and order, and only under the fear of death and damnation did they continue to follow their captain. In the wilderness they had the opportunity to apply their desires in a collective form of leverage, where the overland march leveled their chances for survival.

Overall, English, American, and Portuguese narratives each reaffirmed the place of status and authority in shipwreck. However, the Portuguese were more rebellious than English and American sailors. Hierarchy was maintained by the Portuguese, but it required a far greater struggle with individuals who felt less of a sense of community.

Gender

Despite differences in origin and time, narratives from England, America, and Portugal demonstrated that gender perceptions persisted across cultural lines. Similar to English and American narratives, the Portuguese accounts rarely provided women with a sense of identity. In some accounts, both Anglo-American and Iberian, gentlemen sheltered women and situated them in protected environments, and women accepted the constraints of patriarchal leadership. Much like women in English and American accounts, those in Portuguese narratives served to provide a sympathetic focus. Portuguese women may have been heroic during the crises for their loyalty to families, but they rarely survived.

Historically women were forgotten in accounts of Portuguese exploration. Neither in New World voyages nor in those to Asia did women appear as participants. Only in rare instances were they mentioned, and then almost as if by accident. Historical scholarship ignored women's presence except as possible concubines or prostitutes, perpetuating the myth that men alone conquered the world.[39] Women, however, did sail the seas and often experienced shipwrecks.[40]

An examination of eight narratives from the *Histório Trágica-Marítima* revealed the presence of Iberian women in six accounts, though in only four did authors provide them with specific titles or names. The few women mentioned in the published accounts were from the upper classes and accompanied male gentlemen. Few women were sent to Asia from Portugal, but their presence reflected a trend in which magistrates or other officials often brought spouses and children to the colonies.

Despite their silence, women played an important role in shipwrecks. Their presence minimized the events' chaotic possibilities and reinforced a sense of order and stability. In British and American narratives women appeared early in the tales and almost immediately became "guardians of virtue." Women, according to these accounts, prayed throughout the ordeals, giving thanks to God as well as their blessings to others on board.

Portuguese accounts brought women into the stories only when all hope was lost and the passengers and crews abandoned ship. On its voyage from Cochin to Lisbon in 1589, the *São Thomé* hit rough weather. With shipwreck imminent and "the boat being finally lowered, it went round to the stern of the ship in order to take from the gallery the women who were there, with the Religious and the gentlemen."[41] In 1559, when the *Garça* began to sink off the Cape of Correntes, Capt. Francisco Barreto, former viceroy of India, "agreed to tranship to the *Aguia* the women and children and all the other useless mouths."[42] These instances were the first indications of women on board. These narratives not only excluded women from physically helping but, unlike the English and American accounts, also regarded them as burdens unable or unwilling to provide spiritual assistance.

In Anglo-American narratives women rarely made it off the ships alive and did so only when time allowed. Men preserved themselves, choosing life over honor. Women who did survive were "ladies" rather than servants or soldiers' wives. The Portuguese narratives went further in maintaining women's place of honor during shipwrecks. In several instances the captains or leading officers explicitly stated that the women and children should go first, even fighting male passengers and crews to assure the women's safety. The captain of the *São Paolo* (1560) was one such gentleman. He "stood by the side with a drawn sword in his hand, preventing anyone from getting into the skiff until all the women and children had been safely disembarked ashore."[43] As in English and American narratives, women and children were allowed to leave ahead of men, but only if time allowed. The massive, deep-drafted Portuguese vessels often used in the *carreira da India* tended to remain intact for several hours, if not days, when grounded, thereby allowing time for the "useless mouths" to disembark safely.

In the Portuguese accounts, as in American and English accounts, the crews removed upper-class women first. Once Dona Mariana and Dona Joanna de Mendoça were safely off the *São Thomé*, the crew of the lifeboat did not stay to pick up others who might need assistance. Dona Joanna gave her two-year-old daughter to her nurse while she entered the boat. However, the nurse refused to let the child go, "saying that unless they took her in also she would not give up the child." Rather than allow the child and the nurse into the boat, the sailors pulled away. Dona Joanna's child, along with the nurse and the other female servants and slaves, went down with the *São Thomé* the next day.[44] Only occasionally might a lower-class female find access to life rafts, and even then she rarely made it through the ensuing struggle to survive the African wilds.

The overall impressions of women in Portuguese narratives differed from those in American and English accounts. In English and American accounts the women were treated as treasures, objects to protect and admire, while the Portuguese portrayed women, as in the *Aguia*, as "useless mouths," recognizing that women did not help in the active sailing or saving of the ships.[45] On the *São Paulo* (1560) one faction of sailors suggested that they should kill the women and children and try to go overland; they uttered "a thousand other similar invectives against the women, as also against those who had allowed them to embark in Portugal."[46] Before abandoning the *São João Baptista* off the Cape of Good Hope in 1622, the master suggested that only a small party should attempt the overland trek. It was "idle talk of going with a column of women and children for so great a distance over such rugged country." The master suggested leaving all unnecessary individuals behind. The men did not follow this course of action, but such words demonstrated how little regard sailors paid women in a crisis situation.

The sailors of the *São Paulo* did have a point, however, and rightly feared that the women would slow them down. Women were a burden on the overland treks that frequently followed Portuguese shipwrecks. Diogo do Couto, narrator of the *São Thomé*, described their trek: "They went on their way with great toil to the women, whose feet were already blistered and wounded, which forced them to go so slowly that on the third day's march some persons wished to push ahead, not daring to travel so leisurely."[47] Upper-class women, unaccustomed to the rigors of an all-day march and with little food and water, usually proved a hindrance to survival.

Yet not all women slowed down the men. For example, the only woman from the *São João*, the captain's wife, Dona Leonor, "though she was a delicate young noblewoman she walked along those rough difficult pathways like any strong countryman."[48] She walked from the outset and apparently did not slow the remaining survivors. Her example, however, was an anomaly when compared to accounts of other Portuguese women.

Authors of the Portuguese narratives limited their discussions of women to those of the upper classes. Elite women, and the gentlemen protecting them, expected to maintain their standing through the use of litters for the treks in Africa. Despite some reluctance among the crew members, this move was generally accepted by all members of the surviving parties. In several narratives sailors and servants built litters or hammocks to transport upper-class women before heading into the wild. Survivors of the *São Thomé*, the *Santo Alberto*, the *São João*, and the *São João Baptista* used litters. Slaves, when available, carried them, though in their absence common sailors shouldered the load. The litters offered women not only relief from physical exertion but also protection from the environment and shielded them from interacting with the lower classes. Despite the survivors' precarious situations, class and gender frequently remained intact, allowing upper-class women to remain privileged individuals.

Such perceptions worked well until starvation and exhaustion overtook those carrying the litters. In such instances men generally refused to carry the women regardless of threats or bribes. The captain of the *São João Baptista* offered eight thousand cruzados to anyone willing to carry the women. Not one individual stepped forward, and indeed several said that they "could carry them no further, even though they were given all the treasures in the world. . . . they were ready to forego all that had been promised them for their past labours."[49]

The slaves, weakened by hunger and exhaustion, refused to carry the women from the *Santo Alberto*. The captain bribed several sailors with one thousand cruzados, which, given the previous amount, appears to have been a bargain. Sixteen grummets accepted and agreed to carry the women to their destination at the river of Lourenço Marques.[50]

Although survivors tried to maintain order, sometimes the stories became ones of negotiation rather than maintaining a solid social framework.[51] Upper-class men too eventually gave in to this reality and refused to carry the women, forcing the women to carry their own weight. Women lost their privileged status and had to come to earth and walk along with the remaining survivors.

Women's involvement in the narratives increased once they left the litters. The narrative of the *São João Baptista* was one of the more descriptive accounts concerning the plight of women and children who could no longer keep up. Early in the story a young girl had a litter, but the slaves soon refused to carry it any farther. Her father had died on the ship, and she had "no one but her little brother to impress upon the captain the great cruelty of leaving a young and beautiful damsel." The captain and other officers helped her along for a while, but no one offered to carry her permanently, although the other women were still in their litters. She finally asked Father Friar Bernardo for confession and lay down on the ground beside the path. There she covered "herself with a skirt of black taffeta that she wore, and every now and then as the people passed her by she uncovered her face and said: 'Ah! Cruel Portuguese, who have no pity on a poor young girl, a

Portuguese like yourselves, and leave her to become food for beasts.'"[52] The others made their way past, ignoring her pleas, and she was not mentioned again in the narrative.

As was the case with Anglo-American narratives, such scenes created drama and sympathy. The remaining women of the *São João Baptista* faced the challenge of walking or being left behind. Burdened with small children and unable to keep up, Beatriz Alvarez chose to remain with her two sons and a daughter, along with the mother of another woman and others too weak to continue.[53] The author related, "It was the most pitiful sight ever witnessed, and whenever I think of it I cannot restrain my tears." Eventually the one remaining woman in the group could no longer keep up, and she too was left behind. According to the narrative, "it was most pitiful to see a young and beautiful woman, whiter and fairer than a Fleming . . . now in the power of Kaffirs, and shedding bitter tears."[54] The inclusion of such information demonstrated the physical weakness of women, increased the narratives' drama and emotion, and acted as a justification for why women failed to survive.

On the *São Thomé*, Dona Joanna Mendoça was a widow who was returning from Goa to Portugal to enter a convent. Her survival was amazing as Dona Joanna faced the march unprotected, "for there was not among all those people a single one bound to her by any tie, who could help her in such necessity." However, a virtuous man, Bernardim de Carvalho, "seeing her weary and alone, . . . drew near and gave his hand to assist her, with all the respect due to a woman so dead to the things of this world, that on the very day she stepped ashore she put on the habit of St. Francis, and cut off her beautiful hair, sacrificing it to God." She was pitiful for being alone and was sure to die until Bernardim stepped up to protect her.[55]

Though Dona Joanna's plight was precarious, her honor remained intact because she was sexually unattainable, having pledged her virtue to God. "This gentleman served her with such love and respect, seeing her mortification, that forgetting his own hardships, he thought only of hers, so that no father or brother could have done more."[56] Rather than from sexual motivation, his assistance came from a familial perspective; like a father, Bernardim sacrificed everything for her, and later in the narrative he died from exhaustion and illness. For his assistance and protection Bernardim was honored in the narrative, as he alone "served her throughout the whole journey with such respect, honor, and virtue."[57] With her family absent, Bernardim acted as the male patriarch, protecting and providing for Dona Joanna, and removed any sense of danger to her being and her reputation.[58]

After Bernardim's death Dona Joanna remained honorable when she found protection with Dona Mariana, a daughter of one of the other survivors, Gregorio Botelho, "with whom she lodged for the sake of propriety." Throughout the narrative Dona Joanna remained in the company of Dona Mariana and was never alone.[59] If the narrative is read at face value, Dona Joanna reflected the ideals of the Virgin Mary, staying chaste and giving herself to a convent and thus a moral way of life. The author's insistence on her public honor, however, possibly minimized any actions that might have besmirched her reputation. If Dona Joanna had had sex, she would have been akin to a common prostitute, "out of control" of her respectability and morality and therefore unworthy of honor.[60]

Survivors of shipwreck reasserted their own societies, always watchful and protective of women's morality and behavior. In elite Iberian society honor was assessed by one's peers.[61] Part of the honor system required elite women always to be with proper chaperones, and unguarded women left opportunities for dishonorable behavior and intrusion by men.[62] In English and American narratives daughters, wives, and sisters typically had male family members to protect them during the chaos of shipwreck, demonstrating that women were not alone. Husbands, fathers, and brothers became tragic heroes as they attempted to save innocent loved ones. Part of the sympathy in relation to family revolved around the accepted male responsibility to shelter, clothe, and feed his family, or his failure to do so.[63]

Narratives overall maintained traditional forms of gender and social hierarchy. Behavior exhibited by women during and after shipwrecks reflected understood limits of female actions and placed women in predictable gender roles. Yet when the time came, survival for the elite meant quick adaptation, and those who clung to traditional structures were soon left behind.[64] When their status could no longer protect them, upper-class women had to walk like the others or be abandoned to die. In the end money and birth no longer held sway, and all survivors became involved in a struggle to stay alive.

In shipwrecks a lack of privacy for women created a larger public sphere in which their status and virtue were closely watched. The increased surveillance of such a trying public realm further threatened honor as it was a social construct, needing constant maintenance through reputation and behavior.[65] In most narratives, with the help of male authors, women persevered with their names and honor, though not always their lives, intact.

Religion

As with English and American narratives, the Portuguese accounts portrayed shipwrecks and storms as allegorical stories of salvation and redemption. "To be cast out of the ship is to be cast out of the community of belief, to be temporarily excommunicated."[66] Much like the Anglo-American accounts, religion remained central to survival; and as with Puritan and evangelical accounts, God's benevolence and wrath were present and intimately connected to individual behavior and chances for survival.

English and American narratives rarely mentioned the presence of clergy on board ships, with only an occasional minister appearing. The stories instead relied on lay individuals, especially women, to perform necessary spiritual tasks. On Portuguese ships, however, members of the clergy were always present. Indeed several religious orders sent missionaries to Asia.[67] These individuals appeared regularly throughout the narratives. For example, the *Santo Alberto* carried an Augustinian friar named Pedro da Cruz and a Dominican friar, Brother Pantaleão, on its 1593 voyage to Lisbon; the *São Thomé* had aboard Friar Nicolau do Rozario of the Order of Preachers and Friar António, a Capuchin lay brother.[68] In addition women traveled the ocean as nuns or novices when they sailed to enter convents. Unlike the limited terms of viceroys and governors, these men and women left for Asia for their lifetimes, though some missionaries returned to Lisbon and were shipwrecked on the return voyages, as evidenced by the *História Trágico-Marítima.*[69]

Often members of the clergy provided physical and spiritual assistance during voyages and in shipwrecks. For example, on the *São Paulo* the Jesuit fathers Manuel Álvarez and João Roxo made "clysters [enemas] and applied them to the sick with their own hands . . . which was a great remedy to us all." The narrator stated, "Without these Religious, our tribulations, both spiritually and temporal, would have been doubled."[70] Rather than have women administer to the men, the male religious figures acted as benevolent caretakers.

Even after shipwrecks clergy kept sailors, soldiers, officers, and passengers hopeful by focusing on the ability of God to redeem and to intercede on their behalf. Manuel Álvarez, a Jesuit on board the *São Paulo,* prevented the survivors from disintegrating into various factions. He warned them that on "all the other great ships which were wrecked in the region of the Cape of Good Hope . . . one of the things which led to the total death and destruction of the survivors was the discord which prevailed among them. Let us not divide our forces . . . since we are all neighbors and all brothers. . . . Therefore I hope and believe in the great mercy of Christ and in his holy name and passion, that those of us who die here will all go to Heaven, as his knights and his martyrs, for thus will Our Lord choose us for glory and for his better service."[71] Members of the clergy acted as leaders and provided focus that minimized fear or despair. In doing so they were integral to the survivors' overall success.

Regardless of nationality, at moments of crisis sailors and passengers prayed to God for mercy. For example, during a terrible storm Capt.

Nathanael Peirce, aboard the *Portsmouth* (1756), advised the passengers to "endeavour to secure their eternal Happiness in the next, by looking unto Jesus Christ their merciful Redeemer for sincere Repentance of all their Sins, and Salvation thro' his Blood."[72] No matter the time period or nationality, the narratives proclaimed great trust in the benevolence of a higher being.

In keeping with the nation's Catholicism, Portuguese narratives, unlike English and American ones, emphasized the intercession of the Virgin Mary, calling upon her guiding grace for survival.[73] Several men and women remained stranded on the *São Thomé* after the lifeboat removed the officers and ladies. Expecting death at any moment, the sailors, servants, and passengers "had placed on the top-gallant-poop a beautiful altar-picture of Our Lady, round which were gathered all the slave-women, who with disheveled hair were piteously wailing and begging that Lady for mercy."[74] In another account Jorge d'Albuquerque comforted his comrades by nailing up two pictures, one of "Our Lord Jesus Christ crucified and the other Our Lady," on the mast for all to look upon. D'Albuquerque went on to state that all should take comfort "knowing how much He suffered for us; and since He is all-merciful and all-powerful, He will deliver us. . . . and the more so, since we have as mediatrix and intercessor the Most Holy Virgin Mary our Lady Queen of the Angels, through whose intercession, prayers and merit, I hope and trust that we will see ourselves delivered from this peril."[75] In Catholicism images of saints were important because they became "points of contact with a higher reality and were most helpful for a dying person who was just about to cross over into that other realm."[76] The posting of such images provided a focal point for victims of shipwreck to rally around and to perhaps find comfort or hope in their final hours. Protestant accounts, of course, did not venerate saints or use their images to console themselves.

The Portuguese accounts added a unique dimension to the place of religion in crisis. Most English and American narratives lacked a long trek overland or detailed their interactions with native inhabitants. In Portuguese accounts, however, this phase was important for detailing the spiritual and physical trials of shipwrecked Europeans. Upon landing, the survivors erected crosses or other Christian monuments, which not only reflected their religious beliefs but also "established primacy and possession" of the territory where they landed.[77] When survivors from the *Santo Alberto* were settled for the night, "several pious persons erected an altar between two rocks, on which they placed a crucifix with two lighted candles."[78] The Portuguese and the various religious orders considered themselves bearers of "superior religion and superior culture," spreading the word of a Catholic God to heathens.[79]

To demonstrate his appreciation for the kindness shown by natives, Nuno Velho, captain-major of the *Santo Alberto*, gave the chief a "cross off the rosary which he had round his neck." He told him that "this was the sacred pledge of friendship which he would leave with him." The "savage" took the cross and kissed it, after which Velho had a larger cross made. According to the narrative, he said, "That upon that tree the author of life overcame death with his own death, and thus it was a cure for death, and health for the sick; and by virtue of that sign the great emperors had conquered and the Catholic kings now overcame their enemies; and so excellent a gift he offered and gave it to him, that he might place it before his hut. And every morning, on coming out, he should reverence it by kissing it, and adore it on his knees; and when health was wanting to his subjects, or rain for his fields, he should confidently ask for it, for a God and Man who died upon the cross to redeem the world would grant it."[80]

As a by-product of shipwreck the Portuguese erected a cross "in the centre of heathendom" and brought the word of Christ to the wilds of Africa. In a similar situation survivors of the *São João Baptista* discovered a survivor from Java who had sailed on the *Santo Alberto*. Upon seeing the Portuguese, this individual "kissed the crucifixes which we wore and made the sign of the cross." In response the Portuguese felt "a great joy. . . . to see in such remote regions and among such barbarous people a man who knew God and the instruments and figures of the passion of Christ."[81] Symbols were important markers distinguishing the Portuguese from other groups and provided focal points both for national identity and for spiritual assistance and hope.

Following the importance of the crucifix in Catholic narratives, one account provided details of a miracle that occurred during the "Shipwreck Suffered by Jorge d'Albuquerque Coelho." In the middle of a great storm d'Albuquerque ordered "to be thrown into the sea a cross of gold, in which was inserted a fragment of the Holy Wood of the True Cross and many other relics." This cross was tied with green silk and weighted with a large nail. When the storm abated, d'Albuquerque ordered the men to raise the cross, whereupon it fell upon the deck "quite untied and free, wrapped up in a little piece of cotton. All of us were astounded on seeing this miracle, and we gave many thanks to our Lord for comforting and encouraging us with so great a miracle. . . . to show us that He would miraculously deliver us from shipwreck."[82] For the Portuguese, this deliverance had no other explanation except to provide a reward for d'Albuquerque's piety.

In Catholicism participation in public rituals and formalities is an important sign of a person's submission to God's will. These public displays certainly appeared in the shipwreck narratives through the use of ritual, relics, and confessions. Such symbols were lacking in English and American accounts and appeared only occasionally in Anglican narratives. In general, English and American narratives focused on personal relationships between individuals and God that rested on faith rather than on outward signs of belief mediated through clergy.

However, in general the narratives, whether English, American, or Portuguese, reaffirmed God as an all-powerful being. Submission to God's will was important to those facing death. Only with God could these individuals survive. "Those who entrusted themselves wholeheartedly to the salvational system of the church, would have no need to fear death and the afterlife."[83] Alvaro Gonçalves, the boatswain's father aboard the *Santo Alberto,* could no longer continue and when dragged from his son, "dismissed him with a blessing, and remained, having confessed himself, like a good Christian very resigned to the will of God."[84] Dom Paulo de Lima, in giving up during his march and "committing himself to the hands of God and whatever might be His will, begged them to leave him alone."[85] Both of these men were prepared for death and in their total submission to God accepted their final moments.

In Portuguese accounts those experiencing shipwrecks and the ordeals of overland treks constantly remained faithful to God and often gave praise to his benevolence in seeing them through various crises. The narrators consistently inserted accounts of survivors relying on God's will to bring them home. For example, upon reaching land survivors of the *Santo Alberto* "greeted each other with tearful embraces. . . . gave thanks to God Our Lord for the great mercies he had shown them on the day of His miraculous incarnation."[86] Throughout the "Wreck of the *São João Baptista,*" survivors evoked the will of God and of the Virgin Mary, implying that their survival depended on higher graces.

Since God controlled all actions, both positive and negative, shipwreck could represent a reward or a punishment. The American William Whitwell, in his 1770 sermon, stated, "Storms and tempests are his usual methods of reproof and punishment to those who do business on the mighty waters."[87] Across the seas this theme resonated as well with Dom Paulo de Lima, a passenger of noble rank who, "being a good Christian and fearing God, thought that this disaster was caused by his sins."[88] The narrator of the wreck of the *São Thomé* described how those on the sinking ship tried to make rafts to sail to shore, but since "God our Lord had chosen those people to perish in that place, all the rafts foundered. It is certain that this must have been a punishment from God."[89] God determined who would live and who would die based on a person's sinfulness or piety.

Portuguese Catholics were like English and American Anglicans in believing that humans had some power to atone for previous sins or to bring about God's favorable intentions. The captain of the *Aguia,* when it came time to throw overboard various goods, stopped his men when they came across "some fardels of indigo which formed part of a charitable gift that the king made each year by way of alms . . . for the upkeep of the church of the monastery of Nossa Senhora da Graça at Lisbon." He did not allow them to throw this indigo over because it belonged to Our Lady, "in whose favor he trusted for the salvation and preservation of his ship."[90] Unwilling to chance her disfavor, he did all he could to please his heavenly Lord and Lady.

Unlike in English and American accounts, for the Portuguese, confessions to priests were desired, if possible. Confession allowed an individual to "face death with a clean soul."[91] On the *São João Baptista* the clergy "who were passengers on board went about exhorting all the others to repent of their sins, making processions and scourging themselves nearly every day. . . . all joined in with many tears, both high and low alike."[92] Aboard the *São Thomé,* "Friar Nicolau do Rozario, of the Order of Preachers, refused to embark in the boat without first confessing all those who remained on the ship; for he did not wish that so many people who were deprived of all corporal consolations should also lack those of the soul."[93] This ceremony was extremely important and especially so in shipwreck when the possibility of death was evident.

Similar to the English and American accounts, many Portuguese narratives ended with the survivors reaching "civilization," or at least ports with Catholic churches. While English and American narratives concluded with authors giving thanks to God or specific individuals involved in the rescues, the survivors did not march in procession to the nearest churches. The Portuguese narratives stressed that public performance was necessary and recounted the need to make an open declaration of thanksgiving.

In Portuguese narratives the last paragraphs often described how survivors proceeded to nearby churches to give thanks for their return and salvation. The "Wreck of the *Santo Alberto*" ended with, "Here they all disembarked and went in procession with the Dominican friars—who, being advised of their arrival, awaited them on the shore—to the Chapel of Nossa Senhora do Baluarte, giving thanks to JESUS our Redeemer, and to the most holy Virgin his Mother, for their extraordinary favours and singular rewards received from their divine and liberal hands in this their shipwreck and journey."[94] Upon their safe landing at Mozambique, the survivors of the *São João Baptista* went to the Chapel of Our Lady of the Bulwark "carrying a wooden cross before us, and chanting the litanies with great devotion. After we had given thanks to God for all His many mercies in bringing us to the Christian land, Father Fr Diogo delivered a pious discourse, reminding us of the numerous hardships from which God had delivered us and of the obligation we were all under to lead exemplary lives thenceforth."[95]

The survivors of the *São Thomé* made it to Sofala, where they went in procession to the Dominican Church of Our Lady of the Rosary.[96] Fulfilling their promises made during shipwreck, the survivors continued their thanksgiving in a public ceremony by which they reiterated their submission to a higher being for all to see and be moved.

As a final note the narrator of the *São Paulo* ended his story with an admonition directly aimed at the readers. Using a psalm found in many English and American narratives, he exhorted his audience to remain good Christians: "They that go down to the sea in ships, that do business in great waters; these see the works of the lord and his wonders in the deep. For he commandeth and raiseth the stormy wind, which lifteth up the waves thereof. They mount up to the heaven, they go down again to the depths; their soul is melted because of trouble. They reel to and fro, and stagger like a drunken man, and are at their wits' end. Then they cry unto the lord in their trouble, and he bringeth them out of their distress. He maketh the storm a calm, so that the waves thereof are still. Then they are glad because they be quiet; so he bringeth them unto their desired haven."[97] Perhaps as a final warning against greed and the failure of the Portuguese to retain their empire, the author added, "Rather than plow the sea in search of riches," individuals should "live on land like good Christians, obeying the law of God within the fold of the Holy Mother Church of Rome."[98] He warned those who wished to go to sea that they should put their trust in Mary, queen of the angels, rather than lady fortune.

For the Portuguese, the "shipwreck narrative is bound up negatively, in the project of a nation's self-construction and identity as it attempts to move beyond the limits of the *pátria* or home country."[99] The Portuguese narratives were ambivalent. If read carefully they explained why the empire fell apart. Greed, carelessness, and laziness caused the loss of many lives on the *carreira da India*, as well as valuable goods necessary for maintaining Portugal's commerce. In many ways the stories were antiexpansionist, demonstrating the failure of the Portuguese to hold and preserve an overseas empire adequately.

At the same time, however, these stories pointed to a glorious past when the Portuguese proudly demonstrated their superiority, even in the face of disaster.[100] Within the narratives, "the tellers of various tales focus their attention on the maritime catastrophes and the human tragedies that ensued, and only in isolated circumstances do they relate these mishaps to the slow sinking of the Portuguese ships of state. . . . nowhere does an author launch into a broadside against the mercantile character of his countrymen."[101] While these Portuguese narratives did reveal "cracks in the empire," they were ultimately positive. Rather than exposing the nation's weaknesses, Portuguese shipwreck narratives, much like English and American narratives, demonstrated the perseverance and superiority of a nation's people. Despite problems, the ultimate survivors possessed a significance reflective of their national identity.

In Portuguese shipwrecks women and men attempted to maintain the contours of Iberian society. They held firmly to standards of hierarchy, status, and honor, going to great lengths to maintain a semblance of routine society. In shipwreck narratives women took advantage of litters to establish their privileged positions while relying on male protection for personal and public honor. For upper-class men, status and duty often remained intact, though they lost some power that ended in a renegotiation of hierarchy.

Honor was fluid and never stable because it relied on public understanding and agreement. Women in shipwrecks tried to survive with both their lives and reputations intact. When choices between honor and life emerged, women chose the former, dying with dignity and virtue intact. The ability to adapt meant survival, but many women were unable to make such a transition. Few survived the arduous adventures, but their presence and behavior when living not only added drama but also created Marian role models for readers. Religion, with an emphasis on Marianism, strengthened gender distinctions that transformed women into martyrs or self-sacrificing virgins.[102] Crisis did allow for some relaxation of standards, and women could overstep traditional boundaries and take over when men were absent, though never permanently, and these women often paid with their lives.

Order was constantly renegotiated throughout the ordeals. While English and American narratives emphasized that the captains remained in control, the Portuguese accounts revealed the fragility of their status. Common sailors attempted to assert their authority, and though in many instances they proved initially able, this threat to hierarchy never remained solid, and traditional order was again reaffirmed.

Religion in the Portuguese narratives took a commanding role, from the survivors praying for Mary's intercession to a comparison of their sufferings with Jesus's sacrifice. Shipwreck was not random but occasioned by both human error and human sin, primarily the latter. Though pilots or captains might have navigated incorrectly, the ultimate punishment came about from God. The narratives went to great lengths to demonstrate the close relationships between sin and divine wrath and between survival and higher intervention. The narratives made interesting stories for those in Portugal, where, from the safety of their homes, readers could enjoy and revel in the wonders of God's benevolence.[103] Without having to undergo any physical trial themselves, audiences learned powerful lessons regarding behavior and salvation. Those who remained loyal and pious had received spiritual and physical assistance from their beliefs, while those who died had confessed their sins, knowing that they were now prepared to meet the afterlife with clean souls. As did the English and American narratives, the Portuguese accounts too used the potentially chaotic event of shipwreck to demonstrate the persistence of social order, keeping Iberian society spiritually and socially safe.

EPILOGUE

Though shipwrecks often occurred out of sight of land, they nonetheless affected those at home. Friends and families lost loved ones, and merchants and owners faced financial losses when ships went to the bottom of the sea. Official documents, merchandise, diplomats, soldiers, sailors, and passengers who never completed their intended voyages caused a disruption in empires, communication, and lives.

Published material related the ordeals through the survivors' accounts to those sitting safely at home. Playing into aspects of religious faith, romanticism, sentimentalism, and a desire for knowledge at large, shipwreck narratives became a popular form of literature in England and America. The thrill of reading about faraway places, traumatic situations, and brave heroes surely appealed to a broad audience.

Conservative by nature, the accounts maintained a sense of social order that readers and participants recognized as stable and necessary. Written primarily by captains and officers, those used to being obeyed, the narratives presented a message of continued deference. These accounts reiterated that survival came about only by "prompt obedience to captain's orders and attention to duty in moments of crisis."[1] Despite language of egalitarianism and independence in early America, respect for rank and place remained important through the turn of the nineteenth century.[2] Whether shipwrecks were part of God's design or from natural causes, the narratives paralleled society's emphasis on knowing one's place.

Such ranking did not imply despotism or absolute authority. Although questioning a master or slighting superior officers was a form of subverting hierarchy, such measures rarely went to extremes. This minimal dispute gave sailors a voice and allowed their active participation in events. Through such protests sailors formed a level of independence within the daily monotony of sailing that perhaps moderated the level of crisis, obviating the need to mutiny. Negotiations did exist, but the narratives suggested that seamen rarely reached a collective level.[3] The sailors in the shipwreck narratives were not out to change society or to subvert authority permanently but instead looked to only immediate concerns. Mutiny did occur, but the published narratives suggested that this was only temporary and that officers soon regained their status. Most important, such subversion came about only briefly and never threatened society as a whole.

Survival was a two-way street. In shipwrecks captains and crews needed one another to stay alive. Captains required sailors to man longboats, cut down trees, or perform necessary manual labor.[4] During shipwrecks and their aftermath these efforts meant shelter, food, and fire. A leader was necessary, however, for a group to survive. Someone must coordinate survivors and provide a means of hope, and that role often fell to captains and officers. Although someone with navigational skills proved necessary, especially when in an open boat, this knowledge did not always translate into unquestioned authority.[5] Especially on small ships where social standing might not differ widely between officers and crews, authority depended on malleable features of respect and experience.[6]

Shipwreck, to an extent, could level social standing, but it never created a true democracy. No matter the size of the vessel, a good captain learned to balance authority with negotiation to stay in control without appearing weak.[7] At any moment captains understood that their rank and continued status depended on the will of the crew members.

In general, hierarchy did remain stable, even when crews resorted to cannibalism.[8] Directly tied to status by way of race, religion, position, and gender, the sequence in which people were eaten reflected social order. Captains and officers often were the last to go, bettering their chances for coming home, and of penning their versions of the events. Reiterating the need for men and women to remain in their places not only had practical results on a ship but also reflected a conservative response on land. In a time of social change the printed narratives reassured audiences that American society was not falling apart, that even in the worst case scenarios, shipwreck and cannibalism, order remained intact.

Published accounts put forth an ideal that hierarchy, moderation, and remaining within acceptable boundaries were necessary for survival. Rather than promoting a negative portrayal of crisis, shipwreck narratives imparted a conservative image by which status and order remained safe. If lower-class heroes and heroines arose, they did so only temporarily and without threatening social norms. As the American colonies transformed into an independent country, the authors created a traditional understanding of crisis where society remained stable and those who behaved appropriately were assured of making it home.

Above all, published narratives provided a positive outlook. The numerous accounts assured readers that even in shipwreck, societal and cultural norms persisted. Reflecting in turn ideologies such as enlightenment, sentimentalism, and romanticism, the narratives allowed audiences to come to terms with potentially chaotic and life-threatening events. Whether it demonstrated God's will or human error, shipwreck provided an opportunity for individuals to overcome tragedy and to return to the arms of a supportive and sympathetic public. The stories promoted a sense of social order in which proper women were protected by manly gentlemen. The printed accounts stressed a conservative portrayal of society in which each person remained in place and did not overstep understood boundaries. Despite the subject's chaotic nature, the authors of shipwreck narratives spun positive endings in which those who behaved as good role models survived.

Shipwreck accounts were popular stories. They blended fact and fiction to create interesting pieces of literature. This fictional element, however, should in no way diminish their importance. Each account added its own perception of shipwreck and of how individuals should react in times of crisis. Rather than focus on the end product, historians should try to determine what factors contributed to this image.[9] Given this statement, analysis of the narratives for the study occurs on two levels. On the one hand, they were pieces of literature or fiction, meant to be best-selling publications. On the other hand, the narratives were presented to audiences as fact, and readers understood the information as such. Taken together, the two perspectives make the narratives an interesting and useful body of documents. Why did authors and audiences select and perpetuate specific stereotypes within the narratives? What do they say about the society that created them? Following this line of thought, shipwreck narratives should also be seen as part of the larger cultural milieu.

The image of a sailing ship often symbolized empire and sea power, "a seaborne icon of home culture and of the expansive itinerancy of the sovereignty of the king."[10] When a ship sailed in fine weather, then the state of a nation appeared strong and solid. But when shipwreck occurred, the nation no longer looked invincible and instead seemed to teeter on the crest of a wave. The state invested time, money, and men in pursuing maritime ventures, and when ships returned safely, profits ran high. When they never returned, an entire nation felt the repercussions.

England saw its naval superiority emerge in defeating the Spanish Armada and the Dutch in the Anglo-Dutch wars of the mid-seventeenth century. England, France, and other European nations imagined themselves conquering a new world when their ships explored the vast unknown, and Spain tied its future success to the New World *flotas*. But shipwreck did occur. The authors of shipwreck accounts emphasized the ability of a nation's people to overcome adversity. Shipwreck narratives were thus more than jeremiads or prescriptive forms of literature. Indeed, as William Vaughn asserted in 1804, they were "worth recording, from the knowledge they convey, and the examples they produce. They plainly show that hope, perseverance, and subordination, should form the seamen's great creed and duty; as they tend to banish despair, encourage confidence, and secure preservation."[11] The stories not only provided practical guides for survival but also helped individuals understand the nature of the societies in which they lived. As Wharton reminds us, "The sea-deliverance was not merely an adventure story or the occasion for uncommon suffering. It was an experience charged with meaning for both the individual who endured it and the audience who was called to bear witness through the medium of the narrative."[12] Shipwreck narratives articulated the social and cultural elements comprising an ordered society in which its inhabitants either did or did not exhibit correct characteristics of gender, status, and religion.

Although many sailors and passengers experienced shipwrecks, with God's blessing Europeans and Americans explored, conquered, and prospered throughout the globe. They brought home a positive message that reiterated stability and order. Accounts of shipwreck supported a nationalistic image of perseverance and triumph in which each nation proved superior in its capabilities to adapt and survive.

On a less altruistic level the stories were a good read. They brought together various elements of life, death, and everything in between. The popularity of shipwreck narratives reflected what Americans considered as important values and provided a means of disseminating them. First and foremost they demonstrated God's presence and that a level of religion persisted through the eighteenth and nineteenth centuries. Although experiences of shipwreck forced sailors to exist somewhere between the devil and the deep blue sea, these men found outlets of expression while maintaining traditional hierarchies. Even when describing cannibalism, when friends and comrades were forced to consume the dead, the narratives reassured audiences that society remained intact, demonstrating how Americans and the United States would once again prevail to sail the vast high seas.

NOTES

Prologue

1. Logbook from the ship *Cashmere*, October 18, 1838.

2. No comprehensive study of American shipwrecks exists. This estimate is based on insurance records and information taken from particular ports at specific times. Chapter two provides more specific numbers.

3. Landow, *Images of Crisis*, 15–16. See also Fabian, *Unvarnished Truth*, for an examination of personal narratives in the nineteenth century. Blum, *View from the Masthead*, presents an analysis of literacy among sailors.

4. Huntress, *Checklist of Narratives*, 28. This list is by no means complete, and there is some speculation that this tale may be fiction. Another popular narrative is that of the raft of the *Medusa*. Huntress's *Checklist of Narratives* shows publications in London, 1818; France, 1824; Dijon, 1824; Edinburgh, 1827; New Haven, 1834; Boston, 1836; London, 1839; Boston, 1839, 1842: Tours, 1846; Boston, 1850, 1851; London, 1853; London, 1853; New York, 1855, 1856; Boston, 1857; Philadelphia, 1857; New York, 1860; and London, 1864. The tale continues to be published today.

5. Of sixty narratives traced to their original authors, captains wrote twenty-two, officers authored six, and passengers added another fourteen. Sailors penned only seven, and one slave supposedly wrote his account. The remaining authors are unknown. If subsequent editions or printings are included, captains wrote twenty-seven accounts, officers wrote six, and passengers authored eighteen. The number written by sailors remains at seven, but the number for which no author has been located increases to seventeen. Eight are attributed to either a slave, a friend, or an editor. These numbers still suggest that a majority, over 60 percent, of the narratives came from officers, captains, or passengers.

6. Huntress, *Narratives of Shipwrecks and Disasters*, xvi. See also Donahue, "Colonial Shipwreck Narratives," 101–31.

7. Wharton, *In the Trough of the Sea*, 9–10, 19. For further analysis, see Pahl, *Paradox Lost*.

8. Masur, *Autobiography of Benjamin Franklin*, 155.

9. Barker-Benfield, *Culture of Sensibility*, 247–48.

10. Bushman, *Refinement of America*, 38–39.

11. From the 1940s to the present decade, several historians have published works pertaining to Native American captivity. Hartman, *Providence Tales,* provides a short but valuable bibliography of research concerning such narratives.

12. I examined one hundred published narratives in addition to numerous poems, sermons, personal letters, logbooks, newspaper accounts, and court and insurance records.

13. Up to this time only a few scholarly works concerning shipwrecks exist, and of those, only Blackmore, *Manifest Perdition,* places shipwreck in a historical context.

14. For example, see Rediker, *Between the Devil and the Deep Blue Sea,* for a strong analysis of radicalism at sea.

Chapter 1: Fact or Fiction

1. Paddock, *Narrative of the Shipwreck of the Ship* Oswego.

2. Captivity narratives made up some of the most popular literature in the seventeenth and eighteenth centuries. See Hartman, *Providence Tales,* 16.

3. Altick, *Victorian Studies in Scarlet,* 50, as cited in Huntress, *Narratives of Shipwrecks and Disasters,* xv.

4. This information comes from archival sources as well as a comparison of narratives listed in Huntress, *Checklist of Narratives,* and Huntress, *Narratives of Shipwrecks and Disasters.*

5. Mather, *Essay for the Recording of Illustrious Providences*; Anonymous, *Remarkable Shipwrecks*; Duncan, *Mariner's Chronicle.*

6. Williams, *Printed Word in Early America,* 20. It is difficult to determine who actually read or owned specific books, and available evidence is sporadic at best. Some books were mentioned in estate inventories, but street literature is especially difficult to trace as it was reused and often discarded, being of little or no value. See Hall, *Worlds of Wonder,* 249.

7. Lockridge, *Literacy in Colonial New England,* 38–42.

8. Wroth, *Colonial Printer,* 14–17, 20; Mott, *American Journalism,* 6. New England colonies relied on Massachusetts printers until the eighteenth century.

9. Oswald, *Printing in the Americas,* 188.

10. Oswald, *Printing in the Americas,* 2; Mott, *American Journalism,* 6–7.

11. See Wroth, *Colonial Printer,* for information.

12. For a general discussion, see Pretzer, "Quest of Autonomy and Discipline," 26–34; Davidson, *Revolution and the Word,* 16; and Mott, *Golden Multitudes,* 77.

13. Stiverson and Stiverson, "Colonial Retail Bookstore," 152, 172.

14. Winans, "Bibliography and the Cultural Historian," 182; Reilly, "Boston Book Trade," 97; Hall, "Uses of Literacy," 8–9, 30; Davidson, *Revolution and the Word,* 22–23, 27–28. Eventually circulating libraries came into use and allowed individuals to check out books without buying them, permitting a greater audience to read printed material.

15. Stiverson and Stiverson, "Colonial Retail Book Trade," 172–73; Brown, "From Cohesion to Competition," 303. Most families owned only the Bible, although other reading material might include almanacs or newspapers.

16. Hall, "Uses of Literacy," 10.

17. Pretzer, "Quest of Autonomy and Discipline," 37–40. Tied in with this, of course, were the transportation and industrial revolutions that allowed greater communication.

18. Brown, "From Cohesion to Competition," 304–5.

19. Williams, *Printed Word in Early America*, 273–74.

20. Winship, "Publishing in America," 66–102; Oswald, *Printing in the Americas,* 8; Mott, *American Journalism,* 47; Wroth, *Colonial Printer,* 128. By the 1820s the printer was no longer the small artisan workshop. See Pretzer, "Quest of Autonomy and Discipline," 22; Davidson, *Revolution and the Word,* 18; and Reilly, "Boston Book Trade," 90–99.

21. Davidson, *Revolution and the Word,* 30–31.

22. Rose, *Voices of the Marketplace,* xxi.

23. "Loss of His Majesty's Ship *Phoenix,*" 162–63.

24. Ditz, "Shipwrecked," 76.

25. Duncan, *Mariner's Chronicle* (1834), vi.

26. "Loss of the Brig *Tyrrel,*" 133. Despite these efforts, only Purnell survived.

27. Downs, *Brief and Remarkable Narrative,* iii–iv. However, he did not specify where the money would be going!

28. Paddock, *Narrative of the Shipwreck of the Ship* Oswego. This was quite a statement for a man who claimed to have only "a common education." He was sailing from New York to Cork in 1800 when he wrecked off the coast of South Barbary.

29. Anonymous, *Strange News from Plymouth.*

30. Bligh, *Narrative of the Mutiny on the* Bounty, 26–27.

31. Thomas, *Remarkable Shipwrecks,* 125–32.

32. Williams, *Printed Word in Early America,* 102, 127.

33. Hartman, *Providence Tales,* 111.

34. Paddock, *Narrative of the Shipwreck of the Ship* Oswego.

35. It was abridged to an essay titled "Compassions Called For: An Essay of Profitable Reflections on Miserable Spectacles; To which is added, a faithful relation of Some late, but Strange Occurrences that called for an awful and unusual Consideration; Especially the Surprising Deliverance of a Company lately Shipwreck'd on a Desolate Rock on the Coast of New-England, Boston: 1711."

36. Wharton, *In the Trough of the Sea,* 142–43; Huntress, *Checklist of Narratives;* Roberts, *Boon Island.* This list is by no means complete, with additional editions printed in both America and England.

37. Winans, "Bibliography and the Cultural Historian," 182.

38. Burch, "Sink or Swim," 28; Lincoln, "Shipwreck Narratives," 158. See discussion in Davidson, *Revolution and the Word.*

39. Tebbel, *History of Book Publishing,* 139–43; Williams, *Printed Word in Early America,* 136.

40. Botein, "Anglo-American Book Trade," 50.

41. Gilreath, "American Book Distribution," 163–64; Hall, "Uses of Literacy," 2; Brown, *Knowledge Is Power,* 290.

42. Reilly, "Boston Book Trade," 121. Many printers were often postmasters, helping to disseminate their printed newspapers or literature. See Mott, *American Journalism*, 60–61.

43. Gilreath, "American Book Distribution," 123; Brown, *Knowledge Is Power*, 32–33, 40–41; Wroth, *Colonial Printer*, 213–24. William J. Gilmore conducted an exhaustive study of print culture in rural New England. He found similar trends of formal and informal modes of access. Conduits for travel and communication such as roads, bridges, and geography; proximity to printing presses and bookstores; and frequency of itinerant sellers or local authors all played roles concerning availability and exposure to printed materials. See Gilmore, *Reading Becomes a Necessity of Life*, especially 155–88.

44. Stiverson and Stiverson, "Colonial Retail Book Trade," 138.

45. Stiverson and Stiverson, "Colonial Retail Book Trade," 139.

46. Huntress, *Checklist of Narratives*. There may have been one narrative published in Wilmington, Delaware, in 1788.

47. Hartman, *Providence Tales*, 21–22.

48. Burnham, *Captivity and Sentiment*, 42.

49. Thacher, *Sermon Preached at . . . the Internment of Eight Seamen*. This quote comes from Job 1:19 and concerns the death of Job's children: "And, behold, a great wind came from the wilderness and struck the four corners of the house, and it fell upon the young men, and they are dead. And I only have escaped alone to tell you."

50. Williams, *Printed Word in Early America*, 52.

51. Hall, *Worlds of Wonder*, 22–23; Williams, *Printed Word in Early America*, 52–53, 56.

52. Hartman, *Providence Tales*, ix, x, 2; Williams, *Printed Word in Early America*, 65.

53. Wharton, "Revolutionary and Federal Periods," 50–51.

54. Halttunen, *Murder Most Foul*, 3, 82. Although Karen Halttunen's study focuses on murder narratives, the same influences behind their creation also affected published shipwreck accounts.

55. Hartman, *Providence Tales*, 26–28, 146.

56. Walling, *Wonderful Providence of God*.

57. Holden, *Narrative of the Shipwreck*, 14–15. And so Horace went to sea.

58. Saunders, *Narrative of the Shipwreck*, 7–8.

59. Bailey, *God's Wonders in the Great Deep*, 3.

60. Deane, *Narrative of the Shipwreck of the* Nottingham Galley (1711), 18.

61. Halttunen, *Murder Most Foul*, 5.

62. MacAndrew, *Gothic Tradition*, 40.

63. "Loss of the *Halsewell*," 199. This narrative was first published in 1786 and became a popular addition to numerous volumes throughout the early nineteenth century.

64. Harrison, *Melancholy Narrative*, 24. The foremast man soon died.

65. Edgar Allan Poe and Herman Melville used the same tactics for their fictional works. The shipwreck of the *Peggy* influenced Poe's *Narrative of Arthur*

Gorden Pym; the whale from the narrative of the *Essex* became the basis for Melville's white whale in *Moby-Dick.* See Wharton, *In the Trough of the Sea,* 22, 26.

66. McLoughlin, *Revivals, Awakenings, and Reform,* 140; May, *Enlightenment in America,* 64, 65.

67. LeBeau, *Religion in America,* 109; Gaustad, *Religious History of America,* 141.

68. Wharton, *In the Trough of the Sea,* 21.

69. Allen, *Narrative of the Shipwreck,* 5.

70. Bushman, *Refinement of America,* 38, 81–82; Halttunen, *Murder Most Foul,* 66. Signs of sensibility included crying and fainting, to demonstrate a delicate constitution. See MacAndrew, *Gothic Tradition,* 36.

71. Peirce, *Account of the Great Dangers,* 11, 12. "The reason he borrowed one of the Men's shoes to drink out of was, because he saw them drink in the same manner; and had none of his own."

72. Peirce, *Account of the Great Dangers,* 14.

73. Harrison, *Melancholy Narrative,* 2.

74. Halttunen, *Murder Most Foul,* 79–81.

75. MacAndrew, *Gothic Tradition,* 27.

76. Clark, *Short Account of the Shipwreck of Capt. Joshua Winslow.*

77. Bradley, *Authentic Narrative.* Keith Huntress suggests that this narrative is fictional. He could find no English editions and no record at Lloyd's, and some of the narrative appears to copy Riley's *Sufferings in Africa,* which was a popular best seller at that time. See Huntress, *Checklist of Narratives,* 109–10.

78. Blackmore, *Manifest Perdition,* 14.

79. Wharton, *In the Trough of the Sea,* 56–64. The original letter no longer exists, but Increase Mather included a version in his *Essay for the Recording of Illustrious Providences,* and a larger version is in the British Library and published in the *Letters from New England.* The quotes were taken from the British library manuscript, 56–57.

80. Wharton, *In the Trough of the Sea,* 15–18.

81. Lockridge, *Literacy in Colonial New England,* 72–101.

82. Williams, *Printed Word in Early America,* 77–78, 80.

83. Dickinson, *God's Protecting Providence;* Andrews and Andrews, *Jonathan Dickinson's Journal,* 24. By 1699 the frontispiece was changed to read, "and most iminent Danger, Evidenced in the Remarkable Deliverance of Robert Barrow, with divers other persons."

84. Hall, "Uses of Literacy," 35.

85. Cross, *Social History of Leisure,* 54, 57.

86. "Loss of the American Ship *Hercules,*" 56.

87. Mott, *American Journalism,* 55.

88. Anonymous, *Shipwreck Stories,* 101. This goes on to detail a story of two lovers whose fathers conspired to keep them apart by sending the young man on a voyage in 1807. Maria wanted to disguise herself and go on board, but her lover opposed, stating, "You are not aware of the perils and difficulties which sailors encounter. A rude wave might wash thee overboard, and a storm create a thousand

apprehensions. Think, my love if the vessel should founder, if all hands should, on an emergency, be commanded to labour at the pumps, what a dreadful task would be thine: How should I tremble to see thee on a tossing raft in the swelling waves: How should I grieve to see thee labouring beyond thy strength?" Upon hearing the news, the unhappy Maria was overcome, and "though alive, when this account was written, has, in all probability, by this time, ascended to heaven, where her's, and the spirit of her lover, have met—to part no more." The tale ends with an admonishment to unthinking fathers who try to control their children's lives (103–5).

89. Bushman, *Refinement of America*, 281.

90. Halttunen, *Murder Most Foul*, 83.

91. Burnham, *Captivity and Sentiment*, 46; Gora, "Literature of Colonial English Puritanism," 150–51; Lincoln, "Shipwreck Narratives," 166.

92. "Loss of the American Ship *Hercules*." Lascars are people of East African or Asiatic origin who worked on British ships.

93. "Loss of the American Ship *Hercules*," 59–60.

94. Samson, "Personal Narratives," 84; Miskolcze, "Don't Rock the Boat," 6.

95. Hall, *Worlds of Wonder*, 81; Gora, "Literature of Colonial English Puritanism," 145.

96. The frontispiece for the 1700 edition states, "Printed in Philadelphia, reprinted in London, and sold by T. Sowle, in White-Hart-Court in Gracious-Street, 1700."

97. Huntress, *Checklist of Narratives*, 107.

98. Duncan, *Mariner's Chronicle*, 1804. Huntress suggests that Duncan's compilation "was probably the most popular source for other compilers of later years" and that American authors "probably stole material from this set" (*Checklist of Narratives*, 47–48).

99. Miskolcze, "Don't Rock the Boat," 18, 134.

100. Williams, *Printed Word in Early America*, 201; Miskolcze, "Don't Rock the Boat," 133.

101. Kerber, *Women of the Republic*, 260–61. Specifically see the chapter "We Own That Ladies Sometimes Read," concerning women and books in the early republic. See also Miskolcze, "Don't Rock the Boat," 112.

102. Burnham, *Captivity and Sentiment*, 42–43; Miskolcze, "Don't Rock the Boat," 4, 100.

103. See the introduction in Burnham, *Captivity and Sentiment*.

104. "Burning of the *Kent*," 320.

105. Barker-Benfield, *Culture of Sensibility*, 215, 228.

106. Huntress, *Narratives of Shipwrecks and Disasters*, xv–xvi; Bailey, *God's Wonders in the Great Deep*; Paddock, *Narrative of the Shipwreck of the Ship* Oswego.

107. They were picked up at 35° 52' latitude, 61° 2' longitude, west. See Bailey, *God's Wonders in the Great Deep*.

108. Fuller, *Voyages in Print*, 6, 11.

109. Anonymous, *Remarkable Shipwrecks*, iii.

110. Anonymous, *Remarkable Shipwrecks*, 273–75.

111. Davidson, *Revolution and the Word*, 260.

112. Brown, "From Cohesion to Competition," 304–5.

113. Halttunen, *Confidence Men and Painted Women*, 193–94. Literature played an important role in creating a sense of propriety and of how to behave, and it reiterated ideals of hearth and home. See Mintz and Kellogg, "Affectionate Family," 193.

114. Shepard, *History of Street Literature*, 26–28, 30; Weiss, *Book about Chapbooks*, 127.

115. Rose, *Voices of the Marketplace*, 88.

Chapter 2: *The Legalities of Loss, Wreck, and Ruin*

1. The Laws of Oleron date to the twelfth century. They were enacted by Elanor, Dutchess of Guienne, mother of Richard I. Richard subsequently introduced them to England, where later rulers built upon them. This quote is from Peters, *Admiralty Decisions*, vii–ix.

2. The committee consists of volunteers who must piece together incomplete or scattered information to create a comprehensive record. The above count is from their Gloucester Archives Committee, "Chronological List of Men Who Died Fishing from Port Gloucester, Massachusetts," on file with the City of Gloucester, Archives Department, Gloucester, Mass.

3. Essex County, Newburyport, Massachusetts, *Merrimack Marine and Fire Insurance Company;* Marblehead Marine Insurance, "List of Policies and Accounts of Risks, 1803–1830." The 5 percent comes from the latter set of documents and is based on the number of policies, not the number of vessels. See "Complete List of Vessels, Fitted Out of the Port of Providence." Of sixty-five vessels listed, sixteen were known to be either castaway or lost at sea.

4. Throckmorton, *Sea Remembers*, 9–10.

5. There are numerous historical and legal works regarding the admiralty courts in North America. Examples are Goebel, *Law Practice of Alexander Hamilton;* and Ubbelohde, *Vice-Admiralty Courts.*

6. Williams, "Maritime Justice in Colonial Georgia," 30–31. Maritime law concerning shipwreck and general average dates back to ancient and medieval times. For example, see Hammurabi's Code of Laws, circa 1780 B.C. or Rhodian Sea Laws of the Byzantine Empire, as well as the Law of Oleron, 1266. Much of modern maritime law can be traced back to these earlier law codes.

7. Williams, "Maritime Justice in Colonial Georgia," 33; Owen and Tolley, *Courts of Admiralty*, 77–79; Andrews, *Colonial Period*, 222–23. American admiralty courts are based on those of continental Europe and are called "civil law," while common-law courts come from English roots. See Morrison, *Fundamentals of American Law*, 9.

8. Owen and Tolley, *Courts of Admiralty*, 26–28.

9. For an overview of various colonies in the seventeenth century, see Crump, *Colonial Admiralty Jurisdiction.*

10. Andrews, *Colonial Period*, 226.

11. The vice-admiralty courts were not set up at the same time but through the eighteenth century. See Mangone, *United States Admiralty Law,* 25; Crump, *Colonial Admiralty Jurisdiction,* 145–46; Andrews, introduction, 15–19. Ultimately jurisdiction shifted from the governors to the king and finally to the High Court of Admiralty.

12. Williams, "Maritime Justice in Colonial Georgia," 55, 68–70. There is some dispute as to when the colonists began to resent the navigation acts, although most historians contend that the vice-admiralty courts did play a role in inciting revolution. See also Ubbelohde, *Vice-Admiralty Courts.*

13. Ubbelohde, *Vice-Admiralty Courts,* 193.

14. Maraist, *Admiralty in a Nutshell,* 3–4; Casto, "Origins of Federal Admiralty Jurisdiction," 118, 137. The move from state to federal courts fed into larger arguments of centralizing authority and the powers available to the federal government versus the states.

15. Maraist, *Admiralty in a Nutshell,* 183. However, when trying maritime cases, such courts used admiralty procedure, especially after the 1690s (185).

16. Morrison, *Fundamentals of American Law,* 9–14.

17. Owen and Tolley, *Courts of Admiralty,* 17; Ubbelohde, *Vice-Admiralty Courts,* 18–20. An individual could not file in rem in common-law courts. Additionally juries rarely understood admiralty law and were easily swayed by popular opinion; thus they were less likely to follow the law strictly. See Andrews, introduction, 60.

18. Ubbelohde, *Vice-Admiralty Courts,* 20, 159. This was not a unanimous decision, and in some colonies certain types of cases (such as insurance) were more favored in the common-law courts.

19. Several excellent works exist on the areas of prize and revenue. Owen and Tolley, *Courts of Admiralty;* Ubbelohde, *Vice-Admiralty Courts;* Goebel, *Law Practice of Alexander Hamilton;* and Andrews, *Colonial Period,* are but a few.

20. Conkling, *Jurisdiction, Law, and Practice,* 72; Andrews, introduction, 25.

21. "Letter to Mr. Barton from John Hebden, Master of the Ship *Margaret.*"

22. Conkling, *Jurisdiction, Law, and Practice,* 76, 105; Owen and Tolley, *Courts of Admiralty,* 3; Dana, *Seaman's Friend,* 223. On the other hand, gross misconduct, such as habitual drunkenness or desertion, allowed owners to withhold wages legally; see Conkling, *Jurisdiction, Law, and Practice,* 92–94; and Andrews, *Colonial Period,* 253–54.

23. Peters, *Admiralty Decisions,* 54–55.

24. Dana, *Seaman's Friend,* 220. Because owners did not insure wages, sailors had every interest in returning ships safely to port. See also Steel, *Ship-Master's Assistant,* 162; and Conkling, *Jurisdiction, Law, and Practice,* 102, 105, 109, 274–75.

25. Clarke, *American Ship-Master's Guide,* 304; Dana, *Seaman's Friend,* 222.

26. Owen and Tolley, *Courts of Admiralty,* 14. This dates back several hundred years.

27. *Negligence Cases in Suffolk County Court, Wood Conta Chantrell,* 159–63. In an interesting side note, Sarah Snelling, wife of one of the victims, sued Chantrell

because the collision left Sarah and her children, "being but one-handed wilbe forced to rely upon the towne for maintainance." The jury found for the defendant (166).

28. Clarke, *American Ship-Master's Guide*, 294. This is an excellent example of the differences between the common-law courts and admiralty jurisdiction.

29. Maraist, *Admiralty in a Nutshell*, 125–26. If an owner abandoned a vessel for a set period of time, then the ship was considered as found and therefore not subject to salvage. The rescuer then became the owner rather than merely awarded salvage. See Conkling, *Jurisdiction, Law, and Practice*, 280–81.

30. Conkling, *Jurisdiction, Law, and Practice*, 274–77; Clarke, *American Ship-Master's Guide*, 295.

31. Hough, *Reports of Cases*, 233–34. The rest of the decree reads as follows:

> It appears to me by the account of the provost marshal of the Sales of the Said Goods saved that the Gross amount of the said sales is £63.8.6; . . . And I further order and decree that one Moiety of the neat amount of the Sales of the said Goods saved amounting to £20:3:5.1/2 be paid to the owner or owners of the said Brigantine and the other Moiety or half part thereof to the Libellant for the use of himself & the owner of the said Pettiauger called the *Mary* as a Recompense for the risque & Trouble of saving the said Goods.
>
> Out of which I order and Decree that there be paid to the Libellants proctor and Advocate for services in this Cause the sum of Twelve pounds To the Register of this court the sum of £7.2.2^d for his fees & services in this Cause and to the provost Marshall for his commissions on the sale of the s^d. Goods and collecting the amount of the sales & filing the accounts thereof & after the Rate of five per Cent on the s^d Sales the Sum of £3:3:5 & for his Notice fees 5/ And to the Libell^t. for Storage & Cart hire 11/ amounting in the whole to £23:1:7^d.

32. Conkling, *Jurisdiction, Law, and Practice*, 284, 288. However, Steel asserts that "in cases of wreck, the rate of salvage is not fixed, but must be reasonable and this to be ascertained by three justices of the peace"; the price depended on the cost of goods saved, the danger, the amount of time and energy, etc. (*Ship-Master's Assistant*, 234).

33. Andrews, introduction, 91–92; Ubbelohde, *Vice-Admiralty Courts*, 13; Williams, "Maritime Justice in Colonial Georgia," 62.

34. Andrews, introduction, 92; Williams, "Maritime Justice in Colonial Georgia," 62. According to Ubbelohde, "if he presented no answer, the fourth reading of the proclamation amounted to a decree for the libelant by default" (*Vice-Admiralty Courts*, 13).

35. Andrews, introduction, 93–94; Ubbelohde, *Vice-Admiralty Courts*, 13; Owen and Tolley, *Courts of Admiralty*, 15, 17.

36. Andrews, introduction, 94–95. "In the infancy of commerce, [this payment] was usually made by some portion of the specific articles saved or recovered' (Clarke, *American Ship-Master's Guide*, 294).

37. Clarke, *American Ship-Master's Guide,* 294; Steel, *Ship-Master's Assistant,* 234.

38. In this case the salvors were granted two-fifths. *Report of Cases,* 32–36.

39. Andrews, introduction, 62; Andrews, *Colonial Period,* 254.

40. Blunt, *Shipmaster's Assistant,* 270–78. According to Steel, *Ship-Master's Assistant,* the sheriffs, justices, mayors, constables, or officers of the customs determined and provided assistance and if they refused would receive a one-hundred-pound fine (233).

41. Blunt, *Shipmaster's Assistant,* 270–78. Going back several centuries, in the Laws of Oleron (1266), article 31 stated, "When survivors reached shore thinking they will find hope, but instead meet with people barbarous, cruel, and more inhuman than mad dogs, who to gain their monies, apparel, and other goods, do sometimes murder and destroy these poor seamen; in this case the lord of that country ought to execute justice on such wretches, to punish them as well corporally as pecunarily, to plunge them into the sea till they be half dead, and then to have them drawn forth out of the sea, and stoned to death" (Peters, *Admiralty Decisions,* Apendix, xlix-1). Rhodian Sea Laws of the Byzantine Empire also have certain acts punishable by death.

42. Appeals went through various procedures, depending on which court plaintiffs brought the maritime cases. See Owen and Tolley, *Courts of Admiralty,* 18; and Blunt, *Shipmaster's Assistant,* 271–72. New Jersey also outlined a means to prevent further wrecks. For instance, if anyone put up lights to strand a vessel purposefully, that person could be fined up to one thousand dollars and/or imprisoned up to one year. Anyone who assisted in preserving a wreck was entitled to salvage, and any unclaimed money after the time prescribed by the Act of March, 1820, had to be paid to trustees of the school fund.

43. Harrison, *Melancholy Narrative,* 47. As with maritime law, marine insurance has a long history. Sea loans date to Greek and Roman antiquity, though true insurance contracts did not come about until much later. Commendas and sea loans allowed investors to pull together money and capital to fund voyages. Examples of each can be found in Lopez, *Medieval Trade in the Mediterranean World,* 168–84.

44. Dover, *Handbook to Marine Insurance,* 2–3, 13–14.

45. Dover, *Handbook to Marine Insurance,* 40–43; Insurance Company of North America, *Episodes of History,* 9.

46. Dover, *Handbook to Marine Insurance,* 25–38, 61. There were problems of gambling and "gambling policies" from which several underwriters wished to disassociate themselves.

47. Gillingham, *Marine Insurance in Philadelphia,* 17–18, 42; Goebel, *Law Practice of Alexander Hamilton,* Vol 1: 399. During the war British occupation and various regulations affected the level of shipping and the need for insurance.

48. Dover, *Handbook to Marine Insurance,* 29; Goebel, *Law Practice of Alexander Hamilton,* Vol. 1: 403–5.

49. Dover, *Handbook to Marine Insurance,* 29. Also created in the same year was the Insurance Company of the State of Pennsylvania; see Gillingham, *Marine*

Insurance in Philadelphia, 117; and Insurance Company of North America, *Episodes of History,* 29.

50. Dover, *Handbook to Marine Insurance,* 45–47. Almost any history book will provide a list of the various trade and navigation acts of the seventeenth and eighteenth centuries.

51. Goebel, *Law Practice of Alexander Hamilton,* 2:430–31. In general, English and American colonial policies were very similar but did have differences. For example, in the colonies the period of time in which proof of loss must be made by the assured ranged from about thirty days to three months, while in England there was no clause and the time rested only on custom; see 395–96.

52. Goebel, *Law Practice of Alexander Hamilton,* Vol 1: 413–17.

53. Goebel, *Law Practice of Alexander Hamilton,* Vol 1: 416–17. The paragraph is from a vessel policy for the brig *Nancy* in 1795 and from a cargo policy for the ship *Brutus* in 1799. The policies go on to outline payments in case of loss and action necessary if a dispute should arise concerning any loss on the policy.

54. Different ports may represent differing levels of risk and therefore a change in the premiums. Today additional policies cover the owner against personal injury or wrongful death. Premiums are the "payments from the assured in consideration of the assumption of the risk by the insurer" (Dover, *Handbook to Marine Insurance,* 63). A shipwreck case could come to court if it occurred under circumstances not fitting with the contract. See Dover, *Handbook to Marine Insurance,* chap. 4, "Substantive maritime Law: Contracts for Carriage of Goods"; and Maraist, *Admiralty in a Nutshell,* 12–13.

55. Steel, *Ship-Master's Assistant,* 162, 217.

56. There is evidence that the vessel was not going to New York, as presented by the position of the wreck at the time it foundered, but this information is highly questionable. The case became more confusing as there were actually three policies up for dispute. Goebel, *Law Practice of Alexander Hamilton,* Vol 2: 755.

57. The verdict was unknown. Goebel, *Law Practice of Alexander Hamilton,* Vol 1: 755. It was common to find that most cases lacked a recorded final verdict. Marcus Rediker studied approximately twenty-two hundred cases, and in many instances the records no longer existed; See Rediker, "Society and Culture," 7.

58. Clarke, *American Ship-Master's Guide,* 353; Campbell, "Marine Note of Protest," 53; Conkling, *Jurisdiction, Law, and Practice,* 155. In both American and English courts, a peril of the sea is usually placed under an act of God. Technically when a ship wrecks, the first contract ends, but the master does have a duty to try to deliver the goods to the contract's port of destination; Conkling, *Jurisdiction, Law, and Practice,* 173.

59. Blunt, *Shipmaster's Assistant,* 152.

60. Harrison, *Melancholy Narrative,* 55–56. This statement was part of a larger sworn protest before David Elias and Robert Shank, notaries public.

61. Paddock, *Narrative of the Shipwreck of the Ship* Oswego, 1. He also added that "she was a good ship of 260 tons, four years old, and a fast sail."

62. Conkling, *Jurisdiction, Law, and Practice*, 164–65; Clarke, *American Ship-Master's Guide*, 332; Steel, *Ship-Master's Assistant*, 214—see a detailed summary of seaworthiness on 251; Blunt, *Shipmaster's Assistant*, 207, 221. Law regarding negligence did not take shape until the nineteenth century; see Whitmore, *Colonial Laws of Massachusetts*, lvii. See also *Negligence Cases in Suffolk County Court*, 3, *Silva v. Low*.

63. "Letter to Andrew Dunlap."

64. Clarke, *American Ship-Master's Guide*, 311; Conkling, *Jurisdiction, Law, and Practice*, 158–59, 170. "Violence which human prudence could not foresee, nor human strength resist, may be considered as a loss in the meaning of such a policy" (Blunt, *Shipmaster's Assistant*, 207).

65. Cargo policy for the ship *Peggy*, *Ms Hicks Papers*, cited in Goebel, *Law Practice of Hamilton*, vol 1: 451–52.

66. Bilton, *Captain Bilton's Journal*.

67. Harrison, *Melancholy Narrative*, 6.

68. Conkling, *Jurisdiction, Law, and Practice*, 630. Conkling provides an in-depth discussion concerning evidence used in various proceedings regarding whether depositions were taken in writing or to be oral and in open court.

69. "Papers of William Sohier," the attorney papers, cover only the questions and none of the answers. They seem to be fairly standard, and other depositions contained similar questions. It is included because it provides a look at what questions were important and the type of information needed to determine whether the ship wrecked due to peril of the sea. On file at Peabody Essex Museum, Salem, Massachusetts.

70. "Papers of William Sohier," attorney papers concerning admiralty cases: "Interrogatives to be exhibited, to be examined in behalf of the plaintiffs in a said institute by Whipple of the Boylston Insurance Company at the court of Common Pleas in the county of Suffolk, January 1830."

71. Conkling, *Jurisdiction, Law, and Practice*, 643. In general the courts disqualified those with an interest in the event from testifying, but this issue depended on a wide range of circumstances.

72. Blunt, *Shipmaster's Assistant*, 153; Campbell, "Marine Note of Protest," 54.

73. Steel, *Ship-Master's Assistant*, 225.

74. Protest for Schooner *Hope*, 1805. The *Hope* soon hit heavy gales, and in early January the crew tried to pump, but the ballast of sand prevented the pumps from working. "All crew agreed to leave and boarded the *Commerce* (which was nearby) and arrived at Liverpool on January 8th."

75. Campbell, "Marine Note of Protest," 46; Conkling, *Jurisdiction, Law, and Practice*, 683.

76. "The above written protest as by the aforesaid Master and two of his men viz. Edmund Cox and Noah Parker, published and declared before mee: the Truth of what is above declared . . . John Stanford Record[r] of his Majesty's colony of Rhode Island and Providence Plantations." This case went through several actions and counteractions; each was found in favor of the defendant. See *Negligence Cases*

in Suffolk County Court, 277–85. New Inlet allowed vessels to sail from Pamlico Sound into the Atlantic.

77. *Negligence Cases in Suffolk County Court*, 282.

78. Campbell, "Marine Note of Protest," 46–55.

79. "The ship must be preserved by the action of sacrifice. If the ship subsequently wrecks (due to another cause) the property saved from the second accident shall contribute to the loss sustained by those whose goods were cast upon the former occasion"; see Steel, *Ship-Master's Assistant*, 225–26. This principle is not known in common-law courts, but as it developed under marine insurance it began to evolve in the common-law courts; see Owen and Tolley, *Courts of Admiralty*, 12.

80. Allen, *Narrative of the Shipwreck*, 4. In most narratives the crews cut down masts and rigging as means of lightening the ships as well as reducing windage (surface of the vessel exposed to the wind), helping to keep the vessels in an upright position.

81. Abbott, *Treatise*, 385; Clarke, *American Ship-Master's Guide*, 285; Maraist, *Admiralty in a Nutshell*, 133–35; Goebel, *Law Practice of Alexander Hamilton*, 454; Dover, *Handbook to Marine Insurance*, 703. Once they reached an agreement, the underwriters signed the adjustment and all compensation was considered final.

82. Clarke, *American Ship-Master's Guide*, 345. This is not always correct; in New York one may or may not abandon in cases of stranding.

83. Clarke, *American Ship-Master's Guide*, 345. The goods may remain, but if they cannot be carried to their designated port, the voyage is lost.

84. If they refused, the case could go to litigation where either side might try to prove a breach of contract or that the ship and cargo represented only a partial loss and therefore could not be abandoned. See Park, *Marine Insurances*, 98, 143, as cited in Goebel, *Law Practice of Alexander Hamilton*, 520–21. Essentially in abandonment the insurers become owners and are subsequently liable for all repairs, etc., after the loss; see Blunt, *Shipmaster's Assistant*, 148.

85. There is no indication of what happened to the ship or whether it was sold or not. See "Letter to Mr. Barton from John Hebden, Master of the *Margaret*."

86. Goebel, *Law Practice of Alexander Hamilton*, 453.

87. Blunt, *Shipmaster's Assistant*, 211.

88. Steel, *Ship-Master's Assistant*, 215.

89. Clarke, *American Ship-Master's Guide*, 337.

90. *Suggestions to Masters of Ships*, 1–8. These are only a few of the suggestions. By the 1840s such suggestions expanded from merely telling masters what to do legally to informing sailors on how to survive shipwreck. See Brady, *The Naval Apprentice's Kedge Anchor* (1841).

Chapter 3: God, Nature, and the Role of Religion in Shipwreck

1. Logbook, *Duke*, 1748.

2. Anonymous, *Mariner's Chronicle*, viii.

3. Mather, *Essay for the Recording of Illustrious Providences*, 21. The passage continues: "They that go down to the Sea in Ships, that do Business in Great Waters;

These see the Works of God, and his Wonders in the Deep. For he commandeth, and raiseth the stormy Wind, which lifteth up the Waves thereof. They mount up to Heaven, they go down again to the Depth, their Souls is melted because of Trouble. They reel to and fro, and stagger like a drunken Man, and are at their Wits end. Then they cry unto the Lord in their Trouble, and he bringeth them out of their Distresses. Oh that men would praise the Lord for his Goodness, and for his wonderful Works to the Children of Men! Psalms 107: 23–31."

4. Wharton, "Colonial Era," 32–35. See Kverndal, *Seamen's Missions,* for a thorough analysis of religion and sailors in the nineteenth century.

5. Donahue, "Colonial Shipwreck Narratives," 102.

6. Butler, *Awash in a Sea of Faith,* 56, 106; Brown, *Knowledge Is Power,* 16–17; Noll, *Old Religion,* 41; Ahlstrom, *Religious History,* 132, 152.

7. Rhoden, *Revolutionary Anglicanism,* 11.

8. Greven, *Protestant Temperament,* 179, 191.

9. Hall, *Worlds of Wonder,* 104–5; Miskolcze, "Don't Rock the Boat," 22; Wharton, *In the Trough of the Sea,* 17; Lincoln, "Shipwreck Narratives," 160.

10. Miller, *New England Mind,* 29.

11. Mather, *Essay for the Recording of Illustrious Providences.*

12. Bailey, *God's Wonders in the Great Deep.*

13. Miller, *New England Mind,* 31.

14. Peirce, *Account of the Great Dangers,* 12, 14.

15. Miller, *New England Mind,* 30.

16. Landow, *Images of Crisis,* 17–18; Johnson, "Humiliation Followed by Deliverance," 244–45.

17. Bartholomew, "Relation of the Wonderful Mercies of God," 123.

18. Thacher, "Some Part of a Letter," 60.

19. Donahue, "Colonial Shipwreck Narratives," 104.

20. Greven, *Protestant Temperament,* 87.

21. Ryther, "Sea-Dangers," 128, 133.

22. Johnson, "Humiliation Followed by Deliverance," 240–42.

23. Miskolcze, "Don't Rock the Boat," 22.

24. Thacher, "Some Part of a Letter," 3.

25. Thacher, "Some Part of a Letter," 59.

26. Steere, "Monumental Memorial of Marine Mercy," 133–40.

27. Donahue, "Colonial Shipwreck Narratives," 106–7.

28. Clark, *Short Account of the Shipwreck of Capt. Joshua Winslow.*

29. Brown, *Dr. Brown's Sermon,* 25–26, 42.

30. Zuckerman, "Identity in British America," 118–19.

31. Bailey, *God's Wonders in the Great Deep,* 9.

32. Donahue, "Colonial Shipwreck Narratives," 109.

33. Thacher, "Some Part of a Letter," 63.

34. Donahue, "Colonial Shipwreck Narratives," 109.

35. Bailey, *God's Wonders in the Great Deep,* 22.

36. Anonymous, *True and Particular Narrative of the Late Tremendous Tornado.*

37. Greven, *Protestant Temperament*, 13.

38. Greven, *Protestant Temperament*, 14, 192, 198.

39. Donahue, "Colonial Shipwreck Narratives," 110.

40. Strachey, "True Reportory of the Wracke . . . of Sir Thomas Gates Knight," 36.

41. Bilton, *Captain Bilton's Journal*, 7. The vessel is unnamed.

42. Deane, *Narrative of the Shipwreck of the* Nottingham Galley, 2. By the 1836 edition, this was changed to "I presently called all hands down to the cabin, where we continued a few minutes, earnestly supplicating the mercy of heaven; but knowing that prayers, alone, were in vain, I ordered all up again to cut the masts by the board" (Thomas, *Remarkable Shipwrecks*, 207).

43. Donahue, "Colonial Shipwreck Narratives," 111.

44. Downs, *Brief and Remarkable Narrative*, iii, iv.

45. Harrison, *Melancholy Narrative*, 29. The crew refused to pray, saying that there "was not time to pray."

46. Harrison, *Melancholy Narrative*, 11–13. The men floated helplessly for days and eventually ate a servant. They were in the process of sacrificing another when the *Susanna* discovered them and transported them to safety.

47. Donahue, "Colonial Shipwreck Narratives," 117–18.

48. "Extract of a Letter from Madeira." Capt. Thomas Cottiman was bound from Liverpool to South Carolina when the accident occurred.

49. "Loss of His Majesty's Ship *Phoenix*," 154–69. This last statement fits well with the Anglican emphasis on duty and place.

50. Harrison, *Melancholy Narrative*, 39. He goes on to thank Gov. Arthur Holdwordth, friend to Captain Evers, and all those who provided assistance or sympathy to him or any of his men.

51. Clarke, *Naufragia*, xi.

52. Greven, *Protestant Temperament*, 227, 230.

53. Downs, *Brief and Remarkable Narrative*, 13.

54. Deane, *Narrative of the Shipwreck of the* Nottingham Galley, 4, 24.

55. See Langman, *True Account of the* Nottingham Galley, for an overview. See also Wharton, *In the Trough of the Sea*, 161–66.

56. Langman, "True Account," 172.

57. Wharton, "Revolutionary and Federal Periods," 62.

58. Walters, *American Deists*, 26.

59. McLoughlin, *Revivals, Awakenings, and Reform*, 99.

60. Walters, *American Deists*, 31, 33, 44.

61. Donahue, "Colonial Shipwreck Narratives," 115.

62. Vaughn, *Narrative of Captain David Woodard*, xiii.

63. Paddock, *Narrative of the Shipwreck of the Ship* Oswego.

64. Vaughn, *Narrative of Captain David Woodward*, xxiii, xxiv.

65. Hartman, *Providence Tales*, 6.

66. "Loss of the Brig *Tyrrel*," 138.

67. Donahue, "Colonial Shipwreck Narratives," 115.

68. "Loss of the Brig *Tyrrel*," 141.

69. "Loss the *Halsewell*," 206.

70. Wharton, *In the Trough of the Sea*, 20.

71. Halttunen, *Murder Most Foul*, 38.

72. Paddock, *Narrative of the Shipwreck of the Ship* Oswego, 26.

73. Paddock, *Narrative of the Shipwreck of the Ship* Oswego, 30. The general consensus on the ship was in favor of going to shore, at which time the men hoisted the boats for shore.

74. Donahue, "Colonial Shipwreck Narratives," 115–16; Wharton, "Revolutionary and Federal Periods," 50. New ideas altered humans' hierarchy in the universe and thus shifted their place in the cosmic order. See Landow, *Images of Crisis*, 23.

75. Walters, *American Deists*, 29.

76. Walters, *American Deists*, 10.

77. "Loss of the American Ship *Hercules*"; Thomas, *Remarkable Shipwrecks*, 57; *Narrative of the Loss of the Ship* Hercules; Anonymous, *Wonderful Escapes*, 28.

78. Abrams, *Natural Supernaturalism*, 101–2.

79. Noll, "Rise and Long Life of Enlightenment," 101; Walters, *American Deists*, 38; Donahue, "Colonial Shipwreck Narratives," 117; Butler, *Awash in a Sea of Faith*, 216. Revolutionary enlightenment was optimistic, romantic, and fervent. Believers looked to a golden age. See May, *Enlightenment in America*, 153–54.

80. McLoughlin, *Revivals, Awakenings, and Reform*, 119.

81. LeBeau, *Religion in America*, 115–16; McLoughlin, *Revivals, Awakenings, and Reform*, 105.

82. Gaustad, *Religious History of America*, 132–33.

83. Noll, Bebbington, and Rawlyk, *Evangelicalism*, 6.

84. Noll, *Old Religion*, 51; LeBeau, *Religion in America*, 49.

85. LeBeau, *Religion in America*, 98; Hatch, *Democratization of American Christianity*, 5.

86. LeBeau, *Religion in America*, 59–60, 67; Matthews, *Toward a New Society*, 28. By becoming virtuous, Americans placed themselves in opposition to the corrupt British. See Butler, *Awash in a Sea of Faith*, 200–201.

87. Noll, *Old Religion*, 63.

88. Hatch, *Democratization of American Christianity*, 6, 11.

89. Dexter, *Narrative of the Loss of the* William and Joseph, 45.

90. Whitwell, *Discourse*, 7.

91. Miskolcze, "Don't Rock the Boat," 100; Cott, *Bonds of Womanhood*, 138, 146.

92. Douglas, *Feminization of American Culture*, 4.

93. Saunders, *Narrative of the Shipwreck*, 10–12.

94. Saunders, *Narrative of the Shipwreck*, 1–38.

95. Douglas, *Feminization of American Culture*, 8.

96. Saunders, *Narrative of the Shipwreck*, 1–38.

97. Ahlstrom, *Religious History*, 426–27; Matthews, *Toward a New Society*, 40–42.

98. Whitwell, *Discourse*, 18. He goes on to discuss the need to give to poor widows and orphans: "By as correct an account as could be taken in the *Essex Gazette*,

Jan 1768 to Jan 1770 the town lost 23 vessels, leaving 70 widows and 155 fatherless children" (15).

99. Rediker, *Between the Devil and the Deep Blue Sea*, 173.

100. Harrison, *Melancholy Narrative*, 11.

101. Rediker, *Between the Devil and the Deep Blue Sea*, 175, 179.

102. Whitwell, *Discourse*, 14. Another class of narratives that appeared in the early nineteenth century included reduced versions of longer or previous accounts collected together in one book. Religion played almost no part in these stories, and they read similarly to newspaper accounts with the bare facts presented. Providence occupied a minor place with few words of thanks to God's intervention. The authors probably published the accounts to be interesting, relying on their popularity to make money.

103. Wharton, *In the Trough of the Sea*, 9.

104. Miskolcze, "Don't Rock the Boat," 30.

105. Donahue, "Colonial Shipwreck Narratives," 102; Noll, "Revolution and the Rise of Evangelical Influence," 130.

Chapter 4: They Worked Like Horses but Behaved Like Men

1. Vaughn, *Narrative of Captain David Woodard*, xxii–xxiii.

2. Creighton, "Davy Jones' Locker," 135.

3. This was not just metaphorical. As Daniel Vickers and Vince Walsh remind us, sailors rarely left home on their own; instead they often sailed with friends and neighbors, which extended important kinship ties from land to sea ("Young Men and the Sea," 19).

4. Fletcher, *Gender, Sex and Subordination*, 303; Woodward, "It's a Man's Life," 288, 291, 293; Dowler, "Till Death Do Us Part," 53–71. Several historians and researchers have looked at masculinity within a war or prison environment, and I argue that the same analysis can apply to sailors as well. For example, see Kimmel, *Manhood in America*, 18. In addition Rotundo, *American Manhood*, contains several chapters concerning boy and male youth culture.

5. Fletcher, *Gender, Sex and Subordination*, xvi, 402; Ditz, "Shipwrecked," 73.

6. Fletcher, *Gender, Sex and Subordination*, 122. Narratives by women do exist but were scarce before the nineteenth century.

7. Gorn, "Seafaring Engendered," 220.

8. Kerber et al., "Forum," 573; Kann, *Republic of Men*, 17.

9. Fletcher, *Gender, Sex and Subordination*, 323–25; Foyster, *Manhood in Early Modern England*, 212.

10. Lewis, *American Adam*, 1, 5.

11. Turley, *Rum, Sodomy, and the Lash*, 1. In the world of the self-made man, "Success must be earned, manhood must be proved—and proved constantly" (Kimmel, *Manhood in America*, 23).

12. Kann, *Republic of Men*, 31. Those who did measure up earned status and citizenship in the newly formed United States. Kann points to several types of American manhood—"Aristocratic Manhood," "Republican Manhood," and "Self-Made

Manhood'—that operated simultaneously while incorporating slightly different definitions (12–15).

13. See Kann, *Republic of Men;* Rotundo, *American Manhood;* and Hitchcock and Cohen, *English Masculinities.*

14. Tosh, "Old Adam and the New Man," 233. Rotundo suggests that masculinity shifted from a community-oriented definition to one based on the individual (*American Manhood,* 20).

15. Yet had men behaved as society suggested, there would be no demand for such prescriptive literature. The need to reinforce this ideal indicates that men did not always behave in a truly masculine manner. See Gregory, "*Homo Religiosus,*" 105.

16. Thacher, "Some Part of a Letter," 59. The original letter is lost, but Increase Mather included a version in his *Essay for the Recording of Illustrious Providences* (1684).

17. "Loss of the *Halsewell,*" 198, 201.

18. Carter, *Men and the Emergence of Polite Society,* 97, 104–5.

19. Merish, *Sentimental Materialism,* 39. Rotundo posits pre-1800 masculinity within the framework of "communal manhood' and duty (*American Manhood,* 11–12).

20. Dorsey, *Reforming Men and Women,* 20–21; Dana, *Two Years before the Mast,* 316–17.

21. Logbook, *Sultanna.* The author goes on to state, "So ends this unfortunate day—the most unhappy dismal, gloomy day of all my past life. Alas: that I was born to plough the ocean for a living."

22. "Letter Transcribed for Mr. Brooks." According to Mackay's daughter, the passengers and crew presented Mackay with a silver pitcher embossed with "To Captain H. C. Mackay from his friends the passengers of the ship *Boston* on her first passage May 1828" ("Loss of the *Boston,*" 322–23). For his efforts Captain Mackay received a check for five hundred dollars and a gold watch from Admiral Isaac Coffin, a passenger aboard the *Boston.* Also see Rediker, *Between the Devil and the Deep Blue Sea,* for a labor analysis of the maritime world.

23. "Burning of the *Kent,*" 312–21.

24. Swift, *Genealogical Notes,* 352–53. Of the 105 who sailed from Boston, only 33 lived, and of those, 16 recovered due to the bitter cold and ice; see Downs, *Brief and Remarkable Narrative.*

25. Leach, *Survival Psychology,* 137–42.

26. Barrow, *Mutiny of HMS* Bounty, 140–41. This work was originally published in 1831, published as part of the World's Classics in 1914, and reprinted in 1928.

27. Barrow, *Mutiny of HMS* Bounty, 141.

28. Burch, "Sink or Swim," 43.

29. "Loss of the Ship *Albion,*" 300.

30. Archer responded by saying, "I have done nothing that I suppose any body else would not have done in the same situation" ("Loss of His Majesty's Ship *Phoenix,*" 158). The narrative first appeared in London in 1804 and was subsequently

published in 1810 and 1813. American editions include publications in 1813, 1834, and 1836. See Huntress, *Checklist of Narratives*, 180.

31. "Journal of the Whaling Voyage." The crew later had to abandon ship.

32. Kann, *Republic of Men*, 133–34.

33. Crespel, *Travels in North America*, 44–59. The remaining sections of the story relate their time on the island and subsequent rescue by the *Active*. The ship was also known as the *Renommée* as well as the *Renown*. This work was first published in France in 1742 and 1752, and the first English edition appeared in 1797. See Huntress, *Checklist of Narratives*, 19.

34. The name of the ship is unknown. After these episodes Gardner fell into a stupor and eventually died. See Walling, *Wonderful Providence of God*.

35. Luckily if a leader stepped up and took control, panic could cease as quickly as it had started (Leach, *Survival Psychology*, 30–34).

36. "Loss of the *Peggy*," 193. The first known publication of the narrative of the shipwreck, *Peggy* was in volume four of Duncan, *Mariner's Chronicle* (1804). It next appeared in Thomas's American anthology *Interesting and Authentic Narratives*.

37. "Loss of the American Ship *Hercules*," 57; *Narrative of the Loss of* Hercules. According to Commander Stout, the ship hit a large storm while sailing from Bengal in 1795.

38. Foyster, *Manhood in Early Modern England*, 7.

39. Ditz, "Shipwrecked," 56–57.

40. Deane, *Narrative of the Sufferings;* Wharton, *In the Trough of the Sea*, 157. Other versions include Deane, *Narrative of the Sufferings* (London, 1722, 1726, 1727, 1730, 1738).

41. Deane, *Narrative of the Sufferings*, 157–58; Bales and Warner, *Boon Island*, 39–41.

42. Bales and Warner, *Boon Island*, 42–44; Langman, *True Account of the* Nottingham Galley. Langman wrote his narrative with the boatswain Nicholas Mellon and the seaman George White, and their sworn oaths are appended to Langman's account. One of the reasons this case did not continue was that Langman and some of the crew claimed that the captain wrote a protest while the men were sick and forced them to sign it before they could fully understand the protest's implications. Also see Wharton, *In the Trough of the Sea*.

43. Shoemaker, "Reforming Male Manners," 145. Ditz wrote that "deceitfulness was the most insidious and dangerous of business-related vices" ("Shipwrecked," 68).

44. Langman, "True Account," 159–72; Langman, *True Account of the* Nottingham Galley. Langman's preface for the latter continued, "Our Apprehensions of this made us refuse the Encouragement which was offered us in New-England, and resolve to come home that we might have an Opportunity to lay before the World, and before those Gentlemen and others who have lost their Estates and Relations in this unhappy voyage, the true Causes of our own and their Misfortunes, and how they might, humanly speaking, have been easily avoided, had Captain Dean [*sic*] been either an honest or an able Commander" (207).

45. Langman, "True Account," 159–72. The use of the term "dogs" was common, in addition to "knave" and "rogue." Such references implied that an individual was dishonest and unable to control himself. See Shoemaker, "Reforming Male Manners," 141. Prov. 26:11 reads, "As a dog returneth to his vomit, so a fool returneth to his folly."

46. Foyster, *Manhood in Early Modern England,* 37; Ditz, "Shipwrecked," 55.

47. Warner, "Captain John Deane and the Wreck of the *Nottingham,*" 106–17. Despite or perhaps because of the narrative's popularity, Deane's reputation lay in ruins. He eventually took a post as lieutenant in the Russian naval service for eleven years, then was made commercial consul at St. Petersburg, and finally was given the title commercial consul for the Port of Flanders at Ostend. See Bales and Warner, *Boon Island,* 7–10.

48. Appleby, Jacob, and Jacob, introduction, 7; Plummer, *Telling Sexual Stories,* 176.

49. Barber, "Social Stratification"; Schultz, "Class Society," 208.

50. Nash, *Class and Society,* 3.

51. Nash, *Class and Society,* 18–19; Nash, *Urban Crucible,* 3–4.

52. Nash, *Class and Society,* 7–8.

53. Padgen and Canny, *Colonial Identity,* 138–40.

54. Henretta, "Economic Development," 137.

55. Schultz, "Class Society," 216.

56. Salinger, "Artisans, Journeymen, and the Transformation of Labor," 63–64.

57. Henretta, "Economic Development," 139, 141; Ingersoll, "Riches and Honour," 47.

58. Nash, *Urban Crucible,* 33. They also had the time and resources to focus on the public good (36–37).

59. Main, "Economic Class Structure," 109–13.

60. Nash, *Class and Society,* 18.

61. Frey, "Inequality in the Here and Hereafter," 99; Kulikoff, "Progress of Inequality," 85.

62. Kulikoff, "Progress of Inequality," 59. For example, in Boston the poor, or near poor, constituted 7 percent in 1771, and this had risen to 10 percent by 1790.

63. Wilentz, *Chants Democratic,* 25–26. It must be remembered that wealth did not always translate to status and power.

64. "Loss of the American Ship *Hercules,*" 58–59; *Narrative of the Loss of the Ship* Hercules. This narrative was apparently popular on both sides of the Atlantic. Huntress, *Checklist of Narratives,* 181, shows at least twelve different publications.

65. Norwood, "Voyage to Virginia," 73.

66. Crowell, *Commonplace Book.*

67. Kann, *Republic of Men,* 22–23, 174.

68. Gorn, "Seafaring Engendered," 220.

69. Barker, *Log Book,* 122–24. Not all fit a positive mold: "The bad part of a ship's company are only a few who may be found among what are called waisters, or the after guard, and who may have been worthless characters on shore."

70. Foyster, *Manhood in Early Modern England,* 40–41; Carter, *Men and the Emergence of Polite Society,* 64–65. As Rediker, *Between the Devil and the Deep Blue Sea,* 192, points out, drinking may have acted as an opiate against the everyday harshness at sea. See also Gilje, *Liberty on the Waterfront,* 6, 92.

71. Swift, *Genealogical Notes,* 353.

72. Harrison, *Melancholy Narrative,* 10.

73. Harrison, *Melancholy Narrative,* 45.

74. Kann, *Republic of Men,* 113; Shoemaker, "Reforming Male Manners," 139.

75. Vickers and Walsh, "Young Men and the Sea." Historians such as Frederick Wallace and Samuel Eliot Morison found harsh class relationships, while Nicholas Rule argued that they never existed. In the 1960s Jesse Lemisch and Ralph Davis viewed authority on ships as a social construction (17–18).

76. Rediker, *Between the Devil and the Deep Blue Sea,* 84–85, 89. In the mid-nineteenth century ordinary sailors earned two dollars less than able seamen and boys earned up to two dollars less than ordinary sailors. Essentially experience determined whether a sailor was ordinary or able. An able seaman could repair rigging as well as reef, furl, and steer. See Dana, *Seaman's Friend,* 158–63.

77. Vickers and Walsh, "Young Men and the Sea," 22, 30. Hierarchy on ships varied from vessel to vessel, according to the size of a crew, the number of officers, etc.

78. Dana, *Seaman's Friend,* 158–63; see chap. 5, "Able Seamen."

79. Andrews, *Ships, Money and Politics,* 71; Gilje, *Liberty on the Waterfront,* 70–71.

80. See Nash, *Urban Crucible.* Many of the "merchant princes" had ties to maritime endeavors, coming into contact with sea captains who traveled in the same circles. See Morison, *Maritime History of Massachusetts,* 122.

81. Kulikoff, "Progress of Inequality," 61–62. Once they became rich enough, society accepted owners and captains in the highest circles. See McElroy, "Seafaring in Seventeenth-Century New England," 364.

82. Dana, *Seaman's Friend,* 131–38; see chap. 1, "The Master."

83. Conkling, *Jurisdiction, Law, and Practice,* 314–15. In addition seamen were not "bound to obey any unlawful command' (318). When the fear of desertion ran high, so was the threat of discipline (Lloyd, *British Seaman,* 87).

84. Rediker, *Between the Devil and the Deep Blue Sea,* 212, 222–23. Threats, brutality, and terror were long-standing means of keeping lower classes in order; see Linebaugh and Rediker, *Many-Headed Hydra,* 50–51.

85. Dening, *Mr. Bligh's Bad Language,* 19.

86. Ward, *Wooden World Dissected,* 6–8. However, when the captain's wife was around, he "truly fears her more than a storm . . . but he makes no tiresome stay with her; for after the honey-moon is over, he pretends pressing order from the board' (10).

87. Swift, *Genealogical Notes,* 354.

88. Vaughn, *Narrative of Captain David Woodard,* xxiii.

89. Leach, *Survival Psychology,* 139–42.

90. Conkling, *Jurisdiction, Law, and Practice,* 313–14.

91. Rediker, *Between the Devil and the Deep Blue Sea*, 95–97; Andrews, *Ships, Money and Politics*, 73–74; Rediker, "Motley Crew of Rebels," 158.

92. Bellamy, *Ramblin' Jack*, 225. Obviously this was before he made captain.

93. Rediker, *Between the Devil and the Deep Blue Sea*, 134, 138.

94. Rediker, *Between the Devil and the Deep Blue Sea*, 104–5; Rediker, "Motley Crew of Rebels," 183–84. See also Gilje, *Liberty on the Waterfront*, for a discussion of sailors' ability to assert their liberty.

95. "Loss of the *Peggy*," 188–89.

96. Vaughn, *Narrative of Captain David Woodard*, 234. This was taken from a two-volume piece printed for J. Sewall, Cornwall.

97. Paddock, *Narrative of the Shipwreck of the Ship* Oswego, 98; "Loss of the *Tyrrel*," 132.

98. "Loss of the Brig *Tyrrel*."

99. Paddock, *Narrative of the Shipwreck of the Ship* Oswego.

100. Authorship is difficult to determine as often survivors related their stories to other persons who then published the accounts. Also some narratives did not provide authors or "respectable persons" to indicate who provided the original stories. Many narratives, though not authored by captains or officers, still indicated that these "gentlemen" survived.

101. "Loss of the *Halsewell*," 197.

102. "Loss of the American Ship *Hercules*," 58. The ship eventually struck bottom less than a mile off shore, and the longboat was no longer an issue.

103. "Loss of the Ship *Margaret*," 310.

104. "Loss of His Majesty's Ship *Phoenix*," 166.

105. "Burning of the *Kent*," 320.

106. Ditz, "Shipwrecked," 53.

107. Law, "Torts," 241–42. Law has a discussion of negligence on 239–66.

108. "Loss of the Sloop *Betsy*," 124.

109. Barrow, *Mutiny of HMS* Bounty, 124. Bligh brought the carpenter to court upon their arrival in England. He was found guilty of some of the charges and reprimanded. He was said to be in a madhouse at the time of publishing (142). According to Greg Dening, Bligh was sensitive to any possibility of a person subverting his authority and that "every order was a sign of their relationship to him (Bligh), challenging his authority and changing the landscape of power on his quarterdeck" (*Mr. Bligh's Bad Language*, 60–61).

110. "Burning of the *Kent*," 318–19.

111. Dewar, *Voyages and Travels of Uring*, 130–31.

112. The narrative failed to relate what happened to the ship, whether it stayed together or not. See Paddock, *Narrative of the Shipwreck of the Ship* Oswego, 30.

113. Swift, *Genealogical Notes*, 353.

114. Which was the case, and they were not rescued except by accident the next day. See Bailey, *God's Wonders in the Great Deep*, 20.

115. Downs, *Brief and Remarkable Narrative*, 10–11.

116. Kann, *Republic of Men*, 31.

117. Bolster, *Black Jacks,* 17.

118. Bolster, *Black Jacks,* 33; Bolster, "Every Inch a Man," 149.

119. " Loss of the American Ship *Hercules,*" 62; *Narrative of the Loss of the Ship* Hercules.

120. Paddock, *Narrative of the Shipwreck of the Ship* Oswego, 34.

121. Paddock, *Narrative of the Shipwreck of the Ship* Oswego, 47.

122. Bolster, "Inner Diaspora," 434.

123. Miskolcze, "Don't Rock the Boat," 43.

124. Vassa, *Interesting Narrative of the Life of Equiano,* 150–51.

125. Bolster, "Inner Diaspora," 422; Bolster, *Black Jacks,* 142–44.

126. Bolster, *Black Jacks,* 189–91, 214; Bolster, "Every Inch a Man," 168.

127. Rediker, *Between the Devil and the Deep Blue Sea,* 96.

Chapter 5: To Honor Their Worth, Beauty, and Accomplishments

1. Ward compared ships to women (*Wooden World Dissected,* 4).

2. Various book reviews state these problems. See, for example, Vickers, "Book Review of *Iron Men, Wooden Women,*" 1120; and Druett, "Book Review," 426–27.

3. Dugaw, "Rambling Female Sailors," 181, 183. See also Creighton and Norling, *Iron Men, Wooden Women.*

4. Norling, "Ahab's Wife," 86–87; Cordingly, *Women Sailors,* xiii, 146.

5. Norling, "Ahab's Wife," 89. This was not common until the 1840s.

6. Druett, *Hen Frigates,* 79.

7. Springer, "Captain's Wife," 95; Druett, *Hen Frigates,* 106–8. Sometimes both parents taught the children, each specializing in different subjects. As children got older, parents might send them to live with relatives on land or to boarding schools (Druett, *Hen Frigates,* 116).

8. Druett, *Hen Frigates,* 136–38.

9. Druett, *Hen Frigates,* 39–40, 180–81. Along with Druett, Cordingly provides several instances in the nineteenth century (*Women Sailors,* 110).

10. Druett, *Hen Frigates,* 155.

11. Crane, *Ebb Tide,* 175–77.

12. Druett, *Hen Frigates,* 102–3; Creighton, "Davy Jones' Locker," 135.

13. Druett, *Hen Frigates,* 50–54. We know about the lives of these women from the many journals they wrote. See Springer, "Captain's Wife," 101–2.

14. Druett, *Hen Frigates,* 136.

15. Walby, *Gender Transformations,* 6.

16. Plummer, *Telling Sexual Stories,* 177–78.

17. Cott, *Bonds of Womanhood,* 2; Taylor, *Angel-Makers,* 109.

18. Clarke, *Naufragia,* vii.

19. Treckel, *To Comfort the Heart,* 2, 6; Brown, *Good Wives, Nasty Wenches,* 16, 17, 19; Fletcher, *Gender, Sex and Subordination,* 12, 379–80.

20. Brown, *Good Wives, Nasty Wenches,* 324.

21. Fletcher, *Gender, Sex and Subordination,* 382–83.

22. Berkin and Horowitz, *Women Voices,* 188–90.

23. Fletcher, *Gender, Sex and Subordination,* 397–400.

24. Berkin, *First Generation,* 200–205.

25. Pleck, "Historical Overview of American Gender Roles," 7.

26. Cott, *Bonds of Womanhood,* 146–48.

27. This number cannot be more precise as from several of the narratives it is unknown if all or any of the women survived.

28. Burg, "Women and Children First," 7.

29. Burg, "Women and Children First," 1–2. Lincoln indicates that this concept did not appear before the early nineteenth century ("Shipwreck Narratives," 167).

30. "Burning of the *Kent,*" 316.

31. Saunders, *Narrative of the Shipwreck,* 10.

32. Miskolcze, "Transatlantic Touchstone," 42–43. Taking off slippery shoes while on deck and removing any clothing that might weigh a person down when in the water are known survival techniques. Lincoln brings up the issue of clothing and survival, and rightly so ("Shipwreck Narratives," 170).

33. Ten of fifty-seven newspaper articles concerning shipwreck mentioned women, but only a few provided any detail. Only one of twelve logbooks that directly mentioned shipwreck had any indication of a woman on board.

34. Allen, *Narrative of the Shipwreck,* 19.

35. Miskolcze, "Transatlantic Touchstone," 50–51. She takes her analysis a step further by examining women who were captured by natives after shipwreck and where "female virtue under the threat of moral dissolution" added to the drama (51). See also "Loss of the Ship *Albion,*" 302. Most of the women were listed as cabin passengers, except for the last two, who were listed under steerage passengers. All of the women drowned.

36. "Loss of the *Prince,*" 148. The story was related by one of the lieutenants.

37. Anonymous, *Strange News from Plymouth.*

38. Anonymous, *Strange News from Plymouth,* 3.

39. "Burning of the *Kent,*" 315.

40. "Loss of the *Kent,*" 316.

41. The opportunity never came about, and all the women were lost ("Loss of the *Halsewell,*" 197).

42. Neither of them was given a name, and they were situated only in relation to male family members ("Loss of the Transport, *Harpooner,*" 341, 344–45).

43. "Loss of the *Halsewell,*" 199.

44. "Loss of the Ship *Albion,*" 300. She along with the remaining women, six in all, drowned.

45. Ditz, "Shipwrecked," 79.

46. "Loss of the *Halsewell,*" 195. Howard examined obituaries from the eighteenth century and found that placing women in relation to men was a common theme ("Bright Pattern to All Her Sex," 230–49).

47. "Loss of the *Boston,*" 323.

48. "Loss of the *Halsewell,*" 199.

49. "Loss of the *Halsewell*," 202. The seven women named were all related to the captain or were wives of officers. Later in the narrative two soldiers' wives and three black women were included (since they were lower-class women, the author neglected to provide their names). All of the women died.

50. "Burning of the *Kent*," 312, 317; Duncan, *Mariner's Chronicle*, 1834, 18.

51. Brown, *Good Wives, Nasty Wenches*, 31.

52. Merish, *Sentimental Materialism*, 4.

53. Congers, *Strange News from Plymouth*, 6.

54. Congers, *Strange News from Plymouth*, 7.

55. Miskolcze, "Don't Rock the Boat," 100. "They were an inspiration in adversity" (Lincoln, "Shipwreck Narratives," 170).

56. "Burning of the *Kent*," 315.

57. Kirkham, *Remarkable Shipwrecks*, 16.

58. "Loss of the *Halsewell*," 202.

59. "Burning of the *Kent*," 316.

60. Ellms, *Tragedy of the Seas*, 193–96. The ship is often referred to as *Frances Mary*.

61. "Loss of the *Francis Mary*," 195–96.

62. "Loss of the *Francis Mary*," 196. In a final paragraph, the *Francis Mary* was towed by another ship back to Jamaica, refitted, and sent back to sea. "The putrid remains of human bodies, which had been the only food of the unfortunate survivors, was found on board the vessel."

63. "Loss of the *Francis Mary*," 194–95.

64. Saunders, *Narrative of the Shipwreck*, 9.

65. Saunders, *Narrative of the Shipwreck*, 10.

66. Saunders, *Narrative of the Shipwreck*, 15.

67. Saunders, *Narrative of the Shipwreck*, 18.

68. Ditz, "Shipwrecked," 79–80.

69. Pease, *Ladies, Women, and Wenches*, 115.

Chapter 6: Chaos and Cannibalism on the High Seas

1. Tannahill, *Flesh and Blood*, 173–74.

2. Tannahill, *Flesh and Blood*, 9.

3. Lestringent, *Cannibals*, 10–11. Capt. James Cook and his men encountered cannibalism among the Maori in New Zealand. His men found that the Maori ate flesh for specific purposes and therefore "undermined the unequivocal association of cannibalism with pathology which the polarity between savage and civilized demanded'; see Thompson, "No Chance in Nature," 33.

4. Tannahill, *Flesh and Blood*, 148.

5. Lestringent, *Cannibals*, 182.

6. Otter, *Melville's Anatomies*, 15.

7. Petrinovich, *Cannibal Within*, 6.

8. Perhaps the most terrifying accounts of cannibalism are those that were random. Murder and psychotic behavior in which the perpetrators ate their victims for pleasure might be seen as threatening to social understandings of behavior.

9. Leach, *Survival Psychology*, 87, 90.

10. Meurn, *Survival Guide*, 130. The guide adds that solid food is better than no food at all, even if you lack water.

11. Meurn, *Survival Guide*, 92–93.

12. Tucker, *Great Starvation Experiment*, 64–65. See also Keys, *Biology of Human Starvation*.

13. Tucker, *Great Starvation Experiment*, 134–35, 192. Most experienced some level of edema, which is not often recorded in the shipwreck narratives. This is probably due to the large quantities of water the men were allowed to drink. Their bodies stored the water, while shipwreck victims lacked the possibility of drinking too much freshwater.

14. Meurn, *Survival Guide*, 130.

15. Leach, *Survival Psychology*, 99–103.

16. "Loss of the *Francis Mary*," 298.

17. Meurn, *Survival Guide*, 126, 128. Modern survival books follow this advice and suggest that gum, chewing on cloth, or holding a button in the mouth does reduce thirst (128).

18. Halttunen, *Murder Most Foul*, 66–67.

19. See Crain, "Lovers of Human Flesh," 27; and Simpson, *Cannibalism and the Common Law*, 114–39.

20. Saunders, *Narrative of the Shipwreck*, 13.

21. Petrinovich, *Cannibal Within*, 37. This is only a rough outline, and much of it depends on what was available.

22. Norwood, "Voyage to Virginia," 82. The woman who tried to buy the rat later died.

23. Dornstreich and Morren, "New Guinea Cannibalism," 9.

24. Petrinovich, *Cannibal Within*, 38–39.

25. Although none of these were taken by lot, it is interesting that none of the women and officers died. The last boy, Daniel Jones, was not eaten but thrown overboard, "his blood being bitter." See "Loss of the *Francis Mary*," 297.

26. Grayson, "Timing of the Donner Party Deaths," 223.

27. Hardesty, *Archaeology of the Donner Party*, 47. Though they boiled the bones, fragments remained large and there is no evidence of reuse or of the bones being reduced to a meal, a method often used by Native Americans in times of famine.

28. Hardesty, *Archaeology of the Donner Party*, 111.

29. Breen, "Historic Diary," 55.

30. Grayson, "Timing of the Donner Party Deaths," 124–32. Other disasters involving settlers moving west show similar mortality patterns. See Grayson, "Human Mortality," 185–88; Bartholomew and Arrington, *Rescue of the 1856 Handcart Companies;* Hafen and Hafen, *Handcarts to Zion;* Kimball, *Historic Resource Study;* and Clayton, *Latter-Day Saints' Emigrants' Guide.* Overall seventeen men died and nine survived, six women perished and ten lived, and thirteen of twenty-nine children never made it out of the mountains.

31. Tucker, *Great Starvation Experiment*, 192.

32. Hardesty, *Archaeology of the Donner Party*, 115.

33. Simpson, *Cannibalism and the Common Law*, 122–23.

34. Armstrong, "Slavery, Insurance and Sacrifice," 173.

35. Petrinovich, *Cannibal Within*, 47–48.

36. Norwood, "Voyage to Virginia," 90.

37. Eating an already dead person was not on the same level as killing someone for food and therefore often made the act of cannibalism seem less horrific to readers and traditional society (see Simpson, *Cannibalism and the Common Law*, 122). However, many such instances might not be reported, and one can only guess the order or procedure for those situations (see Petrinovich, *Cannibal Within*, 2–3).

38. Petrinovich, *Cannibal Within*, 3, 50, 56; Barrow, *Mutiny of HMS* Bounty, 119. One conflicting account is of the *Mignonette*, which foundered in the late nineteenth century. The courts tried to prove murder in that the survivors did not unduly suffer. Popular sentiment was split at first, but opinion shifted to support for the crew. See Simpson, *Cannibalism and the Common Law*, 79–80.

39. He also stated to the crew and servants, who supported his wife through this ordeal, that upon arrival at Rotterdam, "tho all the cargo be lost, you shall be plentifully rewarded." The letter was written by J. G. and certified for truth by John Cross and William Atkins, seamen. See Anonymous, *Strange News from Plymouth*, 4–5.

40. Carpinger and the Lady were the only two to survive. The story has a happy ending in that Carpinger managed to save a casket of jewels, and "considering the care and kindness of Carpinger, the Lady seems much to favour him, and when time of mourning is over, will undoubtedly make him Happy in her embraces" (Anonymous, *Strange News from Plymouth*, 7).

41. Simpson, *Cannibalism and the Common Law*, 124–29.

42. Thorton, "From Oregon to California," 52. One person also suggested they give pistols to two people and let them fight until "one or both were slain."

43. Thorton, "From Oregon to California," 55, 61.

44. Thorton, "From Oregon to California," 60.

45. Thorton, "From Oregon to California," 106.

46. The captain went on to add that "in all my days, I never feasted on any thing which appeared so delicious to my appetite,—the piercing sharpness of necessity had entirely conquered my aversion to such food" (Harrison, *Melancholy Narrative*, 16–18; "Extraordinary Famine," 177).

47. Harrison, *Melancholy Narrative*, 17–22; "Extraordinary Famine," 175–77. By this time they had encountered two vessels; one could not approach them due to inclement weather, and the second promised to send over food but instead set all sails and left them without any provisions.

48. Clarke, *Historical Memoirs of Shipwrecks*, x–xi.

49. Armstrong, "Slavery, Insurance and Sacrifice," 177–78.

50. The first mate's boat had separated from the captain's and the second mate's boats.

51. Chase, *Narrative of the Whale-Ship* Essex.

52. "Loss of the Whale Ship *Essex*," 168.

53. Chase, *Narrative of the Whale-Ship* Essex, 71–72.

54. "Extraordinary Famine," 177–78; Harrison, *Melancholy Narrative*, 23–25.

55. Clarke, *Historical Memoirs of Shipwrecks*, x–xi. In another version the crew cut the meat into small pieces and pickled it. They did throw over the head and fingers; see Harrison, *Melancholy Narrative*, 25–26.

56. "Extraordinary Famine," 179.

57. Harrison, *Melancholy Narrative*, 35.

58. Breen, "Historic Diary," 59. Milt made a "logical" choice as he was single and not related to anyone in the party.

59. The following information came from several sources: King, *Winter of Entrapment*; Hardesty, *Archaeology of the Donner Party*; and Grayson, "Timing of the Donner Party Deaths."

60. Those cannibalized included, at Alder Creek Camp, Jacob Donner (sixty-five years old) and Samuel Shoemaker (twenty-five), while Milt Eliot (twenty-eight) was the only recorded victim at the Murphy Cabin. George Keesberg supposedly ate Lavina Murphy (fifty), James Eddy (three), George Foster (four), and Tamsen Donner (forty-five).

61. King, *Winter of Entrapment*, 62–63. Of the ten men, only two made it out alive, and all five women survived. The two men to survive were William Eddy and William Foster. The women were Sara Murphy, Mary Graves, Sara Graves Fosdick, Amanda McCutchen, and Harriet Murphy Pike. Those eaten included Antonio (twenty-three), Lemuel Murphy (twelve), Patrick Dolan (forty), Franklin Graves (fifty-seven), Jay Fosdick (twenty-three), and the two Native Americans, Luis and Salvadore.

62. "Loss of the *Francis Mary*," 296.

63. "Loss of the *Francis Mary*," 297.

64. Saunders, *Narrative of the Shipwreck*, 12–13.

65. Saunders, *Narrative of the Shipwreck*, 15. It was a common belief that blood had to be taken from a new corpse as the fluid quickly coagulated. However, according to Todd C. Grey, M.D., "the extent to which cadaveric blood coagulates is highly variable and even when there is significant clotting a fair amount of the blood remains liquid. In addition, the clotted blood eventually reliquifies" (cited in Thorton, "From Oregon to California," 113, personal communication between Thorton and Grey).

66. "Loss of the *Francis Mary*," 297–98.

67. Thorton, "From Oregon to California," 59.

68. McGlashin, *History of the Donner Party*, 66.

69. Savigny and Corréard, *Narrative of a Voyage to Senegal*, 47.

70. Savigny and Corréard, *Narrative of a Voyage to Senegal*, 65.

71. Savigny and Corréard, *Narrative of a Voyage to Senegal*, 84. The plot was foiled by a few sailors who remained loyal to the officers.

72. McKee, *Deathraft*, 120.

73. "Shipwreck of the *Medusa*," 155.

74. Of the fifteen, five died within a matter of days. Those who made it onto the *Argus* were a captain, one lieutenant, two sub-lieutenants, a sergeant-major, and one black soldier. In addition the midshipman, the surgeon, the master gunner, the pilot, and one sailor made it on board, as well as the geographical engineer, an ex-sergeant, the governor's secretary, and a hospital administrator. See McKee, *Deathraft*, 167; and "Shipwreck of the *Medusa*," 155–56.

75. Petrinovich, *Cannibal Within*, 55. On the *Peggy*, before they pickled the remains of the Negro, "they chopped off the head and fingers, which they threw overboard, by common consent"; see Harrison, *Melancholy Narrative*, 25. Bodies were rarely left to rot but rather were dispatched quickly and processed with available tools. For a discussion of how literary sources dealt with this issue, see Burch, "Sink or Swim."

76. "Loss of the *Francis Mary*," 297–98.

77. Petrinovich, *Cannibal Within*, 212. The sweetness is ascribed to various societies throughout the world.

78. The men divided themselves into three boats with the captain, first mate, and second mate each in charge of a vessel.

79. Chase, *Narrative of the Whale-Ship* Essex, 67.

80. Chase, *Narrative of the Whale-Ship* Essex, 68, 70. The boat originally had six men: one stayed on the island, two died, and three survived.

81. Thorton, *From Oregon to California*, 90–91.

82. Petrinovich, *Cannibal Within*, 6; Leach, *Survival Psychology*, 150.

83. Leach, *Survival Psychology*, 98.

84. Rose, "Anatomy of Mutiny," 570.

85. McKee, "Fantasies of Mutiny," 300.

86. Pratt, "Mutiny," 529–30.

87. Leach, *Survival Psychology*, 108, 115–19.

88. "Loss of the *Nottingham* Galley," 216. Some of this behavior the captain attributed to cannibalism and its effects on dehumanizing the participants.

89. Pratt, "Mutiny," 530.

90. Langman, "True Account," 162, 164. One of the reasons this case did not continue was that Langman and some of the crew claimed that the captain wrote a protest while the men were sick and forced them to sign it before they could fully understand the protest's implications.

91. Pratt, "Mutiny," 530; Rediker, *Between the Devil and the Deep Blue Sea*, 228–29.

92. Dewar, *Voyages and Travels of Uring*, 172–77.

93. Arnold, "All Hands Drunk and Rioting," 233. Alfred Conkling agrees that not all attempts at revolt ought to end in punishment (*Jurisdiction, Law, and Practice*, 98).

94. Dewar, *Voyages and Travels of Uring*, 131–32.

95. Pratt, "Mutiny," 532.

96. According to his account, "the sea rose so high, and broke so terribly, they were frighted and confounded, and stared like Men amaz'd without obeying my orders." They made it back to shore only by the captain's quick thinking, and "When the seamen were got Safety, they swore the most bitter oaths, that they would not go to sea in the Canow anymore"; see Dewar, *Voyages and Travels of Uring,* 130–31.

97. For a discussion of slighting and male speech, see Kamensky, "Talk Like a Man," 19–50.

98. McKee, *Deathraft,* 98–99.

99. McKee, *Deathraft,* 104–6.

100. McKee, *Deathraft,* 107, 119.

101. McKee, *Wreck of the* Medusa, 71.

102. McKee, *Deathraft,* 137–40.

103. Bushman, *Refinement of America,* 39.

104. Fuller, *Mutiny,* xi.

105. McKee, "Fantasies of Mutiny," 301.

106. Andrews, *Ships, Money and Politics,* 71.

107. Armstrong, "Slavery, Insurance and Sacrifice," 181.

108. Halttunen, *Murder Most Foul,* 82.

109. Miskolcze, "Don't Rock the Boat," 133.

110. Thompson, "No Chance in Nature," 37.

111. Harrison, *Melancholy Narrative,* 35, 45.

112. For an alternate interpretation of social order at sea, see Rediker, *Between the Devil and the Deep Blue Sea.* Rediker argues for a constant negotiation and radicalization at sea that created a more flexible definition of status and order.

Chapter 7: Portuguese Narratives: A Comparative Perspective

1. Dias, Prologue to "Voyage and Shipwreck of the *São Paulo,*" 58.

2. Duffy, *Shipwreck and Empire,* 22.

3. Duffy, *Shipwreck and Empire,* 24–25, 36–37. Duffy does an excellent job in outlining the history of each publication. The wrecks in Gomes de Brito's volumes occurred between 1552 and 1602, while the third volume covers a series of wrecks from 1625 to 1651. Boxer, *Tragic History of the Sea,* discusses the confusion and history of the publication of the Portugese narratives, v, vi. Some of the stories were later reprinted by well-known individuals such as Diogo de Couto.

4. For an overview of the history of the *História Trágica-Marítima,* see Duffy, *Shipwreck and Empire;* and Blackmore, *Manifest Perdition.*

5. Duffy, *Shipwreck and Empire,* 46.

6. Blackmore, *Manifest Perdition,* xxi.

7. Boxer, *Portuguese Seaborne Empire,* 59. According to Boxer, one quintal equaled 51.405 kilograms or 130 pounds.

8. Boxer, *Portuguese Seaborne Empire,* 215. Russell-Wood adds the following to the outbound list: "tin, lead, quicksilver, cinnabar, worked and natural coral from the Mediterranean, alumstone, Florentine scarlet cloth, Genoese velvet, red cloth from London and Flanders, French and English linens, Portuguese wine, clocks,

and low-value European goods such as glassware, trinkets, and even playing cards" (*World on the Move*, 132).

9. Pearson, *New History of India*, 140–41. From 1580 to 1640 Portugal was ruled by Spain.

10. Duffy, *Shipwreck and Empire*, 9; Boxer, *Mary and Misogyny*, 74; Boxer, *Portuguese Seaborne Empire*, 59–60; Ley, *Portuguese Voyages*, x.

11. Duffy, *Shipwreck and Empire*, 14–15.

12. Difie and Winius, *Foundations of the Portuguese Empire*, 324.

13. Difie and Winius, *Foundations of the Portuguese Empire*, 200. The trip often covered twenty-three thousand miles, and if one includes the time to load and unload, the round trip lasted approximately eighteen months. See Boxer, *Tragic History of the Sea*, 6.

14. Difie and Winius, *Foundations of the Portuguese Empire*, 201; Russell-Wood, *World on the Move*, 58.

15. Boxer, *Tragic History of the Sea*, 25; Boxer, *Portuguese Seaborne Empire*, 216. The overloading or improperly loading of ships never appeared in British or American accounts.

16. Vaz d'Almada, "Wreck of the *São João Baptista*," 191–92.

17. Disney, *Twilight of the Pepper Empire*, appendix 3.

18. Couto, "Voyage of the *Aguia* and *Garça*," 29. A knee is a "timber fitted for connecting, stiffening, and resisting racking stress in principal structural parts." To careen, the ship was heeled to one side, "whether afloat or aground, in order to make other side of hull below water-line accessible for cleaning, caulking, or effecting repairs." See McEwan and Lewis, *Encyclopedia of Nautical Knowledge*, 72, 270. The definition for não is imprecise but it usually describes a middle–size vessel, with three masts, used in the Middle Ages or Age of Discovery.

19. Smith, "Excavations at Plettenberg Bay," 53. The vessel began to leak on its return voyage to Lisbon, forcing the crew to anchor for repairs. The vessel later foundered in the same bay during a storm.

20. Smith, *Vanguard of Empire*, 136–37. Roger Smith describes a *capitán*'s rank as "more a military than a nautical classification, and as executive director, he was in charge of everything and everyone aboard his ship."

21. "Loss of the *Boston*," 322.

22. Lavanha, "Wreck of the *Santo Alberto*," 111.

23. Duffy, *Shipwreck and Empire*, 123.

24. Couto, "Voyage of the *Aguia* and *Garça*," 32. The officers voted unanimously to steer for land.

25. Swift, *Genealogical Notes*, 354.

26. Couto, "Voyage of the *Aguia* and *Garça*," 33.

27. Luis, "Shipwreck Sufferred by Jorge d'Albuquerque Coelho," 127.

28. Duffy, *Shipwreck and Empire*, 83.

29. Dias, "Great Ship *São Paulo*," 72. Once these individuals, along with some of their parents and trustworthy friends, made it safely ashore, the remainder disembarked before nightfall.

30. Vaz, d'Almada, "Wreck of the *São João Baptista,*" 196. According to the narrative, the master was not a well-liked man. "His death caused sorrow to few and rejoicing to many."

31. Dias, "Great Ship *São Paulo,*" 85–87. Those on land eventually organized themselves and elected António Dias as their captain. Later in the narrative the castaways eventually met up with those on the vessels.

32. "Wreck of the *São Thomé,*" 62, 64.

33. Couto, "Voyage of the *Aguia* and *Garça,*" 37. The crew of the *Garça* overcame the ship's problems and caught up with the *Aguia.* Eventually the *Aguia* began to leak, and the *Garça* crew rescued her passengers and crew.

34. Duffy, *Shipwreck and Empire,* 68–70; Pérez-Mallaína, *Spain's Men of the Sea,* 214.

35. Luis, "Jorge d'Albuquerque," 147.

36. Dias, "Great Ship *São Paulo,*" 72–73.

37. Boxer, *Portuguese Seaborne Empire,* 214. Duffy supports this allegation, citing their brutal treatment at sea and their contempt on land that many had no inclination for obedience (*Shipwreck and Empire,* 74–75).

38. Dias, "Great Ship *São Paulo,*" 73–74. The sailors had every reason to be upset as many knew that the master and second pilot had made off with the boat in an earlier shipwreck.

39. Maura, *Women in the Conquest,* 8–9. Contemporaneous documents reveal a high level of discussion concerning women, especially prostitutes, on ships. This suggests that such women were a real problem on vessels. See Pérez-Mallaína, *Spain's Men of the Sea,* 165–66.

40. Boxer, *Mary and Misogyny,* 64–65; Boxer, *Tragic History of the Sea,* 20; Boxer, *Race Relations,* 58; Coates, *Convicts and Orphans,* 121. Though most women were wives, occasionally prostitutes and orphans might be on ships as well. Obviously it is impossible to determine the number of female servants or slaves as the authors rarely acknowledged their presence. Most Indiamen carried only a small number of women, averaging fifteen to twenty per ship out of several hundred people.

41. Couto, "Shipwreck of the *São Thomé,*" 59.

42. Couto, "Voyage of the *Aguia* and *Garça,*" 40.

43. Dias, "Voyage of the *São Paolo,*" 72.

44. Couto, "Shipwreck of the *São Thomé,*" 59–60.

45. Couto, "Narrative of the *Aguia* and *Garça,* 40.

46. Dias, "Voyage of the *São Paulo,*" 73; Vaz, d'Almada "Wreck of the *São João Baptista,*" 196. The master wanted to leave behind all unnecessary individuals and steal away in the boat. The captain killed him that night, much to the joy of many on the ship.

47. Couto, "Wreck of the *São Thomé,*" 78. Diogo do Couto was not aboard the *São Thomé,* but Couto got his information from various survivors (41).

48. Ley, *Portuguese Voyages,* 253.

49. Vaz, d'Almada, "Shipwreck of the *São Paulo Baptista,*" 210–11.

50. "Shipwreck of the *Santo Alberto*," 137. This river is probably the Maputo or the Tembe in southern Mozambique.

51. Blackmore, *Manifest Perdition*, 68–69.

52. Vaz, d'Almada, "Wreck of the *São Paulo Baptista*," 202–3. She remained true to her people, and ever pious, when she ended with the words, "may Our Lord bring you to your homes."

53. Vaz, d'Almada, "Wreck of the *São Paulo Baptista*." The survivors took the youngest son so "that a whole generation might not perish there" (212).

54. This quote brings up many issues regarding race and gender. See Vaz, d'Almada, "Wreck of the *São Paulo Baptista*," 212, 252. The survivors took her son as well. The first group of women and children left were subsequently killed by blacks who had been left behind (225–27).

55. Lavrin, "Sexuality in Colonial Mexico," 65. Men with stronger wills also provided moral protection for inherently sinful and weak women; see Aarom, *Women of Mexico City*, 261.

56. Couto, "Wreck of the *São Thomé*," 77–78.

57. Couto, "Wreck of the *São Thomé*," 90.

58. Johnson, "Dangerous Words," 131.

59. Couto, "Wreck of the *São Thomé*," 90–100, 104.

60. Twinam, "Honor, Sexuality, and Illegitimacy," 120. Honor for women was seen in chastity and fidelity, while for men honor came through a fight for reputation; see Seed, *To Love, Honor and Obey*, 63.

61. Twinam, *Public Lives*, 338–39; Twinam, "Negotiation of Honor," 73.

62. Lavrin, "Lo Femenino," 159.

63. Brown, *Good Wives, Nasty Wenches*, 31.

64. Duffy, *Shipwreck and Empire*, 75.

65. Twinam, *Public Lives*, 47; Johnson and Lipsett-Rivera, *Faces of Honor*, 7.

66. Blackmore, *Manifest Perdition*, 14. Calvo-Stevenson, *Sinking Being*, demonstrates how colonial Spanish American literature also placed shipwreck in a providential format.

67. Russell-Wood, *World on the Move*, 89, 92.

68. Lavanha, "Wreck of the *Santo Alberto*," 109; Couto, "Wreck of the *São Thomé*," 67.

69. Boxer, *Portuguese Seaborne Empire*, 74.

70. Dias, "Great Ship *São Paulo*," 64–65.

71. Dias, "Great Ship *São Paulo*," 74–75. He further pledged that he would "never leave this island unless we all go together."

72. Peirce, *Account of the Great Dangers*, 12.

73. Blackmore, *Manifest Perdition*, 6–7. Boxer adds that such cult of the Virgin was popular in all overseas colonies (*Mary and Misogyny*, 104).

74. Couto, "Wreck of the *São Thomé*," 63. Obviously all the Portuguese women were on the life raft. At the head of this group of slave women was the nurse who held Dona Joanna's baby, as mentioned above.

75. Luis, "Shipwreck Suffered by Jorge d'Albuquerque," 145.

76. Eire, *From Madrid to Purgatory,* 330.

77. Russell-Wood, *World on the Move,* 2. There is an account of Mrs. Eliza Bradley in which she is held captive in Northeast Africa. This is a fictional account but one that reflected American fears of captivity by Barbary pirates in the early nineteenth century.

78. Lavanha, "Wreck of the *Santo Alberto,*" 137. This being April 15, Maundy Thursday, "Friar Pedro (an Augustinian) recited the Litany, and afterwards preached a sermon suitable to the occasion."

79. Boxer, *Church Militant,* 39.

80. Lavanha, "Wreck of the *Santo Alberto,*" 171.

81. Vaz, d'Almada, "Wreck of the *São João Baptista,*" 228.

82. Luis, "Shipwreck Suffered by Jorge D'Albuquerque Coelho," 137–38.

83. Eire, *From Madrid to Purgatory,* 350.

84. "Wreck of the *Santo Alberto,*" 169.

85. Couto, "Wreck of the *São Thomé,*" 84–85.

86. "Wreck of the *Santo Alberto,*" 114.

87. Whitwell, *Discourse,* 7.

88. Couto, "Wreck of the *São Thomé,*" 59. The quote goes on to state that "he did not seem to be the same man who in such great risks and perils as those in which he previously found himself had never lost a bit of strength and courage, which now completely failed him."

89. The narrator suggested that they could have made larger rafts, large enough to hold everyone along with water and provisions. See Couto, "Wreck of the *São Thomé,*" 61.

90. "Voyage of the *Aguia* and *Garça,*" 31. This church was an Augustinian establishment.

91. Eire, *From Madrid to Purgatory,* 30.

92. Vaz, d'Almada, "Wreck of the *São João Baptista,*" 194.

93. Couto, "Wreck of the *São Thomé,*" 60–61. The friar stayed on board until those in the lifeboat convinced him to swim to the boat, thus leaving all those poor souls on the sinking ship.

94. Lavanha, "Wreck of the *Santo Alberto,*" 186. Boxer adds in a footnote, "Our Lady of the Bulwark (Bastion), in the fortress of São Sebastião at the northern tip of the island, to whom the survivors of the *São João* likewise gave thanks."

95. Vaz, d'Almada, "Wreck of the *São João Baptista,*" 271. "After this, everyone went to seek a vessel in which to go to Goa."

96. Couto, "Wreck of the *São Thomé,*" 99.

97. Dias, "Wreck of the *São Paulo,*" 106.

98. Dias, "Wreck of the *São Paulo,*" 106.

99. Blackmore, *Manifest Perdition,* 40.

100. Boxer, *Portuguese Seaborne Empire,* 144, 146.

101. Duffy, *Shipwreck and Empire,* 166.

102. Perry, *Gender and Disorder*, 41.
103. Blackmore, *Manifest Perdition*, 16–17.

Epilogue

1. Lincoln, "Shipwreck Narratives," 160.
2. Bushman, *Refinement of America*, 39.
3. Kamensky, "Talk Like a Man," 34. Also see Rediker, *Between the Devil and the Deep Blue Sea*.
4. Arnold, "All Hands Drunk and Rioting," 234.
5. Fuller, *Mutiny*, xi.
6. Andrews, *Ships, Money and Politics*, 71.
7. McKee, "Fantasies of Mutiny," 301.
8. Crain, "Lovers of Human Flesh," 42–43.
9. Winks, "Making of the Fugitive Slave Narrative," 113.
10. Blackmore, *Manifest Perdition*, 80.
11. Vaughn, *Narrative of Captain David Woodard*, xviii, xix.
12. Wharton, "Providence," 46.

BIBLIOGRAPHY

Primary Sources

Abbott, Charles. *Treatise of the Law Relative to Merchant Ships and Seaman.* New-buryport, Mass.: Edward, Little and Co., 1840.

Allen, Sarah. *A Narrative of the Shipwreck and Unparalleled Sufferings of Mrs. Sarah Allen, (Late of Boston) on Her Passage in May Last from New York to New Orleans.* 2nd ed. Early American Imprints, second series, no. 36713. Boston: Printed for Benjamin Marston, 1816.

Andrews, Evangeline Walker, and Charles McLean Andrews, eds. *Jonathan Dickinson's Journal or, God's Protecting Providence.* New Haven, Conn.: Yale University Press, 1945.

Anonymous. *A History of the Insurance Company of North America of Philadelphia.* Philadelphia: Press of Review Publishing and Printing Company, 1885.

Anonymous. *The Mariner's Chronicle: Containing Narratives of the Most Remarkable Disasters at Sea, Such as Shipwrecks, Storms, Fires, and Famines; Also Naval Engagements, Piratical Adventures, Incidents of Discovery, and Other Extraordinary and Interesting Occurrences.* Stereotyped by A. Chandler. New Haven, Conn.: Durrie and Peck, 1834.

Anonymous. *Remarkable Shipwrecks: or, A Collection of Interesting Accounts of Naval Disasters; with Many Particulars of the Extraordinary Adventures and Sufferings of the Crews of Vessels Wrecked at Sea, and of Their Treatment on Distant Shore; Together with an Account of the Deliverance of Survivors; Selected from Authentic Sources.* Hartford, Conn.: Andrus and Starr, 1813.

Anonymous. *Shipwreck Stories, Told by Survivors.* Originally published for Thomas Tegg, about 1812. Reprinted, Golden Valley, Minn.: Empire, 1967.

Anonymous. *Strange News from Plymouth, or, A Wonderful and Tragical Relation of a Voyage from the Indies: Where by Extraordinary Hardships, and the Extremities of the Late Great Frost, Several of the Seamen and Others Miserably Perish'd; and for Want of Provision, Cast-Lots for Their Lives, and Were Forced to Eat One Another, and How a Dutch Merchant Eat Part of His Own Children, and Then Murdered Himself because He Would not Kill His Wife; with the Miraculous Preservation of George Carpinger, an English Seaman, and the Dutch Merchants Wife, Now a Shore* at Plymouth; in a Letter to Mr. D. B. of London, Merchant. London: Printed for J. Congers at the Black-Raven in Duck-Lane, 1684.

Anonymous. *A True and Particular Narrative of the Late Tremendous Tornado, or Hurricane, at Philadelphia and New-York, on Sabbath–Day, July 1, 1792: When Several Pleasure Boats Were Lost in the Harbor of the Latter, and Thirty Men, Women and Children, (Taking Their Pleasure on That Sacred Day) Were Unhappily Drowned in Neptune's Raging and Tempestuous Element!!!! ——Tell This Not in Massachusetts! Publish It Not in the Streets of Connecticut! Lest Their Sober-Minded Young Men and Maidens Should Bitterly Reproach Thee in the Day of Thy Calamity, and Triumph over Thee When Thy Desolation Cometh; and Ask of Thee, Where Art Thy Magistrates? Or Do They Bear the Sword of the Lord in Vain?—Where Art Thy Watch Me. ——Have They Deserted Their Watch-Tower? Or Have they Fallen Asleep?* Boston: Printed and sold by E. Russell, n.d.

Anonymous. *Wonderful Escapes!* Dublin: Printed by Richard Grace, Mary-Street, 1822.

Bailey, Joseph. *God's Wonders in the Great Deep: or a Narrative of the Shipwreck of the Brigantine,* Alida and Catherine, *Joseph Bailey, Master, on the 27th of December, 1749, Bound from New York to Antigua; Written by the Master Himself.* New York: Printed and sold by James Parker, and the New Printing Office in Beaver Street, 1750.

Barker, H. M. *The Log Book; or Nautical Miscellany.* London: J&W Robins, 1826.

Barlow, Edward. *Barlow's Journal of His Life at Sea in King's Ships: East & West Indiamen & Other Merchantmen from 1659 to 1703.* Vol. 1. Translated by Basil Lubbock. London: Hurst & Blackett, 1934.

Barrow, Sir John. *The Mutiny and Piratical Seizure of HMS* Bounty: *With an Introduction by Admiral Sir Cyprian Bridge. GCR Humphrey.* 1831. Reprinted, Milford: Oxford University Press, 1928.

Bartholomew, Benjamin. "A Relation of the Wonderful Mercies of God Extended unto Us the 19 of October 1660 in the Ship *Exchange* Being Bound from New-ingland to Barbadoes." In *In the Trough of the Sea: Selected Sea-Deliverance Narratives, 1660–1766,* edited by Donald Wharton. Westport, Conn.: Greenwood, 1979.

Bellamy, Reynell. *Ramblin' Jack: Journal of Captain John Cremer.* London: Jonathan Cape, 1936.

Bilton, Thomas. *Captain Bilton's Journal of His Unfortunate Voyage from Lisbon to Virginia, in the Year 1707.* London: Printed for A. Bettesworth and E. Curll, 1715.

Bligh, William. *Narrative of the* Mutiny on the Bounty, *on Board His Britannic Majesty's Ship* Bounty; *and the Subsequent Voyage of Part of the Crew, in the Ship's Boat, from Tofoa, One of the Friendly Islands, to Timor, a Dutch Settlement in the East Indies.* Philadelphia: Printed by William Spotswood, 1790.

Blunt, Joseph. *Shipmaster's Assistant and Commercial Digest.* New York: E. & G. W. Blunt, 1837.

Bradley, Eliza. *An Authentic Narrative of the Shipwreck and Sufferings of Mrs. Eliza Bradley, the Wife of Captain James Bradley of Liverpool; Commander of the* Sally

Which Was Wrecked on the Coast of Barbary, in June 1818. Boston: Printed by James Walden, 1820.

Brady, William. *The Naval Apprentice's Kedge Anchor; Or Young Sailors' Assistant.* New York: Taylor and Clement, 1841.

Breen, Patrick. "Historic Diary of Patrick Breen." In *Winter of Entrapment,* edited by Joseph King, 204–10. Toronto: P. D. Meany, 1992.

Brown, Andrew. *Dr. Brown's Sermon, on the Dangers and Duties of the Seafaring Life; Preached before the Protestant Dissenting Congregation, at Halifax; and Published at the Desire of the Marine Society, in That Place.* Boston: Belknap and Hall, 1793.

"Burning of the *Kent.*" In *Interesting and Authentic Narratives of the Most Remarkable Shipwrecks,* edited by R. Thomas, 312–20. Hartford: Published by Ezra Strong, 1836.

Cases Argued and Determined in the High Court of Admiralty, edited by George Minot. Boston: Little, Brown and Company, 1853.

Chase, Owen, "Narrative of the Most Extraordinary and Distressing Shipwreck of the Whale-Ship *Essex*" (New York: W.B. Gilley, 1821). In Thomas Philbrick, ed. *The Loss of the Ship* Essex, *Sunk by a* Whale, 13–80. New York: Penguin Group, 2000.

Clark, Jonas. *A Short and Brief Account of the Shipwreck of Capt. Joshua Winslow.* Boston: James Clark, 1788.

Clarke, Francis. *The American Ship-Master's Guide, and Commercial Assistant, Being an Enlargement of the Seamen's Manual.* Boston: Allen, 1838.

Clarke, James Stanier. *Historical Memoirs of Shipwrecks and of the Providential Deliverance of Vessels.* London: Printed for A. K. Newman, 1821.

———. *Naufragia, or Historical Memoirs of Shipwrecks.* London: Printed by I. Gold for J. Mawman, 1805.

Clayton, W. *The Latter-Day Saints' Emigrants' Guide.* St. Louis: Steam Power, 1848.

"A Complete List of Vessels, Fitted Out of the Port of Providence, Which Have Been Taken, Plundered, Cast Away, or Lost at Sea, from the 20th of May, 1756, to the Commencement of the Late War, to the Present Time." *Providence Gazette,* January 21, 1764.

Congers, J. *Strange News from Plymouth in a Letter to Mr. D. B. of London, Merchant.* London: Printed for J. Congerse, 1684.

Conkling, Alfred. *The Jurisdiction, Law, and Practice of the Courts of the United States in Admiralty and Maritime Cases.* 2 vols. Albany: W. C. Little, 1848.

Couto, Diogo do. "Narrative of the Loss of the *Aguia* and *Garça,* 1559–60." In *Further Selections from Tragic History of the Sea,* edited by C. R. Boxer, 189–274. Minneapolis: University of Minnesota Press, 1958.

———. "Narrative of the Shipwreck of the Great Ship *São Thomé* in the Land of Gumos, in the Year, 1589." In *Tragic History of the Sea,* edited by C. R. Boxer, 53–106. Minneapolis: University of Minnesota Press, 1958. Referred to as "Wreck of the *São Thomé*"

Crespel, Emmanuel. *Travels in North America, by M. Crespel, with a Narrative of His Shipwreck, and Extraordinary Hardships and Sufferings on the Island of Anticosti;*

and an Account of That Island, and of the Shipwreck of His Majesty's Ship Active. London: Printed by Sampson Low, 1797.

Crowell, Simeon. "Commonplace Book of Simeon Crowell," 1818–46, 1854–56. Boston: Massachusetts Historical Society, Crowell Collection.

Dana, Richard Henry. *The Seaman's Friend: Containing a Treatise on Practical Seamanship.* Boston: Published by Thomas Groom and Co., 1851.

———. *Two Years before the Mast.* Boston: Houghton Mifflin, 1911.

Deane, Jasper. *Narrative of the Sufferings, Preservation and Deliverance of Capt. John Deane and Company.* London: Printed by R. Tookey, 1711.

Deane, John. *Narrative of the Shipwreck of the* Nottingham Galley, *&C. First Published in 1711: Revised and Re-printed with Additions in 1727, and Now Re-published in 1730, by John Deane, Commander, His Majesty's Consul for the Ports of Flanders.* London?, 1730.

———. *A Narrative of the Shipwreck of the* Nottingham Galley, *&C. First Published in 1711: Revised and Re-printed with Additions in 1727, Re-published in 1730, and Now Propos'd for the Last Edition, during the Author's Life Time; by John Deane, Then Commander, of the Nottingham Galley; but Now, and for Many Years Past, His Majesty's Consul for the Ports of Flanders, Residing at Ostend, 1738.* London?, 1738.

Dexter, Elisha. *Narrative of the Loss of the* William and Joseph *Whaling Brig, of Martha's Vineyard, and the Sufferings of Her Crew for Seven Days on a Raft in the Atlantic Ocean, with Some Remarks upon Whaling.* Boston: Printed by Samuel N. Dickenson, 1842.

Dias, Henrique. "Shipwreck of the *São Paulo* and Itinerary of the Survivors." In *Further Selections from the Tragic History of the Sea, 1559–1565,* edited by C. R. Boxer, 57–108. Minneapolis: University of Minnesota Press, 1958.

Dickinson, Jonathan. *Gods Protecting Providence, Man's Surest Help and Defence in the Times of the Greatest Difficulty and Most Imminent Danger: Evidenced in the Remarkable Deliverance of Divers Persons from the Devouring Waves of the Sea, amongst Which They Suffered Shipwrack; and Also from the More Cruelly Devouring Jawes of the Inhumane Canibals of Florida / Faithfully Related by One of the Persons Concerned Therein, Jonathan Dickenson.* Philadelphia: Printed by Reinier Jansen, 1699.

———. *God's Protecting Providence, Man's Surest Help and Defence, in Times of the Greatest Difficulty, and Most Eminent Danger: Evidenced in the Remarkable Deliverance of Robert Barrow, with Divers Other Persons, from the Devouring Waves of the Sea; amongst Which They Suffered Shipwrack; and Also, from the Cruel Devouring Jaws of the Inhumane Canibals of Florida; Faithfully Related by One of the Persons Concerned Therein, Jonathan Dickenson.* 1699. Reprinted in London and Sold by T. Sowle.

Downs, Barnabas. *A Brief and Remarkable Narrative of the Life and Extreme Sufferings of Barnabas Downs.* Boston: Printed by E. Russell for the author, 1786.

Duncan, Archibald. *The Mariner's Chronicle; or, Authentic and Complete History of Popular Shipwrecks: Recording the Most Remarkable Disasters Which Have Happened on the Ocean to People of All Nations; Particularly the Adventures and*

Sufferings of British Seamen, by Wreck, Fire, Famine, and Other Calamities Incident to a Life of Maritime Enterprise. 6 vols. London: Printed and published by J. & J. Cundee, 1804–8.

————. *The Mariner's Chronicle; or, Authentic and Complete History of Popular Shipwrecks: Recording the Most Remarkable Disasters Which Have Happened on the Ocean to People of All Nations; Particularly the Adventures and Sufferings of British Seamen, by Wreck, Fire, Famine, and Other Calamities Incident to a Life of Maritime Enterprise.* Hartford, Conn., Andrus and Starr, 1813.

————. *Mariner's Chronicle: Containing Narratives of the Most Remarkable Disasters at Sea, Such as Shipwrecks, Storms, Fires, and Famines; Also Naval Engagements, Piratical Adventures, Voyages of Discovery, And Other Extraordinary and Interesting Occurrences.* New Haven, Conn.: R.M Treadway, 1834.

Ellms, Charles. *Tragedy of the Seas.* Philadelphia: Carey and Hart, 1841.

Equiano, Olaudah. *The Interesting Narrative of Olaudah Equiano.* London, 1789.

Essex County, Newburyport, Massachusetts. *Merrimack Marine and Fire Insurance Company Policies, 1803–1804.* Phillips Library, Peabody Essex Museum, Salem, Mass.

Extract of a letter from Madeira dated October 17, 1763. *Providence Gazette,* December 31, 1763.

"Extraordinary Famine in the American Ship *Peggy.*" In *Interesting and Authentic Narratives of the Most Remarkable Shipwrecks,* edited by R. Thomas, 175–79. Hartford: Published by Ezra Strong, 1836.

Gloucester Archives Committee. "Chronological List of Men Who Died Fishing from Port Gloucester, Massachusetts." On file with the City of Gloucester, Archives Department, Gloucester, Mass.

Hammon, Briton. *A Narrative of the Uncommon Sufferings, and Surprizing Deliverance of Briton Hammon, a Negro Man . . . Servant to General Winslow, of Marshfield, in New-England: Who Returned to Boston, after Having Been Absent Almost Thirteen Years; Containing an Account of the Many Hardships He Underwent from the Time He Left His Master's House, in the Year 1747, to the Time of His Return to Boston; How He Was Cast Away in the Capes of Florida; . . . the Horrid Cruelty of the Indians in Murdering the Whole Ship's Crew; . . . the Manner of His Being Carried by Them into Captivity; Also, an Account of His Being Confined Four Years and Seven Months in a Close Dungeon.* Boston: Printed and sold by Green & Russel, 1760. Microfilm.

Harrison, David. *The Melancholy Narrative of the Distressful Voyage and Miraculous Deliverance of Captain David Harrison, of the Sloop* Peggy, *of New York, on His Voyage from Fyal, One of the Western Islands, to New-York . . . the Whole Being Authenticated in the Strongest Manner, by Repeated Depositions, Before the Right Hon. George Nelson, Esq. Lord-Mayor of the City of London, and Mr. Robert Shank, Notary Public.* London: Printed for James Harrison, 1766.

Holden, Horace. *A Narrative of the Shipwreck, Captivity, and Sufferings of Horace Holden and Benj. H. Nute, Who Were Cast Away in the American Ship* Mentor, *on the Pelew Islands, in the Year 1832; and for Two Years Afterwards Were Subjected* to *Unheard of Sufferings among the Barbarous Inhabitants of Lord North's Island.* Boston: Russel, Shattuck, and Co., 1836.

Janeway, James. *Mr. James Janeway's Legacy to His Friends: Containing Twenty Seven Famous Instances of Gods Providences in and about Sea Dangers and Deliverances, with the Names of Several That Were Eye-witnesses to Many of Them; Whereunto Is Added a Sermon on the Same Subject.* London: Printed for Dorman Newman, 1674.

"Journal of the Whaling Voyage to the South Pacific Ocean on Board the Barque *Henry* of Salem and Commanded by Charles Lind, Commenced June 12th 1845." Phillips Library, Peabody Essex Museum, Salem, Mass.

Kirkham, Samuel. *Remarkable Shipwrecks and Chronological Tables.* 2nd ed. Harrisburg, 1824.

Langman, Christopher. *A True Account of the Voyage of the* Nottingham Galley, *John Deane Commander, from the River Thames to New England and Since Our Arrival at London: Near Which Place She Was Cast Away on Boon-Island, December 11, 1710 by the Captain's Obstinacy, Who Endeavour'd to Betray Her to the French, or Run Her Ashore; with an Account of the Falsehoods in the Captain's Narrative; and a Faithful Relation of the Extremeites the Company Was Reduc'd to for Twenty-Four Days on That Desolate Rock, Where They Were Forc'd to Eat One of Their Companions Who Died, but Were at Last Wonderfully Deliver'd; the Whole Attested upon Oath, by Christopher Langman, Mate; Nicholas Mellen, Boatswain; George White, Sailor in Said Ship.* London: Printed for S. Popping, 1711.

———. "A True Account of the Voyage of the *Nottingham*-Galley of London John Dean Commander, from the River Thames to New-England." In *In the Trough of the Sea,* edited by Donald Wharton, 159–72. Westport, Conn.: Greenwood, 1979.

Lavanha, João Baptisa. "Shipwreck of the Great Ship *Santo Alberto,* and Itinerary of the People, Who Were Saved from It, 1593." In *Tragic History of the Sea,* edited by C. R. Boxer, 189–274. Minneapolis: University of Minnesota Press, 1959.

"Letter to Andrew Dunlap, Boston, June 11, 1819." MS 150. Dunlap Papers. Phillips Library, Peabody Essex Museum, Salem, Mass.

"Letter to Mr. Barton from John Hebden, Master of the Ship *Margaret.*" Boston, 1795. Barton Family Papers. Phillips Library, Peabody Essex Museum, Salem, Mass.

Logbook, *Cashmere,* 1838. G. W. Blunt White Library, Mystic Seaport Museum, Mystic, Conn.

Logbook, *Duke,* 1748. Phillips Library, Peabody Essex Museum, Salem, Mass.

Logbook, *Sultanna.* Phillips Library, Peabody Essex Museum, Salem, Mass.

"Loss of His Majesty's Ship *Phoenix.*" In *Interesting and Authentic Narratives of the Most Remarkable Shipwrecks,* edited by R. Thomas, 154–68. Hartford: Published by Ezra Strong, 1836.

"Loss of the *Boston.*" In *Interesting and Authentic Narratives of the Most Remarkable Shipwrecks,* edited by R. Thomas, 321–22. Hartford: Published by Ezra Strong, 1836.

"Loss of the Brig *Tyrrel*." In *Interesting and Authentic Narratives of the Most Remarkable Shipwrecks,* edited by R. Thomas, 131–41. Hartford: Published by Ezra Strong, 1836.

"Loss of the *Francis Mary*." In *Interesting and Authentic Narratives of the Most Remarkable Shipwrecks*, edited by R. Thomas, 295–98. Hartford, Conn.: Published by Silas, Andus and Sons, 1848.

"Loss of the *Halsewell* East Indiaman." In *Interesting and Authentic Narratives of the Most Remarkable Shipwrecks,* edited by R. Thomas, 195–205. Hartford: Published by Ezra Strong, 1836.

"Loss of the *Nottingham* Galley, of London." In *Interesting and Authentic Narratives of the Most Remarkable Shipwrecks,* edited by R. Thomas, 206–18. Hartford: Published by Ezra Strong, 1836.

"Loss of the Peggy" In *Interesting and Authentic Narratives of the Most Remarkable Shipwrecks,* edited by R. Thomas, 187–94. Hartford: Published by Ezra Strong, 1836.

"Loss of the *Prince,* by Fire." In *Interesting and Authentic Narratives of the Most Remarkable Shipwrecks,* edited by R. Thomas, 142–53. Hartford: Published by Ezra Strong, 1836.

"Loss of the Ship *Albion*." In *Interesting and Authentic Narratives of the Most Remarkable Shipwrecks,* edited by R. Thomas, 299–305. Hartford: Published by Ezra Strong, 1836.

"Loss of the American Ship *Hercules*." In *Interesting and Authentic Narratives of the Most Remarkable Shipwrecks,* edited by R. Thomas, 56–88. Hartford: Published by Ezra Strong, 1836.

"Loss of the Ship *Margaret*." In *Interesting and Authentic Narratives of the Most Remarkable Shipwrecks*, edited by R. Thomas, 308–12. Hartford: Published by Ezra Strong, 1836.

"Loss of the Sloop *Betsy*." In *Interesting and Authentic Narratives of the Most Remarkable Shipwrecks,* edited by R. Thomas, 118–30. Hartford: Published by Ezra Strong, 1836.

"Loss of the Transport, *Harpooner*." In *Interesting and Authentic Narratives of the Most Remarkable Shipwrecks,* edited by R. Thomas, 341–44. Hartford: Published by Ezra Strong, 1836.

"Loss of the Whale Ship *Essex*." In *Mariner's Chronicle: Containing the Narratives of the Most Remarkable Disasters at Sea, Such as Shipwrecks, Storms, Fires and Famines; Also, Naval Engagements, Piratical Adventures, Incidents of Discovery and Other Extraordinary and Interesting Occurrences,* 398–402. New Haven, Conn., 1835.

Luis, Afonso. "Shipwreck Suffered By Jorge D'Albuquerque Coelho." In *Further Selections from Tragic History of the Sea,* edited by C. R. Boxer, 109–57. Minneapolis, University of Minnesota Press, 1959.

Mansfield, Helen. "Journal of a Voyage from Charleston toward Liverpool." Letter transcribed for Mr. Brooks from the log of the *Boston* by Mackay's daughter, 1897. Phillips Library, Peabody Essex Museum, Salem, Mass.

Marblehead Marine Insurance. Vol. 12. "List of Policies and Accounts of Risks, 1803–1830" Phillips Library, Peabody Essex Museum, Salem, Mass.

Mather, Increase. *An Essay for the Recording of Illustrious Providences: Wherein an Account Is Given of Many Remarkable and Very Memorable Events, Which Have Happened in This Last Age; Especially in New England.* Boston: Sold by George Calvert, London, 1684.

McGlashin, D. F. *History of the Donner Party.* Truckee, Calif.: Crowley and McGlashin, 1879.

Negligence Cases in Suffolk County Court. Boston: Society, 1933.

Norwood, Henry. "A Voyage to Virginia." In *In the Trough of the Sea: Selected Sea-Deliverance Narratives, 1660–1766,* edited by Donald Wharton, 65–90. Westport, Conn.: Greenwood, 1979.

Paddock, Judah. *A Narrative of the Shipwreck of the Ship Oswego, on the Coast of South Barbary, and of the Sufferings of the Master and the Crew While in Bondage among the Arabs: Interspersed with Numerous Remarks upon the Country and Its Inhabitants, and Concerning the Peculiar Perils of That Coast; by Judah Paddock, Her Late Master.* New York: Published by Captain James Riley, A. Seymour Printer, 1818.

Peirce, Nathanael. *An Account of the Great Dangers and Distresses, and the Remarkable Deliverance of Capt. Nathanael Peirce, Who Sail'd from Portsmouth, in New-Hampshire, Bound for Louisbourg; and Being Taken Up at Sea, Was Carried to Oporto. / Written by Himself.* Early American Imprints, first series, no. 7747. Boston: Printed and sold by Edes and Gill, 1756.

Peters, Richard. *Admiralty Decisions in the District Court of the United States, for the Pennsylvania District.* Vol. 1. Early American Imprints, 2nd series, no. 13364. Philadelphia: Published by William Farrand, 1807.

Prince, Thomas. Logbook, *George and Elizabeth.* 1709. Boston: Massachusetts Historical Society.

Protest for Schooner *Hope,* 1805. D. G. W. Blunt White Library, Mystic Seaport Meseum, Mystic, Conn.

Report of Cases in the High Court of Admiralty. Vol. 1. Philadelphia: Reprinted and sold by James Humphreys, 1800.

Riley, James. *An Authentic Narrative of the Loss of the American Brig* Commerce, *Wrecked on the Western Coast of Africa, in the Month of August, 1815.* 3rd ed. New York: Published by the author, 1818.

Roberts, Kenneth. *Boon Island: Including Contemporary Accounts of the Wreck of the Nottingham Galley.* Hanover, N.H.: University Press of New England, 1996.

Ryther, John. "Sea-Dangers and Deliverances Improved, in a Sermon Preached by John Ryther, Minister of the Gospel." In *Mr. James Janeway's Legacy to His Friends: Containing Twenty Seven Famous Instances of Gods Providences in and about Sea Dangers and Deliverances, with the Names of Several That Were Eye-witnesses to Many of Them; Whereunto Is Added a Sermon on the Same Subject,* edited by James Janeway. London: Printed for Dorman Newman, 1674.

"Saturday, September 20, 1766, taken from the *London Magazine* for June 1766." *Providence Gazette,* September 20, 1766.

Saunders, Ann. *Narrative of the Shipwreck and Sufferings of Miss Ann Saunders.* Providence: Printed for Z. Crossmon, 1827.

Savigny, Henry, and Alexander Corréard. *Narrative of a Voyage to Senegal in 1816.* 1818. Reprinted, Marlboro, Vt.: Marlboro, 1986.

"Shipwreck of the French Frigate *Medusa.*" In *Narratives of Shipwrecks and Disasters, 1586–1860,* edited by Keith Huntress, 142–63. Ames: Iowa State University Press, 1974.

Sohier, William. Papers. Phillips Library, Peabody Essex Museum, Salem, Mass.

Steel, David. *The Ship-Master's Assistant and Owner's Manual: Containing Complete Information, as Well to Merchants, Masters of Ships, and Persons Employed in the Merchant-Service, . . . Relative to the Mercantile and Maritime Laws and Custom; . . . the Eighth Edition, Considerably Improved and Enlarged; the Whole Compiled from Undoubted Authority, and the Acts of Parliament Faithfully Abridged, by David Steel, Jun.* London: Printed for David Steel, 1799.

Steere, Richard. "A Monumental Memorial of Marine Mercy Being an Acknowledgment of an High Hand of Divine Deliverance on the Deep in the Time of Distress, 1688." In *In the Trough of the Sea: Selected Sea-Deliverance Narratives, 1660–1766,* edited by Donald Wharton. Westport, Conn.: Greenwood, 1979.

Stout, Benjamin. *Narrative of the Loss of the Ship* Hercules, *Commanded by Cpt. Benjamin Stout, on the Coast of Caffraria, the 16ᵗʰ of June, 1796: Also a Circumstantial Detail of His Travels through the Southern Deserts of Africa and the Colonies to the Cape of Good Hope; Introduction by John Adams, President of the Continental Congress of America.* New York, 1798. Reprinted New York: Asbel Stoddard, 1800.

Strachey, William. "A True Reportory of the Wracke, and Redemption of Sir Thomas Gates Knight; upon, and from the Ilands of the Bermudas: His Comming to Virginia, and the Estate of That Colonie Then, and After, under the Government of the Lord La Warre, July 15, 1610." In *In the Trough of the Sea: Selected Sea-Deliverance Narratives, 1660–1766,* edited by David Wharton. 28–55. Westport, Conn.: Greenwood, 1979.

Suggestions to Masters of Ships, Approved by the Merchants Underwriters of New York & a List of Agents for Vessels and Cargoes in Distress. New York: R. C. Root, Anthony, & Co. 1859.

Swift, Otis, Amos. *Genealogical Notes of Barnstable Families.* Revised by C.F. Swift (Barnstable, Mass: F.B. & F.P. Goss, 1888).

Thacher, Anthony. "Some Part of a Letter of Anthony Thacher Written in New England and Sent to His Brother Mr. Peter Thacher. . . ." In *In the Trough of the Sea: Selected Sea-Deliverance Narratives, 1660–1766,* edited by Donald Wharton, 56–64. Westport, Conn.: Greenwood, 1979.

Thacher, Thomas. *A Sermon Preached at Lynn, December 11, 1795, at the Internment of Eight Seamen: by Thomas Cushing Thacher, A.M. Minister of the First*

Congregational Society in That Place; Published by Desire. Boston: Printed by Samuel Hall, 1795.

Thomas, R. *Interesting and Authentic Narratives of the Most Remarkable Shipwrecks*. Hartford: Published by Ezra Strong, 1836.

Thorton, J. Quin. "From Oregon to California in 1848." In *Unfortunate Emigrants: Narratives of the Donner Party*, edited by Kristen Johnson, 14–120. Logan: Utah State University Press, 1996.

Towle, Dorothy. *Records of the Vice-Admiralty Court of Rhode Island, 1716–1752*. Washington, D.C.: American Historical Association, 1936.

Turner, William. *A Compleat History of the Most Remarkable Providences, Both of Judgment and Mercy, Which Have Hapned in This Present Age: Extracted from the Best Writers, the Author's Own Observations, and the Numerous Relations Sent Him from Divers Parts of the Three Kingdoms; to Which Is Added, Whatever Is Curious in the Works of Nature and Art; the Whole Digested into One Volume, under Proper Heads; Being a Work Set on Foot Thirty Years Ago, by the Reverend Mr. Pool, Author of the Synopsis Criticorum and Since Undertaken and Finish'd, by William Turner*. London: Printed for John Dunton, 1697.

Uring, Nathaniel. *Voyages and Travels of Captain Nathaniel Uring*. Alfred Dewar, ed. London: Cassell, 1928, originally published 1726.

Vassa, Gustavus. *The Interesting Narrative of the Life of Equiano*. 9th ed. Ed. Vincent Carretta. New York: Penguin Classics, 1995.

Vaughn, David. *The Narrative of Captain David Woodard and Four Seamen, Who Lost Their Ship While in a Boat at Sea*. London: Printed for J. Johnson and S. Hamilton, 1804.

Vaz d'Almada, Francisco. "Treatise of the Misfortune That Befell the Great Ship, *São João Baptista*, 1622. [Shipwreck of the *São João Baptista*]" In *Further Selections from the Tragic History of the Sea, 1559–1565*, edited by C. R. Boxer, 189–274. Minneapolis: University of Minnesota Press, 1958.

Walling, William. *The Wonderful Providence of God: Exemplified in the Preservation of William Walling, Who Was Drove Out to Sea from Sandy-Hook Near New York*. Boston: Reprinted for Francis Skinner, 1730.

Ward, Edward. *Wooden World Dissected*. London: Printed by H. Meere and sold by J. Woodward, 1708.

Whitmore, William. *Colonial Laws of Massachusetts, 1672–1686*. 1660. Reprinted, Boston: Published by order of the City Council of Boston, 1889.

Whitwell, William. *A Discourse, Occasioned by the Loss of a Number of Vessels, with Their Mariners, Belonging to the Town of Marblehead; and Delivered December 17, 1769*. Salem: Printed and sold by Samuel Hall, 1770.

Secondary Sources

Aarom, Silvia Marina. *The Women of Mexico City*. Stanford, Calif.: Stanford University Press, 1985.

Abrams, M. H. *Natural Supernaturalism*. New York: W. W. Norton, 1971.

Ahlstrom, Sydney. *Religious History of the American People.* New Haven, Conn.: Yale University Press, 1972.

Altick, Richard. *Victorian Studies in Scarlet.* New York: W. W. Norton, 1970.

Andrew, Charles M. Introduction. In Doroty Towle, ed., *Records of the Vice-Admiralty Court of Rhode Island,* 1716–1752, 1–80. Washington, D.C.: American Historical Association, 1936.

———. *The Colonial Period of American History.* Vol. 4. New Haven, Conn.: Yale University Press, 1964.

Andrews, Kenneth. *Ships, Money and Politics.* Cambridge: Cambridge University Press, 1991.

Appleby, Joyce, M. Jacob, and J. Jacob. Introduction. In *Origins of Anglo-American Radicalism,* edited by Margaret Jacob and James Jacob, 1–13. London: George Allen University, 1984.

Armstrong, Timothy. *American Bodies: Cultural Histories of the Physique.* New York: New York University Press, 1996.

———. "Slavery, Insurance and Sacrifice in the Black Atlantic." In *Sea Change: Historicizing the Ocean,* edited by Bernhard Klein, 167–85. New York: Routledge, 2003.

Arnold, Allan. "All Hands Drunk and Rioting: Disobedience in the Old Merchant Marine." In *Ships, Seafaring and Society: Essays in Maritime History,* edited by Timothy Runyan, 227–38. Detroit: Published for the Great Lakes Historical Society by Wayne State University Press, 1987.

Baehre, Rainer K. *Outrageous Seas.* Montreal: Carlton University Press, 1999.

Bailyn, Bernard. *The New England Merchants in the Seventeenth Century.* New York: Harper and Row, 1955.

Bales, Jack, and Richard Warner, eds. *Boon Island.* Hanover, N.H.: University Press of New England, 1996.

Barber, Bernard. "Social Stratification." In *Class and Society in Early America,* edited by Gary Nash, 75–88. Englewood, N.J.: Prentice-Hall, 1970.

Barker, Hannah, and Elain Chalus. *Gender in Eighteenth Century England.* London: Longman, 1997.

Barker-Benfield, G. J. *The Culture of Sensibility.* Chicago: University of Chicago Press, 1993.

Bartholomew, R., and L. J. Arrington. *Rescue of the 1856 Handcart Companies.* Provo, Utah: Charles Redd Center for Western Studies, Brigham Young University, 1993.

Batten, Charles, Jr. *Pleasurable Instruction: Form and Convention in Eighteenth-Century Travel Literature.* Berkeley: University of California Press, 1978.

Bebbington, David. *Evangelicalism in Modern Britain: A History from the 1730s to the 1980s.* London: Unwin Hyman, 1989.

Berkin, Carol. *First Generations, Women in Colonial America.* New York: Hill and Wang, 1996.

Berkin, Carol, and Leslie Horowitz, eds. *Women Voices, Women's Lives.* Boston: Northeastern University Press, 1998.

Blackmore, Josiah. *Manifest Perdition*. Minneapolis: University of Minnesota Press, 2002.

Blum, Hester. *A View from the Masthead*. Chapel Hill: University of North Carolina Press, 2008.

Bolster, Jeffrey. *Black Jacks: African-American Seamen in the Age of Sail*. Cambridge, Mass.: Harvard University Press, 1997.

———. "Every Inch a Man: Gender in the Lives of African American Seamen, 1800–1860." In *Iron Men, Wooden Women: Gender and Seafaring in the Atlantic World, 1700–1920*, edited by Margaret Creighton and Lisa Norling, 138–68. Baltimore: Johns Hopkins University Press, 1996.

———. "The Inner Diaspora: Black Sailors Making Selves." In *Through a Nation Darkly: Reflection on Personal Identity in Early America*, edited by Ronald Hoffman, Mechal Sobel, and Fredrika Teute, 419–48. Chapel Hill: Published for the Omohundro Institute of Early American History & Culture, Williamsburg, Virginia, by the University of North Carolina Press, 1997.

Botein, Stephen. "Anglo-American Book Trade before 1776: Personnel and Strategies." In *Printing and Society in Early America*, edited by William Joyce et al., 48–82. Worcester, Mass.: American Antiquarian Society, 1983.

Boxer, C. R. *The Church Militant and Iberian Expansion, 1440–1770*. Baltimore: Johns Hopkins University Press, 1978.

———. *Further Selections from the Tragic History of the Sea, 1559–1565*. Cambridge: Cambridge University Press, 1968.

———. *Mary and Misogyny: Women in Iberian Expansion Overseas*. London: Duckworth, 1975.

———. *Portuguese Seaborne Empire*. New York: Knopf, 1969.

———. *Race Relations in the Portuguese Empire*. Oxford, U.K.: Clarendon, 1963.

———. *Tragic History of the Sea*. 2nd series, no. 112. Cambridge: Cambridge University Press, 1959.

Brown, Kathleen. *Good Wives, Nasty Wenches, and Anxious Patriarchs*. Chapel Hill: University of North Carolina Press, 1996.

Brown, Richard. *Knowledge Is Power*. New York: Oxford University Press, 1989.

Brown, Robert. "From Cohesion to Competition." In *Printing and Society in Early America*, edited by William Joyce et al., 300–309. Worcester, Mass.: American Antiquarian Society, 1983.

Burch, Julie. "Sink or Swim: Shipwreck Narratives, Survival Tales, and Postcultural Subjectivity." Ph.D. diss., University of Michigan, 1994.

Burg, B. R. "Women and Children First: Popular Mythology and Disaster at Sea, 1840–1860." *Journal of American Culture* 20, no. 4 (1997): 1–9.

Burnham, Michelle. *Captivity and Sentiment: Cultural Exchange in American Literature, 1682–1861*. Hanover, N.H.: University Press of New England, 1997.

Bushman, Richard. *The Refinement of America*. New York: Vintage Books, 1993.

Butler, Jon. *Awash in a Sea of Faith*. Cambridge, Mass.: Harvard University Press, 1990.

Calvo-Stevenson, Hortensia. "Sinking Being: Shipwrecks and Colonial Spanish American Writing." Ph.D. diss., Yale University, 1990.

Campbell, John. "A Marine Note of Protest." *American Neptune* 23, no. 1 (1963): 46–55.

Canny, Nicholas. "The British Atlantic World Working towards a Definition." *Historical Journal* 33, no. 2 (1990): 117–57.

Canny, Nicholas, and Anthony Padgen, eds. *Colonial Identity in the Atlantic World, 1500–1800.* Princeton, N.J.: Princeton University Press, 1987.

Carnes, Mark, and Clyde Griffen, eds. *Meanings for Manhood: Constructions of Masculinity in Victorian America.* Chicago: University of Chicago Press, 1990.

Carreta, Vincent, ed. *The Interesting Narrative of the Life of Equiano.* 9th ed. New York: Penguin Classics, 1995.

Carter, Philip. *Men and the Emergence of Polite Society, Britain 1660–1800.* Harlow, U.K.: Pearson Education, 2001.

Cary, John, Julius Weinberg, Thomas Hartstone, and Robert Wheeler, eds. *The Social Fabric: American Life from 1607 to 1877.* 8th ed. Vol. 1. New York: Longman, 1999.

Casey, James. *Early Modern Spain: A Social History.* New York: Routledge, 1999.

Casto, William. "The Origins of Federal Admiralty Jurisdiction in an Age of Privateers, Smugglers, and Pirates." *American Journal of Legal History* 37, no. 2 (1993): 117–56.

Cevallo-Camdau, Francisco, Jeffrey Cole, Nina Scott, and Nocomedes Suarez-Araus, eds. *Coded Encounters: Writing, Gender, and Ethnicity in Colonial Latin America.* Amherst: University of Massachusetts Press, 1994.

Chatteron, E. Keble. *Brotherhood of the Sea.* New York: Longman, Green, 1927.

Coates, Timothy. *Convicts and Orphans: Forced State-Sponsored Colonies in the Portuguese Empire, 1550–1755.* Stanford, Calif.: Stanford University Press, 2001.

Cordingly, David. *Women Sailors and Sailors' Women.* New York: Random House, 2001.

Cott, Nancy. *The Bonds of Womanhood.* New Haven, Conn.: Yale University Press, 1977.

Crain, Caleb. "Lovers of Human Flesh: Homosexuality and Cannibalism in Melville's Novels." *American Literature* 66, no. 1 (1994): 25–53.

Crane, Elaine. *Ebb Tide in New England.* Boston: Northeastern University Press, 1998.

Creighton, Margaret. "Davy Jones' Locker Room: Gender and the American Whaleman, 1830–1870." In *Iron Men, Wooden Women: Gender and Seafaring in the Atlantic World, 1700–1920,* edited by Margaret Creighton and Lisa Norling, 118–37. Baltimore: Johns Hopkins University Press, 1996.

———. "'Women' and Men in American Whaling." *International Journal of Maritime History* 4, no. 1 (1992): 195–218.

Creighton, Margaret, and Lisa Norling, eds. *Iron Men, Wooden Women: Gender and Seafaring in the Atlantic World, 1700–1920.* Baltimore: Johns Hopkins University Press, 1996.

Cross, Gary. *A Social History of Leisure since 1600.* State College, Pa.: Venture Publishing, 1990.

Crump, Helen. *Colonial Admiralty Jurisdiction in the Seventeenth Century.* London: Longmans, Green, 1931.

Davidson, Cathy. *Revolution and the Word: The Rise of the Novel in America.* New York: Oxford University Press, 1986.

Davis, Charles, and Henry Louis Gates Jr., eds. *The Slave's Narrative.* New York: Oxford University Press, 1985.

Davis, Ralph. *The Rise of the English Shipbuilding Industry in the 17th and 18th Centuries.* London: David and Charles, 1972.

Dening, Greg. *Mr. Bligh's Bad Language.* Cambridge: Cambridge University Press, 1992.

Difie, Bailey, and George Winius. *Foundations of the Portuguese Empire: 1415–1580.* Minneapolis: University of Minnesota Press, 1977.

Disney, A. R. *Twilight of the Pepper Empire.* Cambridge, Mass.: Harvard University Press, 1978.

Ditz, Toby. "Shipwrecked; or, Masculinity Imperiled: Mercantile Representations of Failure and the Gendered Self in Eighteenth-Century Philadelphia." *Journal of American History* 81, no. 1 (1994): 51–80.

Donahue, Jane. "Colonial Shipwreck Narratives: A Theological Study." *Books at Brown* 23 (1969): 101–31.

Dorsey, Bruce. *Reforming Men and Women.* Ithaca, N.Y.: Cornell University Press, 2002.

Douglas, Ann. *Feminization of American Culture.* New York: Knopf, 1970.

Dover, Victor. *A Handbook to Marine Insurance.* London: H. F. G. Witherby, 1962.

Dowler, Lorraine. "Till Death Do Us Part: Masculinity, Friendship, and Nationalism in Belfast, Northern Ireland." *Environment and Planning D: Society and Space* 20, no. 1 (2002): 53–71.

Druett, Joan. "Book Review." Review of *Iron Men, Wooden Women: Gender and Seafaring in the Atlantic World, 1700–1920*, edited by Margaret Creighton and Lisa Norling. *William and Mary Quarterly* 54, no. 2 (1997): 426.

———. *Hen Frigates.* New York: Simon and Schuster, 1998.

Duffy, James. *Shipwreck and Empire.* Cambridge, Mass.: Harvard University Press, 1955.

Dugaw, Diane. "Rambling Female Sailors: The Rise and Fall of the Seafaring Heroine." *International Journal of Maritime History* 4, no. 1 (1992): 179–94.

Dye, Ira. "Early American Seafarers." *Proceedings of the American Philosophical Society* 120, no. 5 (1976): 331–60.

Ebersole, Gary. *Captured by Texts: Puritan to Postmodern Images of Indian Captivity.* Charlottesville: University Press of Virginia, 1995.

Eire, Carlos. *From Madrid to Purgatory.* Cambridge: Cambridge University Press, 1995.

Fabian, Ann. *The Unvarnished Truth.* Berkeley: University of California Press, 2000.

Fletcher, Anthony. *Gender, Sex and Subordination in England, 1500–1800*. New Haven, Conn.: Yale University Press, 1995.

Fowler, William. *Rebels under Sail*. New York: Scribner, 1976.

Foyster, Elizabeth. *Manhood in Early Modern England*. New York: Addison Wesley Longman, 1999.

Frey, Sylvia. "Inequality in the Here and Hereafter: Religion and Construction of Race and Gender in the Post-Revolutionary South." In *Inequality in Early America*, edited by Carla Pestana and Sharon Salinger, 87–108. Hanover, N.H.: University Press of New England, 1999.

Fuller, Edmund. *Mutiny! Being Accounts of Insurrections, Famous and Infamous, on Land and Sea, from the Days of Caesar to Modern Times*. New York: Crown, 1953.

Fuller, Mary. *Voyages in Print: English Travel to America, 1576–1624*. Cambridge: Cambridge University Press, 1995.

Gale, John. *Introduction to Marine Insurance*. London: Macmillan, 1937.

Gaustad, Edwin Scott. *Religious History of America*. New York: Harper and Row, 1966.

Gaynham, Henry. *From the Lower Deck*. Barre, Mass.: Barre, 1970.

Gilje, Paul. *Liberty on the Waterfront: American Maritime Culture in the Age of Sail*. Philadelphia: University of Pennsylvania Press, 2004.

———. "Loyalty and Liberty: The Ambiguous Patriotism of Jack Tar in the American Revolution." *Pennsylvania History* 67, no. 2 (2000): 166–93.

Gillingham, Harold. *Marine Insurance in Philadelphia, 1721–1800*. Philadelphia: Patterson and White, Co., private printers, 1933.

Gilmore, William. *Reading Becomes a Necessity of Life*. Knoxville: University of Tennessee Press, 1989.

Gilreath, James. "American Book Distribution." In *Needs and Opportunities in the History of the Book: America, 1639–1876*, edited by David Hall and John Hench, 103–86. Worcester, Mass.: American Antiquarian Society, 1987.

Goebel, Julius, ed. *Law Practice of Alexander Hamilton*. Vols. 2, 4. New York: Columbia University Press, 1969.

Gora, Phillip. "The Literature of Colonial English Puritanism." In *Teaching the Literatures of Early America*, edited by Carla Mulford, 143–52. New York: Modern Language Association of America, 1999.

Gorn, Elliot. "Seafaring Engendered." *International Journal of Maritime History* 4, no. 1 (1992): 219–25.

Grayson, Donald. "Human Mortality in a Natural Disaster: The Willie Handcart Company." *Journal of Anthropological Research* 52, no. 2 (1996): 185–205.

———. "Timing of the Donner Party Deaths." Appendix 3. In *Archaeology of the Donner Party*, edited by Donald Hardesty, 124–32 . Reno: University of Nevada Press, 1997.

Gregory, Jeremy. "*Homo Religiosus:* Masculinity and Religion in the Long Eighteenth Century." In *English Masculinities, 1600–1800*, edited by Tim Hitchcock and Michele Cohen, 85–110. London: Addison Wesley, 1999.

Greven, Philip. *Protestant Temperament*. New York: Knopf, 1977.

Guttridge, Leonard. *Mutiny: A History of Naval Insurrection.* Annapolis, Md.: Naval Institute Press, 1992.

Hafen, L. R., and A. W. Hafen. *Handcarts to Zion: The Story of a Unique Western Migration, 1856–1860.* Lincoln: University of Nebraska Press, 1992.

Hall, David. "Uses of Literacy in New England, 1600–1850." In *Printing and Society in Early America,* edited by William Joyce et al., 1–47. Worcester, Mass.: American Antiquarian Society, 1983.

————. *Worlds of Wonder, Days of Judgment: Popular Religious Belief in Early New England.* Cambridge, Mass.: Harvard University Press, 1990.

Hall, David, and John Hench. *Needs and Opportunities in the History of the Book: America, 1639–1876.* Worcester, Mass.: American Antiquarian Society, 1987.

Halttunen, Karen. *Confidence Men and Painted Women: Study of Middle-Class Culture in America, 1830–1870.* New Haven, Conn.: Yale University Press, 1982.

————. *Murder Most Foul.* Cambridge, Mass.: Harvard University Press, 1998.

Hardesty, Donald. *Archaeology of the Donner Party.* Reno: University of Nevada Press, 1997.

Hartman, James. *Providence Tales and the Birth of American Literature.* Baltimore: Johns Hopkins University Press, 1999.

Hatch, Nathan. *Democratization of American Christianity.* New Haven, Conn.: Yale University Press, 1989.

Henretta, James. "Economic Development and Social Structure in Colonial Boston." *William and Mary Quarterly* 22, no. 1 (1965): 75–92.

————. "Economic Development and Social Structure in Colonial Boston." In *Class and Society in Early America,* edited by Gary Nash, 133–48. Englewood Cliffs: N.J.: Prentice-Hall, 1970.

Heyrman, Christine. *Commerce and Culture.* New York: W. W. Norton, 1984.

Hitchcock, Tim, and Michele Cohen, eds. *English Masculinities, 1600–1800.* London: Longman, 1999.

Hoffman, Ronald, and Peter Albert, eds. *The Transforming Hand of Revolution.* Charlottesville: University Press of Virginia, 1995.

Hoffman, Ronald, Mechal Sobel, and Fredrika Teute, eds. *Through a Glass Darkly: Reflection on Personal Identity in Early America.* Chapel Hill: Published for the Omohundro Institute of Early American History & Culture, Williamsburg, Virginia, by the University of North Carolina Press, 1997.

Hough, Charles Merrill. *Reports of Cases in the Vice-Admiralty Courts of the Province of New York.* New Haven, Conn.: Yale University Press, 1925.

Howard, Stephen. "'A Bright Pattern to All Her Sex': Representations of Women in Periodical and Newspaper Biography." In *Gender in Eighteenth Century England,* edited by Hannah Barker and Elain Chalus, 230–49. London: Longman, 1997.

Howell, Colin, and Richard Twomey, eds. *Jack Tar in History: Essays in the History of Maritime Life and Labour.* Fredericton, N.B.: Acadiensis, 1991.

Huntress, Keith. *Checklist of Narratives of Shipwrecks and Disasters at Sea to 1860.* Ames: Iowa State University Press, 1979.

————. *Narratives of Shipwrecks and Disasters, 1586–1860.* Ames: Iowa State University Press, 1974.

Ingersoll, Thomas. "Riches and Honour Were Rejected by Them as Loathsome Vomit: Fear of Leveling in New England." In *Inequality in Early America,* edited by Carla Pestana and Sharon Salinger, 46–66. Hanover, N.H.: University Press of New England, 1999.

Insurance Company of North America. *Episodes of History in the Stories of the United States and the Insurance Company of North America.* Philadelphia: Insurance Company of North America, 1916.

Jacob, Margaret, and James Jacob. *Origins of Anglo-American Radicalism.* London: George Allen University, 1984.

Johnson, Kristen, ed. *Unfortunate Emigrants: Narratives of the Donner Party.* Logan: Utah State University Press, 1996.

Johnson, Lyman. "Dangerous Words, Provocative Gestures, and Violent Acts." In *Faces of Honor,* edited by Lyman Johnson and Sonya Lipsett-Rivera, 127–51. Albuquerque: University of New Mexico Press, 1998.

Johnson, Lyman, and Sonya Lipsett-Rivera. *Faces of Honor.* Albuquerque: University of New Mexico Press, 1998.

Johnson, Parker. "Humiliation Followed by Deliverance: Metaphor and Plot in Cotton Mather's *Magnalia.*" *Early American Literature* 15, no. 3 (1980/81): 237–46.

Joyce, William. *Printing and Society in Early America.* Worcester, Mass.: American Antiquarian Society, 1983.

Kamensky, Jane. "Talk Like a Man: Speech, Power, and Masculinity of Gender." In *A Shared Experience: Men, Women and the History of Gender,* edited by Laura McCall and Donald Yacovene, 19–50. New York: New York University Press, 1998.

Kann, Michael. *A Republic of Men.* New York: New York University Press, 1998.

Kerber, Linda. *Women of the Republic: Intellect and Ideology in Revolutionary America.* Chapel Hill: Published for the Institute of Early American History and Culture, Williamsburg, Va., by the University of North Carolina Press, 1980.

Kerber, Linda, Nancy Cott, Lynn Hunt, Caroll Smith-Rosenberg, and Christine Stansell. "Forum: Beyond Roles, Beyond Spheres; Thinking about Gender in the Early Republic." *William and Mary Quarterly,* 3rd series, 64 (1989): 565–85.

Keys, Ancel. *Biology of Human Starvation.* Minneapolis: University of Minnesota Press, 1950.

Kimball, Stanley. *Historic Resource Study: Mormon Pioneer National Historic Trail.* Washington, D.C.: National Park Service, 1996.

Kimmel, Michael. *Manhood in America.* New York: Free Press, 1996.

King, Anthony. *Urbanism, Colonialism, and the World Economy.* New York: Routledge, 1990.

King, Joseph. *Winter of Entrapment.* Toronto: P. D. Meany, 1992.

Klein, Bernhard, ed. *Sea Change: Historicizing the Ocean.* New York: Routledge, 2003.

Knight, Franklin, and Peggy Liss. *Atlantic Port Cities*. Knoxville: University of Tennessee Press, 1991.

Kulikoff, Allan. "The Progress of Inequality." In *New American Nation*, vol. 11, *American Society 1776–1815*, edited by Peter Onuf, 51–88. New York: Garland, 1991.

Kverndal, Roald. *Seamen's Missions: Their Origin and Early Growth*. Pasadena: William Carey Library, 1986.

Landow, George. *Images of Crisis*. Boston: Routledge and Kegan Paul, 1982.

Lavrin, Asunción. "Lo Femenino: Women in Colonial Historical Sources." In *Coded Encounters: Writing, Gender, and Ethnicity in Colonial Latin America*, edited by Francisco Cevallo-Camdau, Jeffrey Cole, Nina Scott, and Nocomedes Suarez-Araus, 153–76. Amherst: University of Massachusetts Press, 1994.

———. *Sexuality and Marriage in Colonial Latin America*. Lincoln: University of Nebraska Press, 1989.

———. "Sexuality in Colonial Mexico: A Church Delimma." In *Sexuality and Marriage in Colonial Latin America*, edited by Asunción Lavrin, 47–95. Lincoln: University of Nebraska Press, 1989.

Law, Sylvia A. "Torts," in Alan Morrison, ed., *Fundamentals of American Law*, 239–63. New York: Oxford Press, 1996.

Lax, John, and William Pencak. "The Knowles Riot and the Crisis of the 1740s in Massachusetts." *Perspectives in American History* 10 (1976): 163–216.

Leach, John. *Survival Psychology*. New York: New York University Press, 1994.

LeBeau, Bryan F. *Religion in America to 1865*. New York: New York University Press, 2000.

Lemisch, Jesse. "Jack Tar in the Streets: Merchant Seamen in the Politics of Revolutionary America." *William and Mary Quarterly* 25, no. 3 (1968): 371–407.

———. "Listening to the 'Inarticulate.'" *Journal of Social History* 3 (Fall 1969): 1–29.

Lewis, R. W. B. *The American Adam*. Chicago: University of Chicago Press, 1955.

Ley, Charles. *Portuguese Voyages*. London: J. M. Dent & Sons, 1947.

Lincoln, Margarette. "Shipwreck Narratives of the Eighteenth and Early Nineteenth Century: Indicators of Culture and Identity." *British Journal for Eighteenth Century Studies* 20 (1997): 155–72.

Lloyd, Christopher. *The British Seaman, 1260–1860*. Cranbury, N.J.: Associated University Presses, 1970.

Lockridge, Kenneth. *Literacy in Colonial New England*. New York: W. W. Norton, 1974.

Long, Rowland. *Richards on the Law of Insurance*. 4th ed. New York: Baker, Voorhis, and Co., 1932.

Lopez, Robert and Irving Raymond, translators. *Medieval Trade in the Mediterranean World: Illustrative Documents*. New York: Columbia University Press, 1955.

MacAndrew, Elizabeth. *The Gothic Tradition*. New York: Columbia University Press, 1979.

Main, Jackson T. "Economic Class Structure." In *Class and Society in Early America*, edited by Gary Nash, 100–116. Englewood Cliffs, N.J.: Prentice-Hall, 1970.

Mangone, Gerard. *United States Admiralty Law.* London: Kluwer Law International, 1997.

Maraist, Frank. *Admiralty in a Nutshell.* 2nd ed. St. Paul, Minn.: West, 1991.

Masur, Louis. *The Autobiography of Benjamin Franklin.* Boston: Bedford–St. Martin's, 1993.

Matthews, Jean. *Toward a New Society.* Boston: Twayne, 1991.

Maura, Juan Francisco. *Women in the Conquest of the Americas.* Translated by John F. Deredita. New York: P. Lang, 1997.

May, Henry. *Enlightenment in America.* New York: Oxford University Press, 1976.

Maynard, Steven. "Making Waves: Gender and Sex in the History of Seafaring." *Acadiensis* 22, no. 2 (1993): 144–53.

McCall, Laura, and Donald Yacovone. *A Shared Experience: Men, Women and the History of Gender.* New York: New York University Press, 1998.

McDowell, Linda. *Gender, Identity, and Place.* Minneapolis: University of Minnesota Press, 1999.

McElroy, John William. "Seafaring in Seventeenth-Century New England." *New England Quarterly* 8, no. 3 (1935): 331–64.

McEwan, M. A., and A. H. Lewis. *Encyclopedia of Nautical Knowledge.* Cambridge, Md.: Cornell Maritime Press, 1953.

McKee, Alexander. *Deathraft: The Human Drama of the* Medusa *Shipwreck.* New York: Scribner, 1975.

———. "Fantasies of Mutiny and Murder." *Armed Forces and Society* 4, no. 2 (1978): 293–304.

———. *Wreck of the* Medusa*: Murder, Mutiny and Survival on the High Seas.* New York: Penguin Group, 2007.

McLoughlin, William. *Revivals, Awakenings, and Reform.* Chicago: University of Chicago Press, 1978.

Merish, Lori. *Sentimental Materialism: Gender, Commodity Culture, and Nineteenth Century American Literature.* Durham, N.C.: Duke University Press, 2000.

Meurn, Robert. *Survival Guide for the Mariner.* Centreville, Md.: Cornell Maritime Press, 1993.

Meyerstein, E. *Adventures by Sea of Edward Coxere.* New York: Oxford University Press, 1946.

Miller, Perry. *Errand into the Wilderness.* New York: Harper and Row, 1956.

———. *New England Mind: The Seventeenth Century*, Colume 1. Cambridge: Harvard University Press, 1983.

Mintz, Steven, and Susan Kellogg. "The Affectionate Family." In *The Social Fabric: American Life from 1607 to 1877*, 8th ed., vol. 1, edited by John Cary, Julius Weinberg, Thomas Hartstone, and Robert Wheeler, 191–206. New York: Longman, 1999.

Miskolcze, Robin. "Don't Rock the Boat: Women and Shipwreck Narratives in Early U.S Culture." Ph.D. diss., University of Nebraska, 2000.

———. "Transatlantic Touchstone: The Shipwrecked Woman in British and Early American Literature." *Prose Studies* 22, no. 3 (1999): 41–56.

Morison, Samuel Eliot. *Admiral of the Ocean Sea: A Life of Christopher Columbus.* Boston: Little, Brown, 1942.

———. *The Maritime History of Massachusetts.* Boston: Houghton Mifflin, 1961.

Morris, Richard. *Select Cases of the Mayor's Court of New York City.* Washington, D.C.: American Historical Association, 1935.

Morrison, Alan. *Fundamentals of American Law.* New York: Oxford University Press, 1996.

Mott, Frank Luther. *American Journalism.* New York: Macmillan, 1941.

———. *Golden Multitudes: The Story of the Best-Sellers in the United States.* New York: Bowker, 1960.

Muir, Edward. *Ritual in Early Modern Europe.* Cambridge: Cambridge University Press, 1997.

Mulford, Carla. *Teaching the Literatures of Early America.* New York: Modern Language Association of America, 1999.

Nash, Gary. *Class and Society in Early America.* Englewood Cliffs, N.J.: Prentice-Hall, 1970.

———. *Urban Crucible.* Cambridge, Mass.: Harvard University Press, 1979.

Newman, Simon. "Reading the Bodies of Early American Seafarers." *William and Mary Quarterly,* 3rd series, 55, no.1 (1998): 59–82.

Noll, Mark. *The Old Religion in a New World.* Grand Rapids, Mich.: William B. Eerdmans, 2002.

———. "Revolution and the Rise of Evangelical Social Influence in North Atlantic Societies." In *Evangelicalism: Comparative Studies of Popular Protestantism in North America, the British Isles, and Beyond 1700–1900,* edited by Mark A. Noll, David W. Bebbington, and George A. Rawlyk, 113–36. New York: Oxford University Press, 1994.

———. "Rise and Long Life of Protestant Enlightenment in America." In *Knowledge and Belief in America: Enlightenment Traditions and Modern Religious Thought,* edited by William Shea, Peter Huff, and Lee Hamilton, 88–124. Cambridge: Cambridge University Press, 1995.

Mark A. Noll, David W. Bebbington, and George A. Rawlyk, eds. *Evangelicalism: Comparative Studies of Popular Protestantism in North America, the British Isles, and Beyond 1700–1900.* New York: Oxford University Press, 1994.

Norling, Lisa. "Ahab's Wife, Women in the American Whaling Industry, 1820–1870." In *Iron Men, Wooden Women: Gender and Seafaring in the Atlantic World, 1700–1920,* edited by Margaret Creighton and Lisa Norling, 70–91. Baltimore: Johns Hopkins University Press, 1996.

Onuf, Peter. *New American Nation.* Vol. 11, *American Society 1776–1815.* New York: Garland, 1991.

Oswald, John Clyde. *Printing in the Americas.* New York: The Gregg Publishing Co, 1937. Reprinted by New York: Hacker Art Books, 1968.

Otter, Samuel. *Melville's Anatomies.* Berkeley: University of California Press, 1999.

Owen, David, and Michael Tolley. *Courts of Admiralty in Colonial America.* Durham, N.C.: Carolina Academic Press, 1995.

Padgen, Anthony, and Nichola Canny. *Colonial Identity in the Atlantic World.* Princeton, N.J.: Princeton University Press, 1987.

Pahl, Jon. *Paradox Lost.* Baltimore: Johns Hopkins University Press, 1992.

Payne, Stanley. *Spanish Catholicism.* Madison: University of Wisconsin Press, 1984.

Pearson, M. N. *The New Cambridge History of India: The Portuguese in India.* Cambridge: Cambridge University Press, 1987.

Pease, Jane. *Ladies, Women, and Wenches: Choice and Constraint in Antebellum Charleston and Boston.* Chapel Hill: University of North Carolina Press, 1990.

Pencak, William. *History Signing In.* New York: Peter Lang, 1993.

Pérez-Mallaína, Pablo. *Spain's Men of the Sea.* Translated by Carla Rahn Phillips. Baltimore: Johns Hopkins University Press, 1998.

Perry, Mary Elizabeth. *Gender and Disorder in Early Modern Seville.* Princeton, N.J.: Princeton University Press, 1990.

Pestana, Carla, and Sharon Salinger. *Inequality in Early America.* Hanover, N.H.: University Press of New England, 1999.

Petrinovich, Lewis. *The Cannibal Within.* New York: Aldine de Gruyter, 2000.

Philbrick, Thomas. *The Loss of the Ship* Essex, *Sunk by a Whale.* New York: Penguin Group, 2000.

Pleck, Elizabeth. "An Historical Overview of American Gender Roles and Relations from Precolonial Times to the Present." Center for Research on Women, Wellesley College, Wellesley Massachusetts, 1991.

Plummer, Ken. *Telling Sexual Stories: Power, Change and Social Worlds.* London: Routledge, 1995.

Pratt, Fletcher. "Mutiny—A Study." *U.S. Naval Institute Proceedings* 58, no. 4 (1932): 520–32.

Pretzer, William. "The Quest for Autonomy and Discipline: Labor and Technology in the Book Trade." In *Needs and Opportunities in the History of the Book: America, 1639–1876,* edited by David Hall and John Hench, 13–59. Worcester, Mass.: American Antiquarian Society, 1987.

Purrington, Philip. "Anatomy of a Mutiny." *American Neptune* 27, no. 2 (1976): 98–110.

Rediker, Marcus. *Between the Devil and the Deep Blue Sea.* Cambridge: Cambridge University Press, 1987.

————. "A Motley Crew of Rebels: Sailors, Slaves, and the Coming of the American Revolution." In *The Transforming Hand of Revolution,* edited by Ronald Hoffman and Peter Albert, 155–98. Charlottesville: University Press of Virginia, 1995.

————. "Society and Culture among Anglo-American Deep Sea Sailors." Ph.D. diss., University of Pennsylvania, 1982.

Rediker, Marcus, and Peter Linebaugh. *The Many-Headed Hydra.* Boston: Beacon, 2000.

Reilly, Elizabeth Carroll. "The Boston Book Trade of Jeremy Condy." In *Printing and Society in Early America,* edited by William Joyce et al., 83–131. Worcester, Mass.: American Antiquarian Society, 1983.

————. *Dictionary of American Printers, Printers' Ornaments and Illustrations.* Worcester, Mass.: American Antiquarian Society, 1975.

Rhoden, Nancy. *Revolutionary Anglicanism.* New York: New York University Press, 1999.

Rogers, Alan. "A Sailor by Necessity: The Life of Moses Adams, 1803–1837." *Journal of the Early Republic* 11, No 1 (1991): 19–50.

Rose, Anne. *Voices of the Marketplace.* New York: Twayne, 1995.

Rose, Elihu. "Anatomy of Mutiny." *Armed Forces and Society* 8, no. 4 (1982): 561–74.

Rotundo, Anthony. *American Manhood: Transformations in Masculinity from the Revolution to the Modern Era.* New York: Basic Books, 1993.

———. "Romantic Relationships: Male Intimacy and Middle-Class Youth in the Northern United States, 1800–1900." *Journal of Social History* 23, no. 1 (1989): 1–25.

Runyan, Timothy. *Ships, Seafaring and Society: Essays in Maritime History.* Detroit: Published for the Great Lakes Historical Society by Wayne State University Press, 1987.

Russell-Wood, A. J. R. *A World on the Move.* New York: St. Martin's, 1992.

Salinger, Sharon. "Artisans, Journeymen, and the Transformation of Labor in Late Eighteenth Century Philadelphia." In *New American Nation,* vol. 11, *American Society 1776–1815,* edited by Peter Onuf, 62–84. New York: Garland, 1991.

Samson, John. "Personal Narratives, Journals and Diaries." In *America and the Sea, a Literary History,* edited by Haskell Springer, 83–98. Athens: University of Georgia Press, 1995.

Scammel, G. V. *Ships, Ocean, and Empire.* Ashgate, Vt.: Ashgate, 1995.

Schlesinger, Arthur Meier. *The Colonial Merchants and the American Revolution.* New York: Frederick Unger, 1918.

Schultz, Ronald. "A Class Society? The Nature of Inequality in Early America." In *Inequality in Early America,* edited by Carla Pestana and Sharon Salinger, 203–21. Hanover, N.H.: University Press of New England, 1999.

Seed, Patricia. *To Love, Honor and Obey in Colonial Mexico.* Stanford, Calif.: Stanford University Press, 1988.

Shea, William, Peter Huff, and Lee Hamilton. *Knowledge and Belief in America: Enlightenment Traditions and Modern Religious Thought.* Cambridge: Cambridge University Press, 1995.

Shepard, Leslie. *The History of Street Literature.* Detroit: Singing Tree, 1973.

Shoemaker, R. B. "Reforming Male Manners: Public Insult and the Decline of Violence in London, 1600–1740." In *English Masculinities, 1660–1800,* edited by Tim Hitchcock and Michele Cohen, 133–50. London: Longman, 1999.

Simpson, A. W. B. *Cannibalism and the Common Law.* Chicago: University of Chicago Press, 1984.

Smith, Andrew. "Excavations at Plettenberg Bay, South Africa of the Camp-Site of the Survivors of the Wreck of the *São Gonçalo,* 1630." *International Journal of Nautical Archaeology and Underwater Exploration* 15, no. 1 (1986): 53–63.

Smith, Gaddis. "Agricultural Roots of Maritime History." *American Neptune* 44, no. 1 (1984): 5–10.

Smith, Roger. *Vanguard of Empire.* New York: Oxford University Press, 1993.

Springer, Haskell. *America and the Sea, a Literary History*. Athens: University of Georgia Press, 1995.

———. "The Captain's Wife at Sea." In *Iron Men, Wooden Women: Gender and Seafaring in the Atlantic World, 1700–1920*, edited by Margaret Creighton and Lisa Norling, 92–117. Baltimore: Johns Hopkins University Press, 1996.

Steele, Ian. *The English Atlantic, 1675–1740*. New York: Oxford University Press, 1986.

Stiverson, Cynthia, and Gregory Stiverson. "Colonial Retail Bookstore: Availability and Affordability of Reading Material in Mid Eighteenth Century Virginia." In *Printing and Society in Early America*, edited by William L. Joyce et al., 132–73. Worcester, Mass.: American Antiquarian Society, 1983.

Taylor, Gordon Rattray. *The Angel-Makers: A Study in the Psychological Origins of Historical Change*. London: Heinemann, 1958.

Tebbel, John. *History of Book Publishing in the United States*. Vol. 1. New York: R. R. Bowker, 1972.

Thompson, Peter. "No Chance in Nature: Cannibalism as a Solution to Maritime Famine, 1750–1800." In *American Bodies: Cultural Histories of the Physique*, edited by Timothy Armstrong, 32–44. New York: New York University Press, 1996.

Throckmorton, Peter. *The Sea Remembers: Shipwrecks and Archaeology*. New York: Weidenfeld & Nicolson, 1987.

Tosh, John. "The Old Adam and the New Man: Emerging Themes in the History of English Masculinities, 1750–1850." In *English Masculinities, 1660–1800*, edited by Tim Hitchcock and Michele Cohen, 217–38. London: Longman, 1999.

Treckel, Paula. *To Comfort the Heart: Women in Seventeenth-Century America*. New York: Twayne, 1996.

Tucker, Tod. *The Great Starvation Experiment*. New York: Free Press, 2006.

Turley, Hans. *Rum, Sodomy, and the Lash: Piracy, Sexuality, and Masculine Identity*. New York: New University Press, 1999.

Twinam, Ann. "Honor, Sexuality, and Illegitimacy in Colonial Spanish America." In *Sexuality and Marriage in Colonial Latin America*, edited by Ascunsión Lavrin, 118–55. Lincoln: University of Nebraska Press, 1989.

———. "The Negotiation of Honor." In *The Faces of Honor*, edited by Lyman Johnson and Sonya Lipsett-Rivera, 68–102. Albuquerque: University of New Mexico Press, 1998.

———. *Public Lives, Private Secrets: Gender, Honor, Sexuality, and Illegitimacy in Colonial Spanish America*. Stanford, Calif.: Stanford University Press, 2001.

Ubbelohde, Carl. *The Vice-Admiralty Courts and the American Revolution*. Chapel Hill: University of North Carolina Press, 1960.

Vaughan, Alden. *Roots of American Racism*. New York: Oxford University Press, 1995.

Vickers, Daniel. "Beyond Jack Tar." *William and Mary Quarterly* 50, no. 2 (1993): 418–24.

———. "Book Review of *Iron Men, Wooden Women*," *American Historical Review* 102, no. 4 (1997): 1120.

————. "An Honest Tar: Ashley Brown of Marblehead." *New England Quarterly* 69, no. 4 (1996): 531–53.

Vickers, Daniel, and Vince Walsh. "Young Men and the Sea: The Sociology of Seafaring in Eighteenth-Century Salem, Massachusetts." *Social History* 24, no. 1 (1999): 17–38.

Walby, Sylvia. *Gender Transformations.* New York: Routledge, 1997.

Walters, Kerry. *American Deists.* Lawrence: University Press of Kansas, 1992.

Warner, R. H. "Captain John Deane and the Wreck of the *Nottingham* Galley: A Study of History and Bibliography." *New England Quarterly* 68, no. 1 (1995): 106–17.

Watson, Michael. "Appropriating Empire: The British North American Vice-Admiralty Judges, 1697–1775." Ph.D. diss., University of Ontario, 1997.

Watson, Samuel. "Flexible Gender Roles during the Market Revolution: Family, Friendship, Marriage and Masculinity among United States Army Officers, 1815–1846." *Journal of Social History* 29, no. 1 (1995): 81–106.

Weiss, Harry. *A Book about Chapbooks.* Hatboro, Pa.: Folklore Association, 1969.

Wharton, Donald. "The Colonial Era." In *America and the Sea: A Literary History,* edited by Haskell Springer, 32–45. Athens: University of Georgia Press, 1995.

————. *In the Trough of the Sea: Selected Sea-Deliverance Narratives, 1660–1766.* Westport, Conn.: Greenwood, 1979.

————. "Providence and the Colonial American Sea Deliverance Tradition." *Essex Institute Historical Collections* 119 (1983): 42–48.

————. "The Revolutionary and Federal Periods." In *America and the Sea: A Literary History,* edited by Haskell Springer, 46–63. Athens: University of Georgia Press, 1995.

Wilentz, Sean. *Chants Democratic.* New York: Oxford University Press, 1984.

Williams, John. "Maritime Justice in Colonial Georgia." Ph.D. diss., Auburn University, 1987.

Williams, Julie Hedgepeth. *The Significance of the Printed Word in Early America: Colonists' Thoughts on the Role of the Press.* Westport, Conn.: Greenwood, 1999.

Winans, Robert. "Bibliography and the Cultural Historian." In *Printing and Society in Early America,* edited by William L. Joyce et al., 174–85. Worcester, Mass.: American Antiquarian Society, 1983.

Winks, Robin. "The Making of the Fugitive Slave Narrative: Josiah Hanson and Uncle Tom—A Case Study." In *The Slave's Narrative,* edited by Charles Davis and Henry Louis Gates, 113–46. New York: Oxford University Press, 1991.

Winship, Michael. "Publishing in America: Needs and Opportunities for Research." In *Needs and Opportunities in the History of the Book: America, 1639–1876,* edited by David Hall and John Hench, 61–102. Worcester, Mass.: American Antiquarian Society, 1987.

Wiswall, F. L. *The Development of Admiralty Jurisdiction and Practice Since 1800.* Cambridge: Cambridge University Press, 1970.

Woodward, Rachel. "It's a Man's Life!': Soldiers, Masculinity and the Countryside." *Gender, Place and Culture* 5, no. 3 (1998): 277–300.

Wroth, Lawrence. *The Colonial Printer.* New York: Dover, 1994.

Young, Alfred. "American Historians Confront 'The Transforming Hand of Revolution.'" In *The Transforming Hand of Revolution,* edited by Ronald Hoffman and Peter Albert, 346–494. Charlottesville: University Press of Virginia, 1995.

Zuckerman, Michael. "Identity in British America: Unease in Eden." In *Colonial Identity in the Atlantic World, 1500–1800,* edited by Nicholas Canny and Anthony Padgen, 115–58. Princeton, N.J.: Princeton University Press, 1987.

INDEX

abandoned ships: and marine insurance, 48, 173n84; as salvage, 34–35, 169n29, 169n31

admiralty law, 31, 167n7

Adventure (Steere), 56

African Americans, 6, 93–95, 103. *See also* slaves

Anglicanism, 22, 52, 53, 60

Aguia, 140–41, 152, 192n33

Albion, 77–78, 104, 184n35, 184n44

Alida and Catherine, 19, 26, 27, 93, 166n107, 182n114

Allen, Sarah, 20–21, 48, 101-102

Aquila, 36

authorship, 4, 11–12, 161n5, 182n100

Bailey, Joseph, 19, 26, 27, 54, 57–58, 93

Barreto, Francisco, 139, 143

Bartholomew, Benjamin, 54–55

Benson, Henry, 78

Betsy, 91

Bilton, Thomas, 43, 60

Bligh, William, 14, 77, 91, 182n109

Blunt, Joseph, 37, 49

Boston, 76, 104, 138

Bounty, 14, 77

Bowaniong, 23–24

Bradley, Eliza, 21

Breen, Patrick, 118, 124

Brown, Andrew, 57

Burger, Elias, 35, 169n31

cannibalism: drawing lots for, 20, 118–20, 122, 123, 127, 132, 133; on *Essex*, 122, 126–27; on *Francis Mary*, 108–10, 116, 117, 124–26, 185n62; on *Nottingham Galley*, 19, 189n88; *on Peggy*, 20, 21, 60–61, 121–23, 126, 132–33, 175n46, 187n46, 188n55, 189n75; precursors to, 116–17; for preservation, 113–14; processing body for, 126–27, 189n75; and religion, 68; ritual acts of, 114, 185n3; and social order, 20, 114, 117–18, 121–23, 127, 132, 133, 157, 188n58

captains, 86–87; and balance of power and understanding, 6–7, 24, 89, 91, 132, 139; and maintaining control, 77, 83, 87–89, 91, 139, 182n109; on Portuguese ships, 138, 139–40, 191n20; reputation of, 76–77, 79–81, 90, 128–29; responsibility for ship, 30, 41–42

Carpinger, George, 106–7, 120, 187n40

carreira da India, 134-37, 143, 153

Cashmere, 1

Clarke, James Stanier, 62, 99, 122, 123

Clinton, De Witt, 15

Cochlan, Arthur, 64

Commerce, 25

common-law courts, 30–32, 34, 168n15, 168n18

Condy, Joseph, 16

Corréard, Alexander, 125–26

ABOUT THE AUTHOR

AMY MITCHELL-COOK, an associate professor and chair of the Department of History at the University of West Florida, specializes in maritime history and nautical archaeology. She has published several articles on shipwreck narratives and maritime history.